The Economics of
Taxation

The Economics of Taxation

Bernard Salanié

The MIT Press
Cambridge, Massachusetts
London, England

Originally published in France under the title *Théorie économique de la fiscalité* by Economica, Paris
© 2002 by Economica

This book was set in Palatino on 3B2 by Asco Typesetters, Hong Kong and was printed and bound in the United States of America.

Library of Congress Cataloging-in-Publication Data

Salanié, Bernard.
  [Théorie économique de la fiscalité. English]
  The economics of taxation / Bernard Salanié.
     p.   cm.
  Enl. translation of: Théorie économique de la fiscalité.
  Includes index.
  ISBN 0-262-19486-4 (alk. paper)
  1. Taxation. I. Title.
HJ2307 .S26   2002
336.2—dc21   2002035595

Contents

Foreword

This book is a somewhat expanded translation of my *Théorie économique de la fiscalité*, published by Economica in Paris. It originates in a course taught at ENSAE and at the University of Chicago. I have greatly benefited from the reactions of the students who went through these courses. I thank without implicating Arnaud Buissé, Dominique Bureau, Paul Champsaur, Pierre-André Chiappori, Maia David, Stéphane Gauthier, Anne Laferrère, Guy Laroque, Thomas Piketty, Jean-Charles Rochet, François Salanié, Jean-Luc Schneider, Alain Trannoy, and especially Philippe Choné for their comments on a first version of this text. I am also grateful to Christian Gouriéroux and six anonymous reviewers for their comments.

Introduction

The word "taxation" may take different meanings. In the stricter sense, taxation is the set of taxes that economic agents pay. In the larger sense, it concerns the whole fiscal policy of governments. I will use it in an intermediate sense. In this book, taxation refers both to taxes and to transfers to households. These transfers are usually classified in two categories:

• social insurance, which is linked to contributions (depending on countries: pensions, health, family, and/or unemployment benefits)
• social welfare, which pays benefits that do not depend on earlier contributions (e.g., minimum income benefits or housing subsidies).

This distinction is somewhat artificial as insurance also implicitly redistributes across social classes. Thus health contributions often depend on income, whereas health risks are only weakly correlated with income. Even when benefits are linked to contributions (as is often the case for pay-as-you-go pension systems), the risk may be strongly correlated with income (thus the rich usually live longer than the poor). Here I will include in taxation all taxes and benefits that come between an individual's gross income and his purchasing power. However, I will adopt a microeconomic viewpoint. I will therefore not study, for instance, the use of taxation to stabilize the economy.

Thus defined, taxation is a very rich and varied topic. Governments have resorted to all sorts of taxes in history, all the while invoking reasons that went from simple expediency to enlightened paternalism. Still, one can find common threads. Thus this introduction begins with a brief historical survey. Then it will give some data on taxation in developed countries. Finally, it gives a road map to the rest of the book.

Some History

As far as we know, taxes appeared concomitantly with civilization in Mesopotamia and in Egypt, as can be seen from Sumerian tablets dated 3,500 BC. In these despotic regimes, the king's own resources were not enough to provide a living for his priests, his court, and his army, so he had to resort to taxes. As the use of money was still rare, most of these taxes were paid in kind. Thus the peasants that constituted most of the population must bring to the king a fixed proportion of their crops (e.g., one-fifth in Egypt and one-tenth in Sumer at times).[1] They moreover had to provide labor to maintain public equipments, but also to build pyramids and temples or to work the king's fields.

Athens and Rome went further by taxing sales of land and slaves and raising import duties. They also tried (and mostly failed) to tax capital and property. For many centuries yet, taxes would mostly fall on peasants. The fall of the Roman empire brought its tax system down with it. For a long time each local authority lived mostly on the produce of its own land. The emergence of the feudal system imposed the principle that everyone, from the peasant to the duke, must provide either military service or labor in return for the right to till his land. Monetary taxes now came in addition to labor and in-kind taxes; they could be indirect taxes (paid on transactions of goods) or direct taxes (paid on wealth or on income). Many cities moreover negotiated charters with the king so as to obtain tax privileges.

In several countries the principle of consent was established early: any new tax must be agreed to by the subjects (*n'impose qui ne veult*). The most famous example is the Magna Carta granted by King John of England to his barons in 1215; it stated that no tax could be raised without the consent of Parliament. Much later, this notion of course led to the American War of Independence, with the cry of "no taxation without representation."

The tax systems did not change much until the Industrial Revolution; to obtain higher revenue, governments mostly multiplied taxes on specific goods (called excises) and custom duties, internal (be-

---

1. Given the logistical difficulties at the time, these contributions were often collected by "tax farmers," who owed a fixed amount to the king and might collect twice as much to obtain a tidy profit. This practice of tax farming was due to persist until the nineteenth century.

tween provinces) as well as external. The French Revolution had important consequences, though. In England and in other European countries, the need to finance the Napoleonic wars led governments to create the first modern income taxes. However, these taxes were abolished when peace returned. The increasing influence of liberal ideas on the virtues of free trade translated in the nineteenth century into a notable decrease in custom duties, which reduced tax revenue. To plug this hole, the English prime minister Robert Peel re-established an income tax in 1842. The other countries followed suit, when the yearning for more equality and the need to finance the first elements of the welfare state became stronger. Thus the United States only created an income tax in 1913, after overcoming the constitutional objections of the Supreme Court. Until then, federal tax revenues mostly came from custom duties and the so-called sin taxes on tobacco and alcohol.

The early income taxes were not very progressive: thus the English income tax was proportional to income, beyond a personal exemption. Only in 1909, after a homeric battle with the House of Lords, could Lloyd George created a "surtax" for high incomes. However, the US income tax, which was created later than the English one, was progressive from the start. One should note here that before the First World War, governments only collected a small part of national income: less than 10 percent, or even less than 5 percent in the United States. Even though income taxes were becoming more and more important, their rates seem very small today: the basic rate was a few percentage points of income, and the top rate was everywhere below 15 percent. Given large personal exemptions,[2] only a small percentage of the population (about 2 percent in the United States) actually paid the income tax. The personal income tax thus was a "class tax," just as the corporate income taxes that emerged in the same period.

Two main factors explain the large increase in tax revenue during the twentieth century: the two world wars, and the emergence of the modern welfare state. During each world war, military expenditure reached or passed half of national income in the main warring countries. Some countries financed this explosion in public expenditure by borrowing, but most countries resorted to tax increases. Thus

---

2. For instance, an American taxpayer only paid income tax in 1913 on the fraction of his income that exceeded five times the average income.

the top marginal rate of the income tax reached 77 percent in the United States in 1918. Moreover the Second World War transformed the income tax into a "mass tax" that touched more than half of all households, with the creation of pay-as-you-earn systems in the United Kingdom and the United States. In both countries the top marginal rate became confiscatory at the end of the war (at 94 percent in the United States and no less than 97.5 percent in the United Kingdom!).

One would expect tax rates to go back to normal after each war. As a matter of fact, tax rates did decrease in the 1920s. However, the strong increase of social expenditure took the lead in raising the tax take. The welfare state was born in the Prussia of Bismarck, with the creation of compulsory health insurance in 1883 and a pension system in 1889. Other countries followed suit in the first half of the twentieth century: unemployment benefits were created in the United Kingdom in 1911, in 1927 in Germany, in 1931 in France, and in 1936 in the United States, pension systems in 1909 in the United Kingdom and in 1935 in the United States. The famous Beveridge report consolidated the system in the United Kingdom after 1945. All these reforms contributed to an explosion of social expenditure that can be seen in the strong increase of the share of transfers in public expenditure in all of these countries over the last hundred years.

The value-added tax (VAT) was introduced in France in the 1950s. It has now become a central tool of tax policy in most developed countries, with the exception of the United States. It was institutionalized in the European Union by several directives in the 1970s.

In the 1980s there were spectacular fiscal reforms in several countries, especially in the United States and the United Kingdom after rightist governments came to power. The top marginal rate of the income tax in the United States was 70 percent at the end of the 1980s; it was reduced to 50 percent in 1981, then to 28 percent in 1986. In the United Kingdom, Mrs. Thatcher brought down the top marginal rate from 83 percent[3] to 40 percent. In both countries the rate of the corporate income tax was also lowered.[4] The governments that succeeded President Reagan and Mrs. Thatcher mostly stuck to these changes, even though President Clinton raised the top mar-

3. Not including a surcharge of 15 percent on capital income, which took the marginal rate to 98 percent for some taxpayers.
4. In the United States the tax basis became more comprehensive at the same time, and the final effect was an increase in corporate tax revenue.

Table I
Tax revenue as a percentage of GDP

	1965	1980	1990	1997
US	25.0	27.6	27.6	29.7
Japan	18.3	25.4	30.9	28.8
Germany	31.6	38.2	36.7	37.2
France	34.5	41.7	43.0	45.1
UK	30.4	35.1	36.3	35.4
OECD	25.8	32.8	35.6	37.2
EU15	27.8	36.9	40.3	41.5

ginal rate to 39.6 percent.[5] The main continental European countries have adopted more modest reforms.

Current Tax Systems

As shown in the preceding section, current tax systems are the product of a long evolution marked by historical accidents; not surprisingly, they vary a lot across countries. Steinmo (1993) shows clearly, in the examples of the United States, the United Kingdom, and Sweden, how political systems condition the tax policy of states. There are nevertheless features that are common to large groups of countries.

First consider the developed countries. Table I presents figures from OECD (1999) on the evolution of the share of taxes in GDP for the five largest economies,[6] for the unweighted average of all OECD countries, and for the unweighted average of the fifteen countries that today constitute the European Union. There are clearly large differences, with the United States and Japan in a low-tax group and France a high-tax country; moreover these international differences tend to persist over time. The tax take is procyclical, so one should not make too much of its precise value in individual years. Still, one can see in the table the large expansion in the tax take in the 1970s, followed by a pause starting in the 1980s that actually led to fiscal retrenchment in Japan and the United Kingdom.

Table II shows the breakdown of tax revenue into its main components in these five countries and groups of countries in 1997. The

---

5. The Tax Relief Act of President Bush should lower it to 35 percent in 2006.
6. For Germany, read Western Germany until 1991, then reunified Germany.

Table II
Components of tax revenue

	PIT	CIT	SSC	Property	General	Specific
US	39.0	9.4	24.2	10.7	7.8	6.8
Japan	20.5	15.0	36.9	10.8	7.0	7.6
Germany	23.9	4.0	41.6	2.7	17.6	9.0
France	14.0	5.8	40.6	5.4	17.8	8.8
UK	24.8	12.1	17.2	10.8	19.5	13.9
OECD	26.6	8.8	24.9	5.5	18.0	12.4
EU15	25.5	8.5	28.6	4.5	17.8	11.5

shares of tax revenue from each tax are indicated as PIT personal income tax, CIT corporate income tax, and SSC social security contributions. "General" designates general consumption taxes (including VAT and sales taxes) and "specific" taxes on specific goods and services (mainly excises and custom duties).

The main tax revenue of OECD countries is the personal income tax, with more than a quarter of the tax take. Several countries have reduced the number of tax brackets and the corresponding tax rates in recent years, while others have made more modest changes. As a result the share of the PIT in tax revenue has gone down a bit, but it varies a lot across countries. Other differences persist, for instance, in accounting for differences in household composition. Thus a majority of countries taxes the two members of a couple separately (as in the United Kingdom); taxation may also be joint as in France for married couples, or at the choice of the couple as in the United States and Germany. Children give access to child credits in the United Kingdom and the United States, while France uses income splitting. Finally, note that the income tax is usually deducted directly from the paycheck (the pay-as-you-earn system).

Social contributions are the second largest source of revenue in the OECD, and the largest one in France, Germany, or Japan. Their share of tax revenue has constantly increased, with the increase in social transfers: they represented only 18 percent of the tax revenue in 1965. These social contributions are usually paid as a proportional tax on wages, sometimes under a ceiling as in the United States.

The third largest resource is the "general" consumption tax, which hits all consumption goods; in most OECD countries it is the VAT (but it is the sales tax in the United States). Its share in tax revenue has jumped from about 12 percent in 1965 to 18 percent in 1997. In the form of VAT, it is even more dominant in middle-income countries and less developed countries. It often has several rates, with a reduced rate on necessities, and even a zero rate sometimes (as in the United Kingdom).

On the other hand, the share of excises (specific taxes that are levied on the consumption of a given good, e.g., alcohol, tobacco, and gasoline) has strongly declined over the last thirty years. While these taxes were the main resource of governments until the nineteenth century, they now constitute only 12 percent of the tax revenue in the OECD.

The other two tax resources (the corporate income tax and the property taxes) are usually classified as taxes on capital. The most striking feature of these two taxes is that their share in tax revenue varies enormously across countries. The share of corporate income taxes has been fairly constant across time; this hides a small reduction in rates and a recovery in the taxable basis (profits). In most countries the corporate income tax only hits incorporated firms; the profits of other firms are taxed as part of the personal income of their owners. The computation of the corporate income tax liability of a firm follows a number of rules that concern the treatment of capital gains, depreciation, provisions, and past losses among other things. As a consequence the effective revenue of the tax may be higher in a country where its nominal rate is lower. The double taxation of dividends is another crucial difference across countries. In the "classical system" that prevails in the United States, dividends are taxed by the corporate income tax (as redistributed profits) and then by the personal income tax (as income of shareholders). Most other countries have taken steps to cancel this double taxation.

Property taxes are very diverse. They include among others wealth taxes, taxes on bequests, taxes on gifts *inter vivos*, taxes on capital gains, and taxes on land and housing. Once again, there are strong variations across countries. Perhaps surprisingly, the United Kingdom and the United States tax property more heavily than France or Germany.

To conclude this short survey of current tax systems, we should add that taxation varies even more across less developed countries. The tax take is much smaller there than in developed countries, at around 20 percent of GDP. In transition economies, the tax take has been moving toward OECD levels.[7] Less developed countries lack an efficient tax administration, which orients their tax revenue toward taxes that are easier to collect. Thus indirect taxes constitute two-thirds of their resources, with custom duties bringing in one-third of tax revenue.[8] The personal income tax brings a much smaller share of tax revenue than in OECD countries, and taxes on capital are almost nonexistent, given the difficulty to properly assess the taxable basis of these taxes.

Overview of the Book

In his classic book, Musgrave (1959) distinguished the three main functions of government:

• allocation, to provide public goods and remedy market failures
• redistribution
• stabilization, as pertains to macroeconomic interventions (including automatic stabilizers).

We will set aside here a study of stabilization, which can be found in any good macroeconomic textbook. We will focus on the first two functions.

In the Arrow-Debreu model the second fundamental welfare theorem shows that under some assumptions, every Pareto optimum can be decentralized as a competitive equilibrium of a private property economy where resources have been redistributed through lump-sum transfers.[9] When this theorem applies, the government can choose its preferred Pareto optimum, proceed to the right lump-sum transfers, and let the competitive equilibrium work its magic without any other kind of intervention.

In practice, we observe several phenomena that lead to market failures (e.g., see Salanié 2000). First come public goods: these are by definition the nonrival goods, which one agent can consume without reducing the consumption of other agents. Then the second theorem does not apply any more (technically, consumptions do not add

---

7. Russia is a notable exception: taxes there collect only half of their theoretical revenue, and the tax take is only about 10 percent of GDP.
8. By contrast, tariffs today bring less than 1 percent of tax revenue in OECD countries, as compared to about 15 percent in the early twentieth century.
9. Recall that the defining property of lump-sum transfers is that they only depend on the identity of agents, and not on their economic transactions.

across agents). The optimal production level for the public good cannot be attained without an intervention of government. Moreover these public goods must be financed, which raises the classical *free-rider* problem.

The presence of external effects also implies that the market cannot reach an optimum on its own; corrective taxes are one way to remedy this market failure (as with ecotaxes designed to reduce pollution).

Adam Smith already considered that the prince must provide three categories of public goods to his subjects: defense, justice, and public works, plus a private good subject to externalities: primary education.[10] Even the most liberal thinkers[11] (the so-called libertarians, whose viewpoint is well expressed by Nozick 1974) accept a "minimal state" that provides defense and justice; free-rider problems indeed make it impossible to leave them to the private sector.

Even in the (hypothetical) absence of these market failures, lump-sum transfers are very unlikely to be a practical proposition. Computing the optimal lump-sum transfers requires government to have an extraordinarily detailed information on the characteristics of the economy. One may mention two attempts in history to implement (obviously nonoptimal) lump-sum transfers. The first one is capitation, which levied on each head of household a tax that only depended on its social status (but sometimes also on wealth, which violated the lump-sum character of the tax). The second one is more recent, with the *poll tax* proposed in the United Kingdom by Margaret Thatcher. This aimed at replacing a property tax on housing that depended on the estimated value of property; the poll tax would only have varied across areas. Since taxpayers can still move between communities, once again it was not a strictly lump-sum tax. In any case, the poll tax project led to violent demonstrations in the spring of 1990; it was abandoned and contributed heavily to the later fall of Mrs. Thatcher.

Thus, in order to finance public goods (or publicly provided private goods such as education and health) as well as in order to redistribute, the government must use non–lump-sum transfers, which by definition depend on the decisions of private agents. As a consequence each taxpayer may reduce his tax bill by changing his

---

10. On the other hand, he thought that higher education must be left to the private sector, with teachers paid on a performance basis (*horresco referens*).

11. I use here the word "liberal" in its classical, non-US sense.

behavior, and he will try to do so as long as the game is worth the candle. It is obviously crucial to be able to evaluate the importance of these incentive effects of taxes. Moreover taxes create a bias among the marginal rates of substitution of various agents, which induces social welfare losses. Once again, a good economist should be able to quantify these losses: available studies show that they may amount to between 10 percent and 50 percent of tax revenue, which is considerable. These two themes constitute the essence of the first part of the book, which deals with positive economics.

The second part of this book adopts a resolutely normative stance. It is clear by now that real-world taxes, which are not lump-sum, reduce the inefficiency of the economy. How then is the governement to choose an optimal tax system? We will see how this question can be modeled, and what partial answers can be given.

These two parts are mostly theoretical, even though we try to introduce empirical and institutional elements as needed. However, economic policy questions rarely reduce to simple models. To show how these questions can be studied in the light of the results obtained in the first two parts, we examine in a third and last part three current tax policy debates: low-income support, the consumption tax, and environmental taxation.

A warning is in order here. The positive study of taxation does not reduce to the elements given in the first part of this book. One may want to go beyond the study of the effects of taxation on economic decisions of private agents and to model the way a community decides on its tax system. This question concerns the political economy of taxation, which has developed a lot in the last twenty years. To keep this book from expanding beyond a reasonable length, this aspect will not be studied here. The reader will find references on the *public choice* approach in Hettich-Winer (1997). The book by Persson-Tabellini (2000) gathers different perspectives to give a very complete survey of modern political economy; its chapters 6 and 12 are particularly oriented toward taxation issues.

Reading this book requires the knowledge of microeconomics at the advanced undergraduate level. An appendix presents the main results that are used in the text. Moreover the study of optimal taxation relies on the theory of optimal control. Since this is often not taught in economics curricula, we give the necessary notions in another appendix.

References

Hettich, W., and S. Winer. 1997. The political economy of taxation, ch. 22 of *Perspectives on Public Choice*, D. Mueller, ed., Cambridge University Press.

Musgrave, R. 1959. *The Theory of Public Finance*. McGraw Hill.

Nozick, R. 1974. *Anarchy, State and Utopia*. Basic Books.

OECD. 1999. *Revenue Statistics 1965–1998*. OECD, Paris.

Persson, T., and G. Tabellini. 2000. *Political Economics*. MIT Press.

Salanié, B. 2000. *The Microeconomics of Market Failures*. MIT Press.

Steinmo, S. 1993. *Taxation and Democracy*. Yale University Press.

I

The Effects of Taxation

The first part of this book is dedicated to the study of the economic effects of taxation. Assume, for instance, that government decides to raise the VAT on sales of cars. The political effects of such a measure are predictable: car producers will complain that their sales will decrease, and car buyers will fear a rise in the price of cars. But who does really bear the price of such a rise in VAT, and in what proportions? Chapter 1 studies this question, first in a partial equilibrium, then in a general equilibrium framework.

Another often debated question is that of the disincentive effects of taxation, as in the negative effect of the income tax on labor supply. Any tax measure will prompt agents to change their behavior so as to pay less taxes. We examine in chapter 2 the mechanisms that change the main behaviors. We show there how the social losses induced by taxation can be evaluated. It is very important to understand both of these points well before moving to the discusssion of optimal taxation in the second part of this book.

1   Tax Incidence

In the economic world an economic action, an institution, a law, do not generate only one effect but a whole series of effects. Only the first effect is obvious. It is manifested simultaneously with its cause: it can be seen. The others only unroll in succession. *They cannot be seen*: we are lucky if we can predict them.

Here is the whole difference between a good and a bad economist: the latter only minds the *visible* effect, while the former accounts for both the effect that *can be seen* and those that must be predicted—Frédéric Bastiat, 1850

Who pays taxes? A first answer consists in accepting that it is the (legal) person who signs the check.[12] Then it must be that in the many countries where the income tax is paid as is it is earned (so that the employer sends a check to the tax authorities), firms pay the personal income tax; this clearly is absurd. Assume in this example that the income tax increases; then firms may try to maintain constant labor costs by reducing net wages dollar per dollar. But then some workers will withdraw from the labor market. To keep them on the market, firms must raise net wages back up, which pushes labor costs up. In equilibrium the net wage will be lower than before the tax increase and the cost of labor will be higher: the burden of the tax increase will be shared between firms and workers.

This first, informal argument only holds in partial equilibrium, when the effects of the tax increase on other markets are neglected; in a general equilibrium analysis, one would have to take into account the induced changes in the prices of goods.[13]

---

12. This is often called the *flypaper theory* of incidence: taxes stick where they first come.
13. This whole chapter adopts the comparative statics method by comparing equilibria before and after a tax change; we economists unfortunately do not know enough that we can reasonably model the very complex issues of the dynamic transition from one equilibrium to the other.

The theory of tax incidence aims at characterizing the effect on economic equilibrium of a change in taxes. The changes in prices are a target variable of the theory; ideally (if it were easy to evaluate changes in utilities) the theory should also compare the utilities of all agents before and after the tax change, so as to give a satisfactory answer to this seemingly simple question: How is the tax burden shared among the economic agents?

This chapter studies the real incidence of taxes both in partial equilibrium and in general equilibrium. This issue emerged in partial equilibrium as early as the seventeenth century.[14] Both Smith and Ricardo discussed tax incidence in detail, but their whole analysis was based on supply, since they lacked an adequate concept of demand.[15] The modern analysis of partial equilibium incidence arrived with the marginalists; however, general equilibrium effects then were relegated backstage. The theory of tax incidence in general equilibrium only emerged with Harberger (1962), which we study in detail later in this chapter.

1.1   Partial Equilibrium

1.1.1   The Effect of Payroll Taxes

For a start, let us look at the effect of payroll taxes on the labor market. In most countries, Social Security (which finances pensions in the United States, but also unemployment and health benefits elsewhere) is financed in large part from payroll taxes based on wages. Some of these taxes are "paid" by employers and some by workers. This legal distinction is artificial: the only concepts of wages that matter are that paid by the employer (the gross wage) and that received by the employee (the net wage). Whether the employer "pays" 80 percent or 50 percent or 20 percent of payroll taxes is immaterial to the equilibrium gross and net wages and to the determination of employment.

First consider the labor market for a category of workers sufficiently skilled that the market clears in the long run. Without payroll

---

14. The first, rather crude general equilibrium model is due to the physiocrats in the second half of the eighteenth century.

15. Smith thought, for instance, that since workers are paid a subsistence wage, they cannot bear any of the tax burden: a tax on wages or basic consumption goods must be shifted onto the other social classes. Ricardo was the first to distinguish short-term and long-term incidence, using the Malthusian theory of labor supply adjustments.

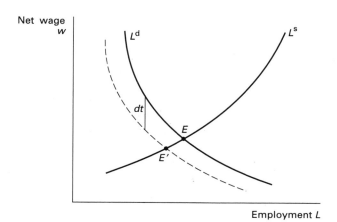

Figure 1.1
Incidence of payroll taxes on skilled labor

taxes, equilibrium is figured by point E on figure 1.1, which is the usual supply and demand graph in the (L, w) plane. Let us now introduce proportional payroll taxes at an infinitesimal rate dt, so that with net wage w, the gross wage now is $w(1 + dt)$. For a fixed net wage, labor demand decreases so that the new equilibrium lies at point E', where both net wage and employment are lower than in E while the gross wage is higher. Thus the burden of payroll taxes is borne both by employers (profits decrease since the cost of labor increases) and by workers (since their net wage decreases). Once again, this analysis does not depend at all on who in practice pays the taxes: it does not matter whether it is the employers, the workers, or any combination of the two.

The precise impact of payroll taxes obviously depends on the elasticities of the demand and supply curves, which are given (in absolute value) by

$$\varepsilon_D = -\frac{wL^{d'}}{L} \quad \text{and} \quad \varepsilon_S = \frac{wL^{s'}}{L}$$

After a payroll tax at rate t is introduced the labor market equilibrium is given by

$$L^d(w(1 + t)) = L^s(w)$$

To simplify, let us start from a situation where $t = 0$; differentiation then gives

$$L^{d'}(dw + wdt) = L^{s'}dw$$

so that

$$\frac{\partial \log w}{\partial t} = -\frac{\varepsilon_D}{\varepsilon_S + \varepsilon_D} \in \ ]-1, 0[$$

Thus the net wage decreases all the more that demand is more elastic relative to supply. Similar calculations show that if we denote the gross wage $W = w(1 + t)$, then

$$\frac{\partial \log W}{\partial t} = \frac{\varepsilon_S}{\varepsilon_S + \varepsilon_D} \in \ ]0, 1[$$

Symmetrically the gross wage increases all the more that demand is less elastic relative to supply. Finally, the fall in employment is given by

$$-\frac{\partial \log L}{\partial L} = \varepsilon_S \frac{\partial \log w}{\partial t} = \frac{\varepsilon_S \varepsilon_D}{\varepsilon_S + \varepsilon_D}$$

since both points E and E' lie on the labor supply curve. Since $ab/(a + b) = 1/(1/a + 1/b)$, the fall in employment is all the larger that demand and supply are more elastic.

Economists usually agree that at least for the male core of the labor market, labor supply is much less elastic than labor demand ($\varepsilon_S \ll \varepsilon_D$). Then the preceding formulas show that the cost of labor hardly changes: workers bear the full burden of payroll taxes.[16] This theoretical analysis is also confirmed in empirical studies. Moreover employment moves very little since labor supply is very inelastic.

Obviously the assumption that the labor market clears may not be adequate for all skill levels. Take, for instance, a country with a minimum wage. Then let us look at the lowest skill levels (those that are affected by the existence of the minimum wage). Assume that the minimum wage is set above the market-clearing wage, as in figure 1.2. Then employment is determined by demand in E, and there is unemployment, as measured by the distance EF. If payroll taxes increase, the net wage stays equal to the minimum wage since it cannot fall further, and the cost of labor increases as the payroll taxes do. Employment is set by labor demand with a higher cost of labor in E' and unemployment increases by the distance $E'E$. This type of

---

16. Whether the taxes are "paid" by employers or by workers.

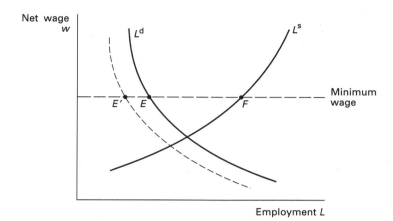

Figure 1.2
Incidence of payroll taxes on unskilled labor

analysis is why many economists in continental Europe have argued for lowering payroll taxes on the low-skilled.

1.1.2   The General Analysis of Partial Equilibrium

The Competitive Case
The analysis of the incidence of the tax on a good (e.g., VAT on cars) is formally identical to that of the impact of payroll taxes on the labor market: identify the net wage to the producer price, the gross wage to the consumer price, and let the demand and supply curves now be drawn for the good under consideration. It follows that the creation (or the increase) of a VAT on cars

• increases the consumer price all the more that the demand for cars is less elastic than the supply of cars

• reduces the producer price all the more that the supply of cars is less elastic than the demand for cars

• reduces the number of cars sold in equilibrium all the more that demand and supply are more elastic.

There are two interesting special cases:

• if demand is much more elastic than supply ($\varepsilon_D \gg \varepsilon_S$), VAT hardly moves the consumer price: the producers bear the whole burden of the tax

• in the polar case where supply is much more elastic than demand ($\varepsilon_S \gg \varepsilon_D$), VAT is entirely shifted to the consumer, who bears the whole tax burden. This is called forward tax shifting.[17]

The rule to remember is that the more inelastic side of the market bears the greater part of the tax burden.

As for the minimum wage on labor markets, one should also consider cases where regulation imposes price floors or price ceilings. For instance, many cities have laws that fix price ceilings for rents. Then an increase in taxes on rents cannot raise rents; in the long run when supply of apartments is elastic, it must result in an increase of demand rationing on the market.

The Monopoly Case

So far we looked at markets where all parties act in a perfectly competitive manner. When producers have some market power, the results may be rather different, as Cournot noticed as early as 1838. For a monopoly, for instance, profit maximization with a demand function D and a cost function C is given by

$$\max_{p}(pD(p) - C(D(p)))$$

which leads to the usual Lerner formula:

$$p = \frac{C'(D(p))}{1 - (1/\varepsilon_D(p))}$$

where $\varepsilon_D(p) = -pD'(p)/D(p)$ is demand elasticity, assumed to be larger than one.

If we introduce a proportional tax at rate t, the identity of the side who "pays" the tax again does not matter. Let p be the consumer price; then the monopoly maximizes over p the profit

$$\frac{p}{1+t}D(p) - C(D(p))$$

which yields the new formula

$$\frac{p}{1+t} = \frac{C'(D(p))}{1 - (1/\varepsilon_D(p))}$$

---

17. *Backward tax shifting* refers to the case where input prices decrease to absorb at least part of the tax burden; partial equilibrium analysis by definition excludes this possibility.

In general, this is a complex equation in p, so it is hard to compute the effect of the tax. In particular, it is quite possible that the consumer price increases by *more* than the amount of the tax,[18] which cannot happen on a competitive market.

Assume, for simplicity, that marginal costs are constant in c; then the competitive supply is infinitely elastic, and one would expect the tax to shift fully onto consumers. It is indeed the case when demand has constant elasticity, since then the right-hand sides of both Lerner formulas coincide.[19] On the other hand, if demand is linear as in $D(p) = d - p$, then the demand elasticity is

$$\varepsilon_D(p) = \frac{p}{d - p}$$

One gets by substituting in Lerner's formula

$$p = \frac{1}{2}(d + c(1 + t))$$

so that the semi-elasticity of price to an infinitesimal tax is

$$\frac{\partial \log p}{\partial t} = \frac{c}{d + c}$$

and both sides of the market bear some of the burden of the tax.

One more *curiosum* should be noted. In the competitive case, collecting a given amount of money as a *specific* tax (in absolute value) or an *ad valorem* tax (proportional to the value of production) changes neither allocations nor incidence. But the choice is no longer irrelevant with a monopoly. First consider the competitive case; let S be the competitive supply function. Then an *ad valorem* tax t yields a producer price p given by

$$D(p(1 + t)) = S(p)$$

and collects $tpS(p)$ for the government. If we replace this tax with a specific tax $\tau = tp$, the new producer price p' is given by

---

18. The reader can check this by assuming constant marginal tax and a demand elasticity that decreases in price.

19. Note that even then, the monoploy bears some part of the tax since that lowers its profits.

$$D(p' + tp) = S(p')$$

and $p' = p$ is an obvious solution. Since the specific tax collects $\tau S(p') = tpS(p)$, neither the producer price nor the government's tax revenue change.

Now consider a monopoly with inverse demand function $P(q)$ and a cost function C. In the no-taxation case, the monopoly's optimum is given by

$$MR(q) = C'(q)$$

where $MR(q) = P(q) + qP'(q)$ is the marginal revenue. If the monopoly pays an *ad valorem* tax at rate t, then marginal revenue decreases by $tMR(q)$, while a specific tax τ of course reduces marginal revenue by τ. Fix a quantity q. Assume that the tax parameters t and τ have been chosen so as to collect the same amount at production level q. Then $tqP(q) = \tau q$ or $\tau = tP(q)$, which implies $\tau > tMR(q)$ since marginal revenue is smaller than price. At given production and tax revenue, the specific tax thus reduces marginal revenue more than the *ad valorem* tax. It follows from figure 1.3 that the quantity produced under a specific tax is lower than under an *ad valorem* tax. For a given tax revenue, an *ad valorem* reduced production less, which is good for social welfare since the monopoly already produces too little. Thus *ad valorem* taxes like VAT should be preferred to specific taxes such as some excises.

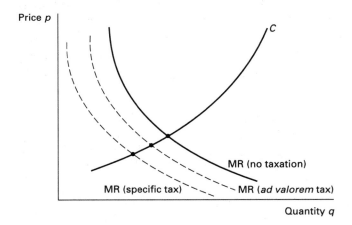

Figure 1.3
Taxation of a monopoly

1.2   General Equilibrium

When we studied the effect of payroll taxes on the labor market, we neglected their effects on the general price level (which feedbacks into labor demand through the production price and into labor supply through the consumer price), but also the possibility of substituting capital for labor (since the cost of capital was exogenous). Our analysis of VAT implicitly set aside the impact of an increase in VAT on incomes and therefore on demand for the good, and also its impact on wages and thus on supply. Moreover we let the money collected sink into a black hole, while in real life it is used to finance public goods or to pay various forms of income. Taking these various effects into account brings us into the world of general equilibrium theory. The founding model in the general equilibrium theory of tax incidence is that of Harberger (1962).

We consider here an economy that produces two goods X and Y from two inputs: labor L and capital K. The technologies have constant returns to scale. The total supply of either input is fixed,[20] but each factor is perfectly mobile across the two sectors. The two goods are consumed by workers, capitalists, and government. To simplify the analysis, we assume that the demand functions for goods only depend on relative prices and on the gross domestic product of the economy. Thus we neglect the impact on demands of the distribution of income. This could be "justified" by assuming that all agents have identical, homothetic preferences,[21] which is of course a bit counterfactual. More realistic analyses take income distribution into account; we will here stick to the assumption of identical homothetic preferences, which makes life much easier.

1.2.1   The No-Taxation Economy

First assume all taxes away. Let $C_X(r, w, X)$ and $C_Y(r, w, Y)$ denote the cost functions in both sectors, where r and w are the prices of capital

---

20. Thus we neglect the influence of prices on the supplies of production factors in the economy. Letting real wages influence labor supply would hardly affect the analysis. Endogenizing the supply of capital is more difficult; we will describe the dynamics of capital accumulation in chapter 6.

21. A preference preorder is homothetic if and only if for all x and y and all positive real numbers λ, $x \sim y$ implies $\lambda x \sim \lambda y$. It is easily seen that with such preferences the demand for each good is proportional to income (the Engel curves are lines that go through the origin). In an economy in which all agents have identical homothetic preferences, an income transfer from one agent to another leaves total demand functions unchanged.

and labor. As returns are constant, both cost functions are proportional to production levels:

$$\begin{cases} C_X(r,w,X) = c_X(r,w)X \\ C_Y(r,w,Y) = c_Y(r,w)Y \end{cases}$$

and the prices of the goods are given by[22]

$$\begin{cases} p_X = c_X(r,w) \\ p_Y = c_Y(r,w) \end{cases}$$

Factor demands are the derivatives of cost functions with respect to factor prices; thus the demand for labor in sector X is

$$L_X = c_{Xw}(r,w)X$$

where c_{Xw} is the derivative of c_X in w.

Equilibrium on factor markets follows:

$$\begin{cases} c_{Xw}(r,w)X + c_{Yw}(r,w)Y = \bar{L} \\ c_{Xr}(r,w)X + c_{Yr}(r,w)Y = \bar{K} \end{cases}$$

where $\bar{K}$ and $\bar{L}$ are the exogenous factor supplies.

Finally, let $X(p_X, p_Y, R)$ and $Y(p_X, p_Y, R)$ denote the Marshallian demand functions; equilibrium on markets for goods is

$$\begin{cases} X(p_X, p_Y, R) = X \\ Y(p_X, p_Y, R) = Y \end{cases}$$

where R is total income, which also equals both GDP ($p_X X + p_Y Y$) and total factor incomes ($w\bar{L} + r\bar{K}$).

The four equilibrium conditions and the two price equations give us six equations, and there are six unknowns: p_X, p_Y, r, w, X, and Y. As usual, one equation is redundant: Walras's law implies that one need only consider equilibrium in three of the four markets. Thus only relative prices can be determined, as is always the case in general equilibrium markets without money.

1.2.2 Introducing Taxes

Let us now introduce, under the guise of redistributive *ad valorem* taxes,

• *ad valorem* taxes on factor prices in both sectors: t_{KX}, t_{KY}, t_{LX}, and t_{LY}
• *ad valorem* taxes on goods: t_X and t_Y.

---

22. This is just the factor price frontier, which states that profits per unit of production are zero.

The taxes on goods could represent VAT, an excise like a gasoline tax or a tax on tobacco, or a *sales tax* as in the United States. Such taxes are usually levied at different rates on different goods. The taxes on labor could be social contributions (a payroll tax) and could be reduced in some sectors for stimulation purposes. The taxes on capital classically resemble the corporate income tax, which does not touch some sectors such as agriculture or housing, but one could also think of other capital taxes.

Let us denote p_X, p_Y the producer prices, and r and w the net-of-tax factor prices. The (producer) price equations then become

$$\begin{cases} p_X = c_X(r(1 + t_{KX}), w(1 + t_{LX})) \\ p_Y = c_Y(r(1 + t_{KY}), w(1 + t_{LY})) \end{cases}$$

The equilibrium conditions on factor markets now are

$$\begin{cases} c_{Xw}(r(1 + t_{KX}), w(1 + t_{LX}))X + c_{Yw}(r(1 + t_{KY}), w(1 + t_{LY}))Y = \bar{L} \\ c_{Xr}(r(1 + t_{KX}), w(1 + t_{LX}))X + c_{Yr}(r(1 + t_{KY}), w(1 + t_{LY}))Y = \bar{K} \end{cases}$$

while equilibrium on goods markets can be written

$$\begin{cases} X(p_X(1 + t_X), p_Y(1 + t_Y), R) = X \\ Y(p_X(1 + t_X), p_Y(1 + t_Y), R) = Y \end{cases}$$

Here R is the new value of total income; it still equals GDP but now includes the tax revenue. The tax revenue T is

$$p_X(1 + t_X)X + p_Y(1 + t_Y)Y = w\bar{L} + r\bar{K} + T$$

where

$$T = rt_{KX}K_X + rt_{KY}K_Y + wt_{LX}L_X + wt_{LY}L_Y + p_X t_X X + p_Y t_Y Y$$

This system of equations in general does not have a closed-form solution. On the other hand, it can be solved numerically so as to study the changes in prices and quantities and the incidence of one of the taxes above in general equilibrium. This approach underlies the *computable general equilibrium*, or CGE models developed after Shoven-Whalley (1972).[23] One can also linearize the system around the existing tax system so as to study infinitesimal changes in taxes, as in Ballentine-Eris (1975). This leads to complex calculations and to conclusions that are hard to interpret, so most of the literature

23. Shoven-Whalley (1984) presents a survey of CGE models.

focused on the effect of introducing infinitesimal taxes in a world originally without taxes. The obvious problem with this approach is that it can only be illustrative. Given the level of taxes in actual economies, nonlinearities can hardly be neglected. Thus any study that aims at realism must use computer simulations.

1.2.3   General Remarks

As described above, the equilibrium conditions call for three remarks. First note that in equilibrium, factors must be paid the same net-of-tax rate in both sectors, since they are perfectly mobile. While this sounds rather obvious, it has important consequences: if, for instance, capital taxation increases in sector X, then the net return of capital must decrease in the whole economy, and not only for capital used in sector X. Otherwise, capitalists would withdraw all of their money from sector X to invest it in sector Y. This would reduce the return of capital in sector Y and increase it in sector X until both are equal again.

This is very much analogous to what happens in the transportation sector. Assume that two cities A and B are only connected by two roads R_1 and R_2. If the government creates a toll on road R_1, in the very short run only motorists who take that road will bear the burden. But soon some of them will turn to the other road. Thus they will congest road R_2 and reduce congestion on road R_1. This equilibrating process will last until the perceived cost of congestion on road R_2 equals the sum of the toll and the cost of congestion on road R_1. In equilibrium, the cost of the toll on R_1 is balanced by the higher cost of congestion on road R_2.

A second remark is that some combinations of taxes are perfectly equivalent. Start from an economy without taxes, and consider raising taxes on both factors at equal rates in sector X: $t_{KX} = t_{LX} = t$. Since c_X and c_Y are homogeneous of degree one in r and w, so that their derivatives are homogeneous of degree zero, the resulting system of equations is

$$
\begin{cases}
p_X & = (1+t)c_X(r,w) \\
p_Y & = c_Y(r,w) \\
c_{Xw}(r,w)X + c_{Yw}(r,w)Y = \bar{L} \\
c_{Xr}(r,w)X + c_{Yr}(r,w)Y & = \bar{K} \\
X(p_X, p_Y, p_X X + p_Y Y) & = X \\
Y(p_X, p_Y, p_X X + p_Y Y) & = Y
\end{cases}
$$

Now abolish these two taxes and replace them with a tax on good X at the same rate t; the new equilibrium system is

$$\begin{cases} p'_X & = c_X(r', w') \\ p'_Y & = c_Y(r', w') \\ c_{Xw}(r', w')X' + c_{Yw}(r', w')Y' & = \bar{L} \\ c_{Xr}(r', w')X' + c_{Yr}(r', w')Y' & = \bar{K} \\ X(p'_X(1+t), p'_Y, p'_X(1+t)X' + p'_Y Y') = X' \\ Y(p'_X(1+t), p'_Y, p'_X(1+t)X' + p'_Y Y') = Y' \end{cases}$$

It is easily seen that the solution of this system is identical to that of the preceding system, substituting only p_X with $p'_X(1+t)$. Thus both tax systems are perfectly equivalent: taxing both inputs at the same rate in one sector is equivalent to taxing the output of that sector at the same rate. It also follows that a proportional and uniform income tax (which would apply the same tax rate to every input in every sector) is equivalent to a uniform VAT on all goods.

The last remark points out a consequence of the assumed inelasticity of total factor supply: a uniform tax on all uses of a factor (e.g., $t_{LX} = t_{LY}$) is entirely borne by that factor. As partial equilibrium incidence theory suggested, it reduces its net-of-tax price one for one and leaves all quantities and after-tax prices unchanged. This is easily seen by rewriting the system of equations as above.

1.2.4   Infinitesimal Analysis

Given the remarks above, we only need to analyze the effects of taxes that are specific to one sector. Harberger's paper studied the incidence of taxing capital in one sector. Since VAT is usually levied at different rates across goods, we will also look at the effect of raising VAT on one of the two goods. We therefore start from an economy without taxes and introduce

- a tax at infinitesimal rate dt_{KX} on the use capital in sector X
- a tax at infinitesimal rate dt_X on the produce of sector X.

The resulting changes in utilities come from both factor incomes and the changes in relative prices. The latter effect is by construction the same for both workers and capitalists, since they have identical preferences. Thus one can study incidence by focusing on factor incomes $w\bar{L}$ and $r\bar{K}$, as we will now do.

The calculations are somewhat tedious,[24] but this is the price to pay to account properly for the complex mechanisms involved in the reequilibration of both factor and goods markets. As in most papers in this literature, we will use *hat calculus*, meaning we will look at variations in growth rates (logarithmic derivatives) as in

$$\hat{z} = \frac{dz}{z}$$

The equilibrium conditions on good markets give $dK_X + dK_Y = dL_X + dL_Y = 0$, whence

$$\begin{cases} K_X \hat{K}_X + K_Y \hat{K}_Y = 0 \\ L_X \hat{L}_X + L_Y \hat{L}_Y = 0 \end{cases}$$

Let us denote $\lambda_{KX} = K_X/\bar{K}$ as the share of sector X in capital use, and similarly denote λ_{KY}, λ_{LX}, and λ_{LY} (so that indeed $\lambda_{KX} + \lambda_{KY} = \lambda_{LX} + \lambda_{LY} = 1$). Then we have

$$\begin{cases} \hat{K}_Y = -\dfrac{\lambda_{KX}}{\lambda_{KY}} \hat{K}_X \\ \hat{L}_Y = -\dfrac{\lambda_{LX}}{\lambda_{LY}} \hat{L}_X \end{cases}$$

Now denote σ_X and σ_Y the elasticities of substitution in production in both sectors. Taking into account the taxation of capital in sector X, we get from the definition of these elasticities

$$\begin{cases} \hat{K}_X - \hat{L}_X = -\sigma_X(\hat{r} - \hat{w} + dt_{KX}) \\ \hat{K}_Y - \hat{L}_Y = -\sigma_Y(\hat{r} - \hat{w}) \end{cases}$$

By substituting the expressions of $\hat{K}_Y$ and $\hat{L}_Y$ found above and solving the resulting two-equation system in $(\hat{K}_X, \hat{L}_X)$, we find, for instance, that

$$\lambda^* \hat{K}_X = (\sigma_X \lambda_{LX} + \sigma_Y \lambda_{LY}) \lambda_{KY} (\hat{w} - \hat{r}) - \sigma_X \lambda_{KY} \lambda_{LX} \, dt_{KX} \qquad (K_X)$$

where we write $\lambda^* = \lambda_{LX} - \lambda_{KX} = \lambda_{KY} - \lambda_{LY}$. Note that λ^* is positive if and only if sector X is less capital intensive than sector Y. Therefore the relative capital intensities of the two sectors will play a crucial role in our results. In order to go further, we need to compute the variation of the relative factor price $(\hat{w} - \hat{r})$ and thus to find other equations. This can be done by expressing $(\hat{X} - \hat{Y})$ in two ways:

---

24. Hurried readers can go directly to the analysis of the net effects.

starting from the production functions or from the demand functions for goods.

Just as in growth accounting, the relative variation of the production of a good is a weighted average of the relative variations of the factors used in its production, where the weights are the factor shares. If we denote $s_{KX} = rK_X/p_X X$ as the share of K_X in the income generated by X and similarly denote s_{KY}, s_{LX}, and s_{LY} (with $s_{KX} + s_{LX} = s_{KY} + s_{LY} = 1$), we have

$$\begin{cases} \hat{X} = s_{LX}\hat{L}_X + s_{KX}\hat{K}_X \\ \hat{Y} = s_{LY}\hat{L}_Y + s_{KY}\hat{K}_Y \end{cases}$$

Using the fact that the sum of the factor shares is one in each sector, this gives

$$\begin{cases} \hat{X} = \hat{K}_X + s_{LX}(\hat{L}_X - \hat{K}_X) \\ \hat{Y} = \hat{K}_Y + s_{LY}(\hat{L}_Y - \hat{K}_Y) \end{cases}$$

We already know how to write $\hat{K}_Y$ as a function of $\hat{K}_X$; we also know how to write the relative variations of factor demands as a function of the relative variations in their costs. Subtracting one equation from the other, we get after some calculations

$$\hat{X} - \hat{Y} = \frac{\hat{K}_X}{\lambda_{KY}} + (s_{LX}\sigma_X - s_{LY}\sigma_Y)(\hat{r} - \hat{w}) + s_{LX}\sigma_X \, dt_{KX}$$

Using equation (K_X) and rearranging, we finally get

$$\lambda^*(\hat{X} - \hat{Y}) = (\sigma_X a_X + \sigma_Y a_Y)(\hat{w} - \hat{r}) - \sigma_X a_X \, dt_{KX} \qquad (1)$$

where we introduced two new positive parameters

$$\begin{cases} a_X = s_{KX}\lambda_{LX} + s_{LX}\lambda_{KX} \\ a_Y = s_{KY}\lambda_{LY} + s_{LY}\lambda_{KY} \end{cases}$$

The second way to write $(\hat{X} - \hat{Y})$ consists in using the demand functions for the goods. Once more, assume that preferences are identical and homothetic. Then demands for X and Y are proportional to income, with proportions that are identical across agents:

$$\begin{cases} X_i(p_X, p_Y, R_i) = R_i x\left(\dfrac{p_X}{p_Y}\right) \\ Y_i(p_X, p_Y, R_i) = R_i y\left(\dfrac{p_X}{p_Y}\right) \end{cases}$$

and the variation in relative demand is unchanged by income effects when R varies since

$$\frac{X}{Y} = \frac{\sum_i X_i(p_X, p_Y, R_i)}{\sum_i Y_i(p_X, p_Y, R_i)} = \frac{x(p_X/p_Y)}{y(p_X/p_Y)}$$

Given this assumption on preferences, the relative change in demands therefore only depends on the relative change in aftertax prices (which includes dt_X):

$$\hat{X} - \hat{Y} = -\varepsilon_D(\hat{p}_X + dt_X - \hat{p}_Y) \tag{2}$$

where ε_D is the difference between the price elasticities of the demands for X and Y, or

$$\varepsilon_D = -\frac{\partial \log(X/Y)}{\partial \log(p_X/p_Y)}$$

This equation introduces a new unknown, with the relative change in prices. But, by differentiating the price equations $p_X = c_X(r(1 + t_{KX}), w)$ and $p_Y = c_Y(r, w)$, we can compute

$$\hat{p}_X = s_{KX}(\hat{r} + dt_{KX}) + s_{LX}\hat{w}$$

and

$$\hat{p}_Y = s_{KY}\hat{r} + s_{LY}\hat{w}$$

whence by subtracting

$$\hat{p}_X - \hat{p}_Y = s^*(\hat{w} - \hat{r}) + s_{KX}\, dt_{KX} \tag{3}$$

where $s^* = s_{LX} - s_{LY}$ is positive if and only if the income share of labor is larger in sector X than in sector Y. Now note that

$$s^* = s_{LX}s_{KY} - s_{LY}s_{KX}$$

and

$$\lambda^* = \lambda_{LX}\lambda_{KY} - \lambda_{LY}\lambda_{KX}$$

By expanding the factors, we can check that

$$s^* = \frac{wr\overline{LK}}{p_X p_Y XY}\lambda^*$$

so that the product $s^*\lambda^* > 0$ always. Thus the parameter s^* has the same interpretation as λ^*: it is positive if and only if X is less capital intensive than Y.

Substituting equation (3) in equation (2), we finally get

$$\hat{X} - \hat{Y} = -\varepsilon_D(s^*(\hat{w} - \hat{r}) + s_{KX}\, dt_{KX} + dt_X) \tag{4}$$

Combining (1) and (4) then gives $(\hat{w} - \hat{r})$; the final equation is

$$D(\hat{w} - \hat{r}) = (\sigma_X a_X - \varepsilon_D \lambda^* s_{KX})\, dt_{KX} - \varepsilon_D \lambda^*\, dt_X$$

where $D = \sigma_X a_X + \sigma_Y a_Y + \varepsilon_D \lambda^* s^*$ is always positive, since $\lambda^* s^* > 0$. The changes in relative prices and relative demands can then easily be computed by using the equations obtained above. We will now discuss the main results. Remember that only relative prices are determined in equilibrium. Thus, if $\hat{w} - \hat{r} > 0$, it just means that labor income increases more (or decreases less) than capital income.

First a general remark: there are two categories of effects. One acts through the relative demands for goods and is called the volume effect. The second acts through the relative factor demand; it is called the factor substitution effect. These categories are easy to identify: volume effects depend on ε_D, while factor substitution effects depend on σ_X and σ_Y. Thus the taxation of capital within X leads to an increased use of labor for a given production level (it is the factor substitution effect) but also to a change in the relative prices of X and Y, which depends on the relative capital intensity of both sectors and which in turn affects the demands for goods (it is the volume effect) and thus the factor demands again.

The Effects of Taxing Capital

In this paragraph we assume $dt_X = 0$, and we examine the impact of $dt_{KX} > 0$. Looking at the equation for $(\hat{w} - \hat{r})$ shows two things:

- if X is more capital intensive than Y, then $\lambda^* < 0$, and therefore $\hat{w} - \hat{r} > 0$
- such is also the case if $\varepsilon_D = 0$.

In the former case, the factor substitution effect (which always yields a relative decline in capital income) is seconded by the volume effect: the increased cost of capital in sector X tends to increase the relative price of X, and thus to decrease the demand for the factor in which X is the more intensive sector, which happens to be capital. This reduces the relative price of capital. In the latter case, there is no volume effect. The factor substitution effect directly reduces the relative income of capital.

Contrary to what might be thought a priori, it is quite possible that taxing capital in X increases its relative income. Such is the case if X is more labor intensive and has a production function with almost complementary factors (σ_X then is close to 0). Then taxing capital also impacts labor; the factor substitution effect is zero and the volume effect tends to increase r/w. It can indeed be proved that if X is more labor intensive, then the relative price of X increases and its relative demand decreases. This apparently counterintuitive result is entirely due to substitution effects in the demands for goods.

What can we say about tax incidence? If $\hat{w} = \hat{r}$, then the relative income of capital is constant, and both factors bear the burden of the tax proportionately to their shares in income. The tax is neutral in that sense. If $\hat{w} > \hat{r}$ (resp. $\hat{w} < \hat{r}$), the tax bears more (resp. less) on capital than on labor. Elementary computations show that if the utility function that generates the demands for the goods and the production functions are Cobb-Douglas (so that $\varepsilon_D = \sigma_X = \sigma_Y = 1$), then $D = 1$ and $\hat{w} - \hat{r} = \lambda_{KX} \, dt_{KX}$. Since only relative prices are determined in equilibrium, we can normalize w to one (which amounts to expressing the prices and incomes in wage units) so that $\hat{w} = 0$. Then we can write

$$dr\bar{K} = -rK_X \, dt_{KX}$$

The left-hand side is the variation (in terms of the price of labor) of the income of capitalists and the right-hand side is minus the tax revenue. Thus when the economy is well described by Cobb-Douglas functions, the capitalists bear the whole burden of the tax.[25] Harberger's simulations suggested that such was indeed the case in the United States, but the much richer CGE models that have been built since then show that this extreme conclusion may not be robust.

In any case, accounting for all of these effects takes us far from the traditional analysis of classical authors, as summed up by John Stuart Mill in his *Principles of Political Economy* (1848, v, iii):

If a tax were laid on the profits of any one branch of productive employment, the tax would be virtually an increase of the cost of production, and the value and price of the article would rise accordingly; by which the tax

---

25. It is in fact possible that the relative income of capital decreases so much that the capitalists bear more than the whole tax burden (start from a Cobb-Douglas economy and make σ_Y go below one). In counterpart, the workers gain from the creation of the tax in such a situation.

would be thrown upon the consumers of the commodity, and would not affect profits.

As we have seen, only in a world without factor substitution effects and volume effects would this conclusion be true: otherwise, capital income certainly changes.

The Effects of VAT

Now assume $dt_{KX} = 0$, and consider some $dt_X > 0$. Its effects are rather simpler, since they only depend on the volume effect. Relative capital income decreases if and only if X is more capital intensive than Y, which is very intuitive: taxing X reduces its net relative price but increases its relative after tax price. The tax therefore reduces relative demand for X, which discourages the use of the factor in which X is the more intensive. The demand for this factor decreases, and so does its relative income.

1.2.5   Final Remarks

Harberger's model gives a good account of the complexity of the reaction of private agents to a tax in general equilibrium, especially through the interaction of factor substitution effects and volume effects. However, neglecting income effects certainly is a rather restrictive assumption, given the tax take in our economies. Moreover the preferences that we assumed for the agents are not realistic. These two drawbacks can be remedied by resorting to more complicated analytical or numerical computations. It is more difficult to go beyond the wholly neoclassical character of the model. This is all the more annoying when it is important to take into account the existence of other distortions in the economy (e.g., the minimum wage for the payroll tax, or imperfect competition in some sectors). The static perspective also is restrictive. If one considers taxes over the whole life cycle of an agent, then the incidence of capital taxation can be rather different, since a given agent may live on labor income when he is young and on capital income when he is old (see Fullerton-Rogers 1993). Finally, we worked in a closed economy. In practice, capital is mobile (less perfectly than is often said) across frontiers, which makes its supply more elastic and therefore must reduce the taxation burden it bears. The final note must be that while we economists are in relative agreement on the incidence of payroll taxes, such is not the case for the corporate income tax.

To conclude this chapter, let us mention the special case of the incidence of taxes on durable goods that are in fixed supply. The simplest example is that of land. Assume that the government creates a yearly tax proportional to the area of land owned by each taxpayer. This new tax reduces the value of land one for one, since the supply of land is assumed to be inelastic. Therefore the agents who own land when the tax is announced bear the whole burden of the tax. On the other hand, future landowners do not bear any burden, since the discounted value of the taxes they have to pay is exactly equal to the decrease in the price they pay for their purchase of land. Thus any change in the expected income flow from a durable good whose supply is fixed is entirely reflected in its price. This effect is called fiscal capitalization; it plays a very important role in the analysis of property taxes.

References

Ballentine, J., and I. Eris. 1975. On the general equilibrium analysis of tax incidence. *Journal of Political Economy* 83: 633–44.

Fullerton, D., and D. Rogers. 1993. *Who Bears the Lifetime Tax Burden?* The Brookings Institution.

Harberger, A. 1962. The incidence of the corporation tax. *Journal of Political Economy* 70: 215–40.

Shoven, J., and J. Whalley. 1972. A general equilibrium calculation of the effects of differential taxation of income from capital in the US. *Journal of Public Economics* 1: 281–321.

Shoven, J., and J. Whalley. 1984. Applied general equilibrium models of taxation and international trade: An introduction and survey. *Journal of Economic Literature* 22: 1007–51.

2   Distortions and Welfare Losses

A traditional technicist view of the role of the economist is that his task is to take governmental objectives as given and then to find a way to implement them that minimizes distortions, or equivalently, that reduces the efficiency of the economy by as little as possible. But what are these distortions, and how can they be measured? At a Pareto optimum the marginal rates of substitution of all consumers are equal to the technical marginal rates of substitution of all firms. Under the usual conditions and without taxation, the competitive equilibrium is Pareto optimal since every consumer equates his marginal rates of substitution to the relative prices, while every firm equates its technical marginal rates of substitution to the relative prices. Once taxes are introduced in such an economy, the relative prices perceived by various agents differ: for instance, consumers perceive after-tax prices, while producers perceive before-tax prices. In these conditions equilibrium does not lead to the equality of marginal rates of substitution any more, and it cannot be a Pareto optimum. The price system does not coordinate the agents efficiently any more since it sends different signals to different agents.

To make this discussion more concrete, consider the very simple example of a two-good, one-consumer, and one-firm economy. The consumer's utility function over goods 1 and 2 is given by $U = C_1 C_2$; the firm transforms good 1 into good 2 through a production function $X_2 = X_1/c$. We normalize the price of good 1 to one. The consumer's initial resources consist in one unit of good 1.

Without taxation, the equilibrium is easily computed. Since the technology exhibits constant returns, the price of good 2 must equal c, and the firm makes zero profit. So the consumer's budget constraint is

$$C_1 + cC_2 = 1$$

Maximizing the utility gives $C_1 = \frac{1}{2}$ and $C_2 = 1/2c$, and therefore the utility is $U = 1/4c$. Note that the marginal rate of substitution of the consumer is

$$\frac{\partial U/\partial C_1}{\partial U/\partial C_2} = \frac{C_2}{C_1} = \frac{1}{c}$$

which equals the technical marginal rate of substitution of good 1 for good 2. As expected, the equilibrium coincides with the single Pareto optimum of this economy.

Let us now introduce a specific tax t on good 2; the tax revenue is redistributed to the consumer as a lump-sum transfer T. Since the production function has constant returns, the supply of good 2 is infinitely elastic and the tax is entirely borne by the consumer, so that the consumer price of good 2 is $(c + t)$. The budget constraint becomes

$$C_1 + (c + t)C_2 = 1 + T$$

and we obtain

$$\begin{cases} C_1 = \dfrac{1 + T}{2} \\ C_2 = \dfrac{1 + T}{2(c + t)} \end{cases}$$

Now the marginal rate of substitution of the consumer is

$$\frac{\partial U/\partial C_1}{\partial U/\partial C_2} = \frac{C_2}{C_1} = \frac{1}{c + t}$$

This differs from the technical marginal rate of substitution, which is still $1/c$. The equilibrium is not a Pareto optimum any more: the tax creates a divergence between the relative prices perceived by the consumer and by the firm, which leads to an inefficient allocation of resources in the economy.

By definition, $T = tC_2$ and by substituting for T:

$$\begin{cases} C_1 = \dfrac{c + t}{2c + t} \\ C_2 = \dfrac{1}{2c + t} \end{cases}$$

which gives a utility

$$U(t) = \frac{c + t}{(2c + t)^2}$$

An elementary computation shows that

$$U - U(t) = \frac{t^2}{4c(2c + t)^2}$$

so that the utility loss (due to the fact that the equilibrium is not Pareto optimal) is a second-order term in t. This is called the *deadweight loss* or *excess burden* of the tax.[26]

Note that the loss exists even though the government returns the proceeds of the tax to the consumer (by construction, $T = tC_2$). It is due to the fact that the producer and the consumer do not perceive the same relative prices; the increase in the relative consumer price of good 2 leads to an excessive consumption of good 1 and an inefficiently low consumption of good 2.

This example shows two points that will recur through this chapter. First, the distortions induced by taxes are channeled by the divergences between the prices perceived by the various agents. Second, the resulting welfare losses are second-order terms in the tax parameters. On the other hand, it is not a forgone conclusion that taxing a good leads to an underproduction and/or an underconsumption of that good: the substitution effect may be masked by an income effect in the other direction. For the standard consumption good, such a phenomenon is associated to a Giffen good and can therefore be considered a rarity. However, it is less implausible for labor supply and savings behavior.

We are now going to study the effects of taxes on the main economic decisions:

- effect of the income tax on labor supply
- effect of taxing interest income on savings
- effect of taxes on risk-taking.

We will then seek to quantify the deadweight losses due to taxes.

---

26. Of course, its precise measure depends on what utility function is used to represent preferences.

2.1   The Effects of Taxation

We will focus here on the main economic decisions, those that play a central role in tax policy debates. In each case we will adopt a partial equilibrium viewpoint; for instance, we will neglect the effect of the income tax on workers' wages.

2.1.1   Labor Supply

As you know, wages affect labor supply in an ambiguous way. A higher wage makes work more attractive relative to leisure (by the substitution effect), but it also increases the demand for leisure (by the income effect) if leisure is a normal good. The same effects come into play when looking at the income tax.

The Standard Model

Consider a consumer with utility function $U(C, L)$, where C is consumption of an aggregate good of unit price and L is labor (so that U increases in C and decreases in L). Assume that a proportional income tax at rate t is created so that the budget constraint becomes

$$C \le (1 - t)(wL + \underline{R}) \equiv sL + M$$

where $\underline{R}$ represents nonlabor income (which is taxed at the same rate as labor income). We define $s = (1 - t)w$ and $M = (1 - t)\underline{R}$.

The creation of (or an increase in) the income tax has three effects:

1. by lowering M, it reduces income; in the usual case where leisure is a normal good, this reduces the demand for leisure and thus increases labor supply

2. the decrease in s goes in the same direction since it also reduces income

3. the decrease in s (the relative price of labor), however, makes labor less attractive and thus reduces the supply of labor.

Effects 1 and 2 are income effects, which depend on the average tax rate, while the substitution effect 3 only depends on the marginal tax rate. This hardly matters here since the tax is proportional, but it may become important with a progressive income tax.

To evaluate these effects, start with

$$\frac{\partial L}{\partial t} = \frac{\partial L}{\partial s}\frac{\partial s}{\partial t} + \frac{\partial L}{\partial M}\frac{\partial M}{\partial t}$$

The Slutsky equation is

$$\frac{\partial L}{\partial s} = S + L\frac{\partial L}{\partial M}$$

where $S > 0$ is the Slutsky term, that is, the compensated derivative of labor supply with respect to the net wage:

$$S = \left(\frac{\partial L}{\partial s}\right)_U$$

This yields

$$\frac{\partial L}{\partial t} = -wS - (wL + \underline{R})\frac{\partial L}{\partial M}$$

The first term on the right-hand side is the substitution effect and is clearly negative. The second term comes from the two income effects; it is positive if leisure is a normal good, and it is multiplied by income. This suggests that the income effect is smaller for low-income individuals. Thus the income tax may have more disincentive effects on the poor than on the rich, other things equal.

One could illustrate this formula with a Cobb-Douglas utility function $U = a \log C + (1 - a) \log(\bar{L} - L)$, but it is easy to see that the $(1 - t)$ term in the budget constraint then only reduces utility without modifying labor supply. The income effect and the substitution effect exactly cancel out, and taxation does not change labor supply. As is often the case, the Cobb-Douglas specification is a very special one.[27]

Obviously a proportional tax is a very bad approximation to real-world income taxes. It is nevertheless easy to analyze simple variants. Thus let us create a negative income tax G that is a benefit given given to all individuals independently of their income.[28] Then the after-tax income becomes $(sL + M + G)$; other things equal, the presence of the G term adds an income effect that reduces labor supply. If the negative income tax is financed by increasing t, then the effects described above come into play. For poor individuals, going from a proportional income tax to a negative income tax seems to reduce labor supply unambiguously. This remark, however,

27. It can be checked that if preferences are CES with an elasticity of substitution σ, then the income tax reduces labor supply if and only if $\sigma > 1$.
28. So that the net tax paid is $t(wL + \bar{R}) - G$, which may be negative.

neglects the fact that in most developed countries the poorest households receive large means-tested benefits. These transfers should be
modeled in order to understand the labor supply of the poor.

Criticisms and Extensions

The standard model implicitly assumes that workers can choose
their hours L freely. In fact the number of hours worked may not
be chosen so easily, especially in some European countries where
working hours are regulated and part-time work may not be the
result of a spontaneous choice. Thus it is interesting to look at the
participation decision, that is the choice between not working and
working a conventional number of hours $\underline{L}$. For simplicity, let us
neglect part-time work and assume that the utility function is $U =
u(C) - v(L)$, with $v(0) = 0$; then we must compare $(u((1 - t)(w\underline{L} + \underline{R}))
- v(\underline{L}))$ and $u((1 - t)\underline{R})$. Note that the participation decision is de-
termined by the average and not the marginal tax rate.

The derivative in t of the difference of these two utilities is

$$-(w\underline{L} + \underline{R})u'((1 - t)(w\underline{L} + \underline{R})) + \underline{R}u'((1 - t)\underline{R})$$

Thus it appears that participation decreases in t if and only if
$xu'(x)$ is increasing,[29] which seems reasonable. Progressivity further
reduces the incentive to participate, since the average tax rate is
higher when the individual works than when he does not. This
analysis of the decision to particpate also applies to the decision to
retire, with the *caveat* that pension rights depend on contributions
paid.

One could also reinterpret the standard model by analyzing L as
an effort variable of the individual, something he does to improve
the productivity of his labor input; the resulting problem is formally
identical, so long as effort causes an increase in wages and is costly
in utility terms. This reinterpretation is useful when studying the
optimal taxation problem.

Even if we focus on labor supply, taxation impacts other variables
than hours worked and effort. Consider, for instance, two jobs: job 2
is more painful and therefore better paid than job 1. Then, assuming
again that utility is separable, the individual must compare the
increase in utility from income $(u(W_2(1 - t)) - u(W_1(1 - t))$ in taking

---

29. Equivalently, if and only if the marginal utility of income has an elasticity $-xu''/u'$
that is lower than one.

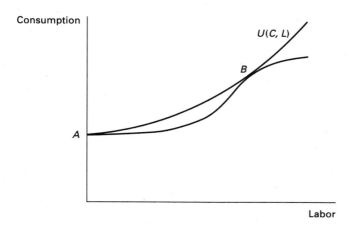

Figure 2.1
Real-world budget constraint

job 2 to the increase in the disutility of labor $(v_2 - v_1)$. Taxation
reduces the first term and leaves the second one unchanged, which
makes job 2 less attractive. Similarly taxation makes household production (tasks that are often but not always done outside of the
market system, e.g., household chores and child care) more attractive, since it is not taxed.

Finally, note that real-world budget constraints are very complex
and nonconvex, given the actual tax-benefit systems. Figure 2.1
illustrates this for a rather typical developed country. The S-shape
represents the fact that the marginal tax rate is high both for low
incomes (where benefits are means tested and more labor income
means less benefits) and for high incomes (given the progressivity of
the income tax). Given such a budget constraint, small tax changes
may induce large changes in labor supply for a given individual
(e.g., a jump from A to B in figure 2.1). In practice, the complexity of
actual real-world tax-benefit systems makes it necessary to resort to
empirical analysis.

Estimates of Labor Supply
The empirical literature on the estimation of labor supply functions
is very rich. So-called structural estimation procedures usually start
from the standard model, where maximizing $U(C, L)$ under the budget constraint $C \leq sL + M$ and the nonnegativity constraint $L \geq 0$
gives the following conditions:

- $L = 0$ if

$$-\frac{U_L'(M, 0)}{U_C'(M, 0)} \geq s$$

This inequality defines an after-tax reservation wage $s_R(M)$ below which the agent refuses to work.

- Otherwise, L is given by

$$-\frac{U_L'(sL + M, L)}{U_C'(sL + M, L)} = s$$

which defines a function $L^*(s, M)$.

These equations lead econometricians to specify the labor supply model as a Tobit model with a latent variable[30]

$$L^* = \alpha + \beta \log s + \gamma \log M + \varepsilon$$

(where ε is an error term) and a labor supply given by

$$L = \max(L^*, 0)$$

Of course, the wage s is only observed when the agent works. So the Tobit model must be estimated jointly with a wage equation that explains wages as a function of characteristics of the agents X and an error term u:

$$\log s = Xa + u$$

As such, this model is not satisfactory. By assuming that the current labor supply only depends on the current wage, it cannot, for instance, account for young executives who work long hours in the hope of a promotion. The model must therefore be inserted in a life-cycle perspective. It also neglects fixed costs of participation linked to transportation costs and/or to the cost of child care, or the difficulties linked to collective choice within a household.

Finally, the model must be adapted for nonproportional taxes, which define a budget constraint

$$C \leq wL + \underline{R} - T(wL + \underline{R})$$

If the marginal tax rate is increasing, then the budget constraint is still convex, as shown on figure 2.2. One can then define a virtual

---

30. The semilogarithmic specification adopted here is only an example.

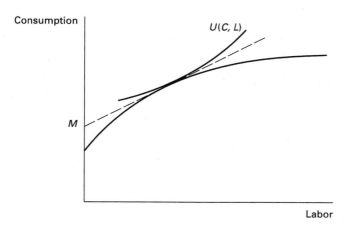

Figure 2.2
Convex budget constraint

wage $s = (1 - T')w$ and a virtual income $M = C - sL$. This way labor supply is also the solution of the program that maximizes utility under the virtual budget constraint

$$C \leq sL + M$$

This brings us back within the standard model, except that s and M depend on L through T' and are therefore endogenous. Then one must estimate the model with the method of instrumental variables or the maximum likelihood method.

In the real world, tax systems unfortunately lead to nonconvex budget constraints such as that in figure 2.1 so that the solution of the maximization program is not characterized by the first-order condition. Then one often has to discretize the choice set for labor supply L (e.g., by considering each of the values $L = 0, 1, \ldots, 60$ hours per week) and to compare the values of utility

$$U(wL + \underline{R} - T(wL + \underline{R}), L)$$

to find the maximum. The parameters of the utility function can then be estimated by the maximum likelihood method and used to evaluate the wage and income elasticities of labor supply.[31]

Given all these complexities, it is not very surprising that estimation results vary across studies. Few doubt that leisure is a normal

---

31. The reader may complete this brief tour by the survey of Blundell-MaCurdy (1999).

good.[32] The compensated wage elastictity of labor supply is more uncertain. It seems to be small for men (somewhere between 0 and 0.2, which yields an uncompensated elasticity close to zero). This is not very surprising: daily observation suggests that most men, at least in the middle part of their lives, participate in the labor force. Moreover their hours often result from collective bargaining more than from individual choice. On the other hand, the labor supply of women is much more wage elastic, especially for married women, for whom the elasticity may be between 0.5 and 1. This striking difference between men and women probably stems from the traditional sexual differentiation of roles within couples: women much more often than men choose to withdraw from the labor force (or to take a part-time job) so as to raise children.

Structural estimates have been criticized because they always rely on a model that may be misspecified. Other authors have resorted to the method of *natural experiments*. This consists, in our case, in comparing the effect of a tax reform on the labor supplies of various subpopulations, some of which are more touched by the reform than others. Thus Eissa (1995) examines the effect of the Tax Reform Act of 1986 (TRA86) in the United States on the labor supply of married women. The most spectacular effect of TRA86 was the reduction of the top marginal rate of the personal income tax from 50 percent to 28 percent. Therefore the reform considerably reduced the marginal rate faced by the wives of high earners; on the other hand, its effect on wives of men with lower wages was much smaller. By comparing the changes in the labor supplies of these two subpopulations of women after TRA86, Eissa estimates that the wage elasticity of the labor supply of women in the first group is about 0.8, which falls in the same ballpark as structural estimates.

Finally, note that empirical studies sometimes use taxable income and sometimes total income. Since labor in the underground economy is by definition not taxed, one would expect that an increase in tax rates induces some agents to leave the legal sector for the underground sector of the economy, at least for part of their working hours. Lemieux-Fortin-Frechette (1994) use a survey on Québec to show that this effect is rather small on the average taxpayer, but that it matters for welfare recipients, who usually face very high marginal withdrawal rates.

---

32. This is confirmed, for instance, by the observation that people who inherit tend to reduce their labor supply (see Holtz-Eakin-Joulfaian-Rosen 1993).

2.1.2   The Effects of Taxation on Savings

In most countries, income taxation bears both on labor income and on income from savings. With perfect financial markets, taxation of labor income only changes the savings rate in that the latter depends on permanent income. We will focus here on the effect of taxation of income from savings on the time profile of consumption over the life cycle. We will therefore start by neglecting the taxation of labor income. We also assume an exogenous interest rate, which neglects general equilibrium effects.

Theoretical Analysis

Consider a consumer who lives two periods and whose labor supply is inelastic. He gets in the first period a wage w, consumes some part of it, and saves the rest according to

$$C_1 + E = w$$

In the second period, he does not work[33] and consumes the net income from his savings. Given an interest rate r and taxation of income from savings at a proportional rate t, his budget constraint in the second period is

$$C_2 = (1 + r(1 - t))E$$

Assuming perfect financial markets, the consumer can save as much as he likes, and the two budget constraints can be aggregated in an intertemporal constraint

$$C_1 + pC_2 = w$$

where p is the relative price of second-period consumption, that is,

$$p = \frac{1}{1 + r}$$

without taxation and

$$p = \frac{1}{1 + r(1 - t)}$$

with taxation.

---

33. Thus the first period could be the active period of life and the second retirement.

As usual, the increase in p due to taxation has two effects:

- an income effect: the increase in p reduces both C_1 and C_2 if consumptions in both periods are normal goods, which increases savings $E = w - C_1$
- a substitution effect: the increase in p makes second-period consumption more expensive and thus tends to reduce savings.

More precisely, denote $U(C_1, C_2)$ the utility function of the consumer.[34] We can write

$$\frac{\partial C_1}{\partial p} = \left(\frac{\partial C_1}{\partial p}\right)_U - C_2 \frac{\partial C_1}{\partial w}$$

Define the intertemporal elasticity of substitution as

$$\sigma = \left(\frac{\partial \log(C_1/C_2)}{\partial \log p}\right)_U$$

First note that since Hicksian demands are the derivatives of the expenditure function $e(p, U)$ with respect to prices, the equality

$$C_1(p, U) + pC_2(p, U) = e(p, U)$$

implies by differentiating in p that

$$\left(\frac{\partial C_1}{\partial p}\right)_U + p\left(\frac{\partial C_2}{\partial p}\right)_U = 0$$

Since by definition

$$\sigma = \left(\frac{\partial \log C_1}{\partial \log p}\right)_U - \left(\frac{\partial \log C_2}{\partial \log p}\right)_U$$

we obtain

$$\sigma = \left(\frac{p}{C_1} + \frac{1}{C_2}\right)\left(\frac{\partial \log C_1}{\partial \log p}\right)_U = \frac{w}{pC_2}\left(\frac{\partial \log C_1}{\partial \log p}\right)_U$$

and

$$\left(\frac{\partial \log C_1}{\partial \log p}\right)_U = e\sigma$$

where $e = E/w = pC_2/w$ denotes the savings rate.

---

34. We can neglect the disutility of labor since labor supply is assumed to be inelastic.

We also have

$$\frac{\partial C_1}{\partial w} = \frac{C_1}{w} \frac{\partial \log C_1}{\partial \log w}$$

Finally, by substituting within the Slutsky equation and denoting

$$\eta = \frac{\partial \log C_1}{\partial \log w}$$

the income elasticity of first-period consumption, we get

$$\frac{\partial \log C_1}{\partial \log p} = e\sigma - C_2 \frac{p}{C_1} \eta \frac{C_1}{w} = e(\sigma - \eta)$$

Moreover

$$\frac{\partial \log E}{\partial \log p} = -\frac{C_1}{E} \frac{\partial \log C_1}{\partial \log p}$$

whence

$$\frac{\partial \log E}{\partial \log p} = -(1 - e)(\sigma - \eta)$$

which shows the negative substitution effect $(-(1 - e)\sigma)$ and the income effect $(1 - e)\eta$. What is the order of magnitude of the resulting effect? Note that once more, the Cobb-Douglas utility function is not much help since it implies $\sigma = \eta = 1$ and thus no effect of taxation on savings. A reasonable assumption is that preferences are homothetic so that both consumptions are proportional to permanent income $(\eta = 1)$. Choose $e = r = \frac{1}{2}$, which is not absurd since the two periods represent the working life and retirement. Then a 50 percent tax on income from savings increases p by 20 percent and reduces savings by 10 percent multiplied by $(\sigma - 1)$ (to the first order). Thus, to get large effects of taxation on savings, the intertemporal elasticity of substitution has to be rather large. It is even quite possible that taxation increases savings (it is the case if and only if $\sigma < \eta$).

If the consumer is paid wages in both periods, then we must take into account a new income effect as permanent income becomes

$$w_1 + \frac{w_2}{1 + r(1 - t)}$$

This time the consumer may decide to borrow (if his second-period wages are relatively high), which makes imperfections on financial markets relevant. If the interest rate at which he can borrow r^+ is larger than the interest rate paid on his savings r^-, then his budget constraint has a kink at the zero savings point. Under these circumstances some consumers will choose to locate in that point,[35] and the substitution effect does not come into play, at least locally. This clearly reduces the negative influence of taxation on savings.

So far we have neglected the taxation of labor income. If it is taxed at the same rate as income from savings (as is the case for the ideal income tax), w must be replaced with $w(1 - t)$. Then taxation reduces permanent income and thus both consumptions. Since savings this time is $w(1 - t) - C_1$, the way this effect goes depends on the income elasticity η.

The taxation of savings affects not only income but also accumulated savings. Such is the case for wealth taxes, but also for taxes on bequests. Assume that in addition to his consumptions the consumer derives utility from any (after-tax) bequest H he leaves at his death. Then his utility is $U(C_1, C_2, H)$, and given a taxation rate τ on bequests, his second-period budget constraint becomes

$$C_2 + \frac{H}{1 - \tau} = E(1 + r(1 - t))$$

His intertemporal budget constraint becomes

$$C_1 + pC_2 + p'H = w$$

where p is still defined as

$$p = \frac{1}{1 + r(1 - t)}$$

and $p' = p/(1 - \tau)$. With a taxation rate of income from savings fixed at p, by the Hicks-Leontief theorem, the two consumptions can be aggregated within a composite good. The effect of changes on the rate of bequest taxation τ then is formally analogous to that of t on savings. This analysis of bequests is only half convincing, however. Whether bequests are planned or accidental (due to early deaths) is a controversial issue. In any case the taxation of bequests, like wealth taxes, collects very small amounts of tax revenues in most countries.

---

35. They are liquidity constrained: they consume their income within each period.

In the United States the tax on bequest is sometimes called a voluntary tax, as it is fairly easy to avoid.

Empirical Results

In the 1970s econometricians tried to estimate the elasticity of aggregate consumer savings to the after-tax interest rate. Apart from Boskin (1978) who obtained a value close to 0.4, most estimates were close to zero. This quasi-consensus was shaken by a paper of Summers (1981). Using the calibration of a life-cycle model in a growing economy, Summers showed that any choice of parameters compatible with the observed ratio of wealth to income implied a large elasticity of savings to the interest rate. More recent work, however, has showed that Summers's result is fragile.

The literature turned in the 1980s to the estimation of Euler equations derived from the intertemporal optimization of consumers; this yielded values for the intertemporal elasticity of substitution σ. Studies done on macroeconomic data have yielded small values for σ. More credible estimations on individual data suggest that σ is nonnegligible but lower than one (which is its value for a Cobb-Douglas utility function), which implies a very small elasticity of savings to the interest rate.

Finally, many authors have used the existence of investments that are favored by taxation. Most of these studies use data from the United States, where it is possible to use Individual Retirement Accounts (IRA) and 401(k) funds to save into pension funds and deduct the amount saved from taxable income. These funds have been very successful, but the important question is whether the money that went into them would have been saved anyway or not. The studies are not unanimously conclusive, but it seems that total savings was only moderately stimulated by the favorable tax treatment of these funds.

A general lesson of this literature[36] is that taxation is unlikely to have a large impact on total savings, although it clearly plays an important role in determining where the money is invested.

2.1.3   Taxation and Risk-Taking

Taxation is often said to discourage risk-taking, since it confiscates part of the return to risky activities such as setting up a business

---

36. Bernheim (2002) contains a much more detailed discussion.

or investing in shares. Domar-Musgrave (1944) however noted that
taxation transforms government into a sleeping partner who absorbs
part of the risk, which may in fact encourage risk-taking. We will
revisit this argument following Mossin. We will set aside the question of whether such risk-taking as exists in the economy is too large
or too small—popular opinion is that risk-taking is insufficient and
should be encouraged, but there is no good evidence either for or
against this view.

We consider the portfolio choice of investing in a riskless asset that
brings a return r and a risky asset that brings a random return x.[37]
We therefore assume that there exists a safe asset in the economy,
which is an approximation (even the purchasing power of money is
affected by inflation). We also assume that *two-fund separation* holds:
all risky assets may be aggregated in a single composite risky asset.[38]

The investor has a strictly concave von Neumann-Morgenstern
utility function u on wealth strictement concave, meaning that he is
risk-averse. We denote W_0 the initial wealth and W the final wealth.
If a is the proportion of the initial wealth invested in the risky asset,
then

$$W = (1 - \tau)W_0(1 + (ax + (1 - a)r)(1 - t))$$

where τ is the tax rate on wealth and t is the tax rate on asset income.

The investor maximizes $Eu(W)$ in a, which gives the first-order
condition

$$E(u'(W)(x - r)) = 0$$

Taxation enters this expression via final wealth W. The impact
of taxation of wealth is easy to see, since it just multiplies initial
wealth W_0 by $(1 - \tau)$. We know from Arrow (1970) that if absolute
risk-aversion $-u''(W)/u'(W)$ is nonincreasing in wealth,[39] then the
amount invested in the risky asset increases with wealth, which
means in our case that $a(1 - \tau)$ is a decreasing function of τ. To go
further and to conclude that the *proportion a* invested in the risky
asset is reduced by the taxation of wealth, we need to ensure that

---

37. To make the problem nontrivial, we assume that $Ex > r$ and that r lies in the interior of the support of x.
38. Two-fund separation was used for the first time by Tobin (1958). It can be justified
under rather strict assumptions on preferences (see Cass-Stiglitz (1970)).
39. This so-called NIARA (*nonincreasing absolute risk-aversion*) hypothesis is confirmed
by almost all empirical studies.

a increases with wealth. This is only true if relative risk-aversion decreases with wealth, which is not clear from the empirical evidence.

Now assume that wealth is not taxed ($\tau = 0$) and focus on taxation of asset income. The first-order condition is

$$E(u'(W_0(1 + (ax + (1 - a)r)(1 - t)))(x - r)) = 0 \tag{1}$$

Let us differentiate it with respect to t. We get

$$E\left(u''(W)(x - r)\left((x - r)(1 - t)\frac{\partial a}{\partial t} - (ax + (1 - a)r)\right)\right) = 0$$

whence by rearranging

$$-\frac{\partial \log a}{\partial \log(1 - t)} = 1 + \frac{r}{a}\frac{Eu''(W)(x - r)}{E(u''(W)(x - r)^2)} \tag{2}$$

First note an interesting special case: if $r = 0$ (e.g., if the riskless asset is money in a world without inflation), we find that

$$-\frac{\partial \log a}{\partial \log(1 - t)} = 1$$

which shows that $a(1 - t)$ is independent of t and therefore implies that taxation increases a. The intuition is that of Domar-Musgrave: taxation amounts to a participation of government in risk and therefore encourages risk-taking.

When $r \neq 0$, things are slightly more complicated. Taxation of income from the riskless asset indeed reduces wealth and may change the attitude of the investor toward risk. To evaluate the second term in (2), we must define the amount invested in the risky asset $Z = aW_0$ and study how it changes with wealth. Rewriting the first-order condition (1) with this new notation, we get

$$E(u'(W_0(1 + r(1 - t)) + (1 - t)(x - r)Z)(x - r)) = 0$$

or by differentiating with respect to initial wealth W_0,

$$E\left(u''(W)(x - r)\left(1 + r(1 - t) + (1 - t) + (x - r)\frac{\partial Z}{\partial W_0}\right)\right) = 0$$

Rearranging obtains

$$\frac{\partial \log Z}{\partial \log W_0} = -\frac{Eu''(W)(x - r)}{E(u''(W)(x - r)^2)}\frac{1 + r(1 - t)}{a(1 - t)} \tag{3}$$

Substituting (3) in (2) finally yields

$$-\frac{\partial \log a}{\partial \log(1-t)} = 1 - \frac{\partial \log Z}{\partial \log W_0} \frac{r(1-t)}{1+r(1-t)}$$

Assume that $r > 0$. We saw that under the NIARA hypothesis, Z increases in W_0. Therefore there is a new wealth effect that induces an increase in risk-aversion and thus makes risk-taking less appealing than in the $r = 0$ case. Arrow thought that the elasticity of Z in W_0 must be lower than one. If such is the case, then the right-hand side is still positive and taxation must always encourage risk-taking, but Arrow's hypothesis is controverted.

Note that until now we implicitly assumed that the government shared in losses as well as gains. This assumption can be justified if losses can be deducted from gains on other risky assets and the resulting gain is always positive. Otherwise, it is useful to examine the impact of the *no loss offset* rule, whereby the government does not subsidize losses. Then $x(1-t)$ must be replaced with x when $x < 0$; with $r \geq 0$, it does not change the return of the riskless asset. It is easy to see that when t gets close to one, then taxation must always reduce risk-taking: it does not reduce losses and gains become negligible. In general, taking the *no loss offset* rule into account tends to reduce risk-taking relative to the case where the government also takes its share of the losses.

Finally, note that in most countries, capital gains are taxed at a lower rate than interest income. Then one should consider that x and r are in fact $x(1-t')$ and $r(1-t)$, with $t' < t$. If risk-aversion does not vary too much with wealth, then this tends to increase risk-taking relative to a uniform taxation.

These remarks show that the real world is more complex than appears from the model. Moreover taxation of asset income is one of the most intricate areas of existing tax systems. Since household data usually are not very detailed on portfolio holdings, this makes estimating the effect of taxation on the holdings of risky assets very difficult. The survey of Poterba (2002) nevertheless concludes that taxation has substantial effects on how households allocate their wealth.

2.2   Welfare Losses

The preceding section shows that taxes change the economic behavior of private agents in ways that may be more complicated than

popular wisdom suggests. Can we quantify the welfare losses induced by these distortions more generally than in the simple example that opened this chapter?

Conceptually the problem is rather simple. Start from an economy characterized by a tax system t_0 (and maybe other distortions),
with an after-tax price equilibrium p_0. Now change the tax system
to t_1 and denote the new after-tax equilibrium prices p_1. Chapter 1
already studied the incidence problem, that is, who bears the burden
of taxes. Here we focus on welfare losses, also called *deadweight losses*
or *excess burdens*, that is, on the total weight of this tax burden.

Consider a "simple" example where taxes are purely redistributive, with no public good to be financed. Take a consumer i. Given
after-tax prices p and taxes t, his utility can be written from his indirect utility function:

$$\mathcal{U}_i(p,t) = V\left(p, (p-t) \cdot \omega_i + \sum_{j=1}^{Jx} \theta_{ij} \pi_j (p-t) + T_i(t)\right)$$

where the θ_{ij} are his shares of firms' profits π_j and $T_i(t)$ represents the
value of taxes that are redistributed to him. We would like to evalu-
ate a sum of changes in utility such as $\sum_{i=1}^{n}(\mathcal{U}_i(p_1,t_1) - \mathcal{U}_i(p_0,t_0))$ but
this makes no sense in general since utilities are ordinal.

Even if we neglect this first difficulty, computing the $\mathcal{U}_i$ must take
into account all general equilibrium interactions, which seems a
hopeless task. To simplify the problem further, consider a representative consumer with an income R that is unchanged by taxation;
then take $t_0 = 0$ and introduce a tax $t_1 = t$ on some good. The after-
tax prices move from p_0 to p_1 after the introduction of tax t. In the
general case, changes in utility can be evaluated using the equivalent
variation or the compensating variation (e.g., see Salanié 2000, ch. 2).
The equivalent variation equivalent, for instance, is by definition

$$E = e(p_0, V(p_1, R)) - R$$

where $e(p,u)$ is the expenditure function, that is, the amount that
must be spent at prices p to reach utility level u.

The equivalent variation therefore is the amount that must be
given to the consumer before introducing the tax so that he gets
exactly the after-tax utility level (of course, $E < 0$ when $t > 0$). The
consumer thus loses $-E$ from the introduction of the tax, the producers lose $(\sum_j \pi_j(p_0) - \sum_j \pi_j(p_1 - t))$, and the government collects

$tx(p_1, R)$. In these conditions it seems reasonable to define the welfare loss as the sum of what the consumer and the producers lose, minus the tax revenue collected by the government (which may be redistributed). The resulting expression is

$$R - e(p_0, V(p_1, R)) + \left(\sum_j \pi(p_0) - \sum_j \pi(p_1 - t) \right) - tx(p_1, R)$$

This may appear to be a satisfactory solution. However, using the compensating variation instead of the equivalent variation would give a different measure of the consumer's welfare loss and therefore of the social welfare loss. The only case where these two measures coincide is when the marginal utility of some good (denoted m) is constant, or

$$U = u(x) + m$$

As is well known, this amounts to the assumption that there is no income effect. Then the equivalent variation and the compensating variation both equal the Dupuit-Marshall measure of consumer surplus.

Let us now adopt all of these very restrictive assumptions (no general equilibrium effects, no income effect, representative consumer, a starting position with neither taxes nor distortions). We will now examine the effect of introducing an infinitesimal specific tax dt on a good.

In figure 2.3, p represents the consumer price. The tax shifts the supply curve upward by dt. The consumer surplus thus decreases by $ABCD$, the producers' profit by $BCEF$, and the government collects $ADFE$. The social welfare loss is just the (curved) triangle DFC, which has basis dt and height $(-dx)$, where dx is the change in the quantity traded. Since the surface of a triangle equals the half-product of its basis and its height, the social welfare loss is $-dtdx/2$. Note that it is positive whatever the sign of dt, for a subsidy as well as for a tax.

We already know from chapter 1 that

$$\frac{dx}{x} = -\frac{\varepsilon_D \varepsilon_S}{\varepsilon_D + \varepsilon_S} \frac{dt}{p}$$

Since dx is proportional to dt, the deadweight loss is proportional to the square of the tax, as Dupuit noted as early as 1844.

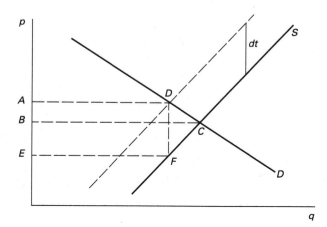

Figure 2.3
Second-order welfare loss

This is often invoked as an argument for *tax smoothing*, the idea that to collect a given revenue, it is better to have several small taxes than one big tax. This idea can be applied to the financing of government expenditure over time: for a given intertemporal tax revenue, it is better to keep tax rates constant (and have a pattern of surpluses and deficits) than to have them vary across years with budgetary needs. Contrariwise, as we will see in chapter 3, this argument should be applied to taxation of several goods with some caution.

Also note that the tax revenue collected by the government is xdt, meaning that the ratio of the deadweight loss to the tax revenue is proportional to the tax rate. To give an order of magnitude, consider the "normal" rate of VAT in the European Union, which is about 20 percent, and assume that demand is unit-elastic. If supply is also unit-elastic, then the deadweight loss is about 5 percent of tax revenue, which is not negligible. If production exhibits constant returns, then $\varepsilon_S = +\infty$ and the deadweight loss goes up to 10 percent of tax revenue. This example, even though it is purely illustrative, shows that the ratio of the deadweight loss to the tax revenue, which is often called the social cost of public funds, takes values high enough that looking for a tax system that minimizes distortions is a useful task.[40]

---

40. Estimates of the social cost of public funds are usually obtained in the literature on CGE models. They vary a lot according to the tax that is studied, but they range from 10 to 50 percent.

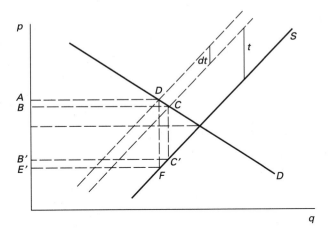

Figure 2.4
First-order welfare loss

What if we start from a tax rate $t > 0$ to go to $(t + dt)$? Then in figure 2.4 the consumer loses $ABCD$, the producers lose $B'C'EF$, and the government collects $AEFD$, instead of $BB'CC'$ before the tax hike. The deadweight loss now is $DFC'C$, which is easily seen to be equal to $-tdx$; thus it is this time of first order in dt.

We saw in this chapter that in general equilibrium and with income effects, there is no universal definition for social welfare losses. Let us, however, close the argument by summing up the very elegant paper by Debreu (1954), which uses the coefficient of resource utilization. Start from an economy without distortions (and thus without taxes) where the vector of initial resources is ω. Now introduce taxes. The new equilibrium leads to utilities U_i. Debreu defines the coefficient of resource utilization $0 < \rho < 1$ as the smallest number r such that in the original economy with initial resources multiplied by r, there exists a Pareto optimum where each consumer i has a utility level at least equal to U_i. We can then define the inefficiency induced by taxes as $(1 - \rho)$, and the social welfare loss by $(1 - \rho)p \cdot \omega$, where p is a price vector that supports the original Pareto optimum. Debreu gives an expression for this social welfare loss that generalizes the expression in $-dtdx/2$ that we obtained in a much more restrictive model. In the very simple example that opens this chapter, it is easy to compute that the coefficient of resource utilization is

$$\rho = \frac{2\sqrt{c(c+t)}}{2c+t}$$

and that the social welfare loss is

$$1 - \rho = \frac{t^2}{(2c+t)(2c+t+2\sqrt{c(c+t)})}$$

whereas surplus analysis gives the approximation

$$\frac{t^2}{8c^2}$$

which is equivalent for small t.

2.3   Conclusion

To conclude this chapter, recall that there are two elasticity concepts: compensated elasticities and uncompensated elasticities. The compensated elasticities only account for substitution effects, while the uncompensated elasticties also take into account income effects. Even lump-sum transfers, which we know induce no distortion and no social welfare loss, create income effects—this is indeed their role in the second welfare theorem. Distortions and social welfare losses are entirely imputable to substitution effects, and therefore their evaluation involves compensated elasticities.[41] On the other hand, the effects of taxation on behavior involve both substitution effects and income effects, and therefore they should be measured using uncompensated elasticities.

References

Arrow, K. 1970. *Essays in the Theory of Risk-Bearing*. North-Holland.

Bernheim, D. 2002. Taxation and savings. In *Handbook of Public Economics*, vol. 3, A. Auerbach and M. Feldstein, eds. North-Holland.

Boskin, M. 1978. Taxation, saving, and the rate of interest. *Journal of Political Economy* 86: S3–S27.

Blundell, R., and T. MaCurdy. 1999. Labor supply: A review of alternative approaches. In the *Handbook of Labor Economics*, vol. 3, O.Ashenfelter and D. Card, eds. North-Holland.

---

41. The analysis in the preceding section assumed away income effects, so that compensated and uncompensated elasticities coincided there.

Cass, D., and J. Stiglitz. 1970. The structure of investor preferences and asset returns, and separability in portfolio allocation. *Journal of Economic Theory* 2: 122–60.

Debreu, G. 1954. A classical tax-subsidy problem. *Econometrica* 22: 14–22.

Domar, E., and R. Musgrave. 1944. Proportional income taxation and risk-taking. *Quarterly Journal of Economics* 58: 388–422.

Dupuit, J. 1844. De la mesure de l'utilité des travaux publics. *Annales des Ponts et Chaussées*, 332–75. Published in English in P. Jackson, ed. *The Foundations of Public Finance*. Elgar, Cheltenham, England, 1996.

Eissa, N. 1995. Taxation and labour supply of married women: The Tax Reform Act of 1986 as a natural experiment. NBER Working Paper 5023.

Holtz-Eakin, D., D. Joulfaian, and H. Rosen. 1993. The Carnegie conjecture: Some empirical evidence. *Quarterly Journal of Economics* 108: 413–35.

Lemieux, T., B. Fortin, and P. Frechette. 1994. The effect of taxes on labour supply in the underground economy. *American Economic Review* 84: 231–54.

Mossin, J. 1968. Taxation and risk-taking: An expected utility approach. *Economica* 137: 74–82.

Poterba, J. 2002. Taxation, risk-taking, and household portfolio behavior. In *Handbook of Public Economics*, vol. 3, A. Auerbach and M. Feldstein, eds. North-Holland.

Salanié, B. 2000. *The Microeconomics of Market Failures*. MIT Press.

Summers, L. 1981. Taxation and capital accumulation in a Life cycle growth model. *American Economic Review* 71: 533–54.

Tobin, J. 1958. Liquidity preference as behavior towards risk. *Review of Economic Studies* 25: 65–68.

II   Optimal Taxation

This second part is dedicated to the study of optimal taxation. This is a very old topic. Smith (*Wealth of Nations*, v, iib) listed four criteria for good taxes:

1. (equity) taxes must be related to each tax payer's ability to pay and/or to the benefits he gets from the state (these obviously do not coincide). Today we would distinguish between horizontal equity and vertical equity. Horizontal equity requires that any two "identical" persons must be treated "identically"—which clearly leaves some room to interpretation. Vertical equity requires that some taxpayers, for instance, because of a higher ability to pay, must pay more than others.

2. taxes must be clearly defined and not arbitrary

3. taxes must be collected in a reasonably painless way

4. taxes must have low costs, both in administrative terms and in terms of the inefficiencies they cause in the economy.

Today we would probably add at least two more criteria:

5. (flexibility) taxes must adapt to economic fluctuations by acting as automatic stabilizers

6. tax incidence should be clear so that taxpayers know who in fact pays taxes.

At this level of generality, the search for optimal taxes seems a daunting task. Economists nevertheless developed in the 1970s a series of models that approaches this question by insisting on the trade-off between equity (point 1) and efficiency (point 4). However, equity is only studied in its vertical meaning, and the inefficiencies that are modeled only concern the distortions induced in the economy, and exclude administrative costs.[42] We will see that this literature nevertheless yielded some useful and sometimes surprising results.

In a perfectly competitive economy, the second welfare theorem tells us that any Pareto optimum can be attained through the right lump-sum redistribution. From this point of view, lump-sum taxes clearly are the optimal form of taxation since they can achieve any redistributive objectives at zero social cost. As we saw in the Introduction, these taxes however are impractical, essentially because the government does not have the information needed to implement them. This is the most important theme in the optimal taxation literature: how much information the government has determines what fiscal instruments it may use. Without lump-sum taxes the government can only tax economic transactions. By doing so, it influences the decisions of private agents, which leads to inefficiencies. The optimal taxation problem then can be stated in simple terms: given the tax revenue that the government has decided to collect, how should it choose the rates of the various taxes to maximize social welfare?

First note that this definition assumes that we can evaluate social welfare, which subsumes many conceptual difficulties such as the interpersonal incomparability of preferences (see Salanié 2000, ch. 1). It seems impossible to discuss redistribution without assuming some form of interpersonal comparability. The literature on optimal taxation cuts through this knot of problems by assuming the existence of a Bergson-Samuelson functional

$$W(V_1, \ldots, V_n)$$

where V_i is the utility index of consumer i. Let x and y denote two vectors of feasible social choices;[43] x is socially preferred to y if and only if

$$W(V_1(x), \ldots, V_n(x)) > W(V_1(y), \ldots, V_n(y))$$

This is clearly a very strong assumption; nevertheless, some qualitative results do not depend at all on the particular choice of the

---

42. These administrative costs are usually nonnegligible; moreover one should add to them the value of the time and money that taxpayers spend to prepare their tax returns and to comply with the law. These *compliance costs* can be ten times higher than the budget of tax authorities. In total, American estimates for the personal income tax suggest that these two categories of costs may amount to 10 percent of the tax revenue.
43. In our applications such vectors will usually represent the consumptions and labor supplies of the various agents.

(increasing and concave) functional W. Note that while the monotonicity of the function W reflects the concern with efficiency, its concavity reflects redistributive objectives. Maximizing W thus does imply a trade-off between equity and efficiency.

There are two types of taxable transactions: consumptions of goods and factor incomes. We speak of indirect taxation for the former and of direct taxation for the latter.[44] First consider the example of taxation on a given good such as bananas. If the tax were nonlinear in the quantity consumed, then consumers would arbitrage between them by sharing purchases equally (if the tax is convex) or by delegating one of them to be the single buyer (if the tax is concave). Thus a nonlinear tax on bananas requires the government to keep a precise tally of the consumption of bananas by a consumer in any given year, which is administratively unfeasible. For this reason taxes on goods are usually linear, and this is the assumption used in the literature.[45] Chapter 3 examines optimal taxation in this setting, using the supplementary assumption that the government can only tax income linearly.

It is relatively easy in fact to collect a nonlinear income tax. Most taxpayers only perceive income from a limited number of sources, and these sources are legally bound to declare the sums they pay. It is therefore possible for government to evaluate precisely for every taxpayer the total income he derives from every factor he owns.[46] Chapter 4 studies the shape of the optimal nonlinear tax on wage income.

The analysis in chapter 3 does not allow for a nonlinear income tax. Chapter 5 shows that the classical results change radically when we add to linear taxes on goods a general nonlinear income tax.

These three chapters only consider wage income. Chapter 6 extends the analysis by studying in what measure it is useful to add a tax on capital income to the optimal tax on wage income.

As was said before, the viewpoint adopted by the literature on optimal taxation may seem simplistic. Chapter 7 presents some of the main critiques of optimal taxation and attempts to evaluate them.

---

44. Some authors include in direct taxation those taxes that can be personnalized and in indirect taxation those that cannot be. This distinction largely coincides with the more traditional one that I use.

45. On the other hand, as we will see in chapter 9, it is quite possible for government to collect a nonlinear tax on total consumption, that part of income that is not saved.

46. This statement should be tempered: it is more tenable for wage income than for other labor income and, especially, for capital income.

3

Indirect Taxation

We assume in this chapter that the government cannot use a non-linear tax on income. The only available tax instruments are linear, possibly differentiated taxes on goods and a linear tax on wages. This approach may seem unduly restrictive, but it played a very important role in the development of theory.

3.1 Ramsey's Formula

The first analysis of this problem is due to Ramsey (1927); his results were rediscovered by Samuelson in a note to the US Secretary of the Treasury (1951, published in 1986). Diamond-Mirrlees (1971b) then extended the Ramsey results to an economy with several consumers. Ramsey's formula is formally identical to that obtained by Boiteux (1956) for the socially optimal pricing of a budget-constrained multi-product monopoly, so it is sometimes called the Ramsey-Boiteux formula.

3.1.1 An Informal Approach

Before moving to the rigourous derivation of Ramsey's formula, let us return to the formulas derived in chapter 2 for the social welfare loss due to a tax on good i in partial equilibrium. If consumer surplus applies, we know that the deadweight loss of a small *ad valorem* t_i on good i is

$$D_i(t_i) = -\frac{p_i t_i\, dx_i}{2} = \frac{\varepsilon_D^i \varepsilon_S^i}{\varepsilon_D^i + \varepsilon_S^i} t_i^2 \frac{p_i x_i}{2}$$

In partial equilibrium, the distortions created on the various markets are, by construction, independent. A tax system $(t_1, \dots, t_n)$ therefore creates a total deadweight loss

$$D(t) = D_1(t_1) + \cdots + D_n(t_n)$$

and collects a tax revenue equal to

$$R(t) = p_1 x_1 t_1 + \cdots + p_n x_n t_n$$

If we minimize $D(t)$ under the constraint that $R(t) = T$ and assuming that expenditure $p_i x_i$ on each good is fixed, we immediately obtain

$$t_i \frac{\varepsilon_D^i \varepsilon_S^i}{\varepsilon_D^i + \varepsilon_S^i} = k$$

where k is the Lagrange multiplier associated to the government's budget constraint. We can rewrite this formula as the famous "inverse elasticities rule":

$$t_i = k \left(\frac{1}{\varepsilon_i^D} + \frac{1}{\varepsilon_i^S} \right)$$

This formula is somewhat surprising: it indeed suggests that optimal indirect taxation is never uniform. It does have its logic: if demand or supply for a good is relatively elastic, taxing it discourages its consumption and production more and thus creates more distortions; it may therefore be better to increase the tax rate on another good whose demand and supply are less elastic.

However, we obtained this formula under very restrictive assumptions, in partial equilibrium and with consumer surplus analysis applied separately on each market. Thus we had to neglect all general equilibrium interactions, but also income effects and cross-elasticities.

3.1.2   The General Model

Now consider the general equilibrium of a simple production economy. The economy consists of I consumer-workers with utility functions $U_i(X^i, L^i)$, where X^i represents consumptions of the n goods and L^i is the supply of labor. For a start, we assume that production has constant returns of the simplest variety: each good is produced from labor alone. Production of a unit of good j requires a_j units of labor so that the production price can only be $p_j = a_j w$ in equilibrium. We choose to normalize $w = 1$; moreover we choose the units of goods so that each a_j equals one, so that all production prices satisfy $p_j = 1$.

Since this is a general equilibrium model, we must specify how the government intervenes in the economy. The government may want to pay civil servants, finance the production of public goods, or purchase private goods. To simplify, we assume here that it just buys T units of labor. Since the wage is normalized to one, the government must collect revenue T. We consider the following taxes:

- linear taxes on goods, which raise consumer prices to $(1 + t_j)$
- a linear tax on wages, so that the after-tax wage is $(1 - \tau)$.

The budget constraint of consumer i, who only owns his labor force, then is

$$\sum_{j=1}^{n} (1 + t_j) X_j^i = (1 - \tau) L^i$$

It is easy to see that in this setting (with no nonlabor income, and no bequests), the tax on wages is equivalent to a uniform tax on goods. Indeed define

$$t_j' = \frac{\tau + t_j}{1 - \tau}$$

Since $1 + t_j' = (1 + t_j)/(1 - \tau)$, we can rewrite the budget constraint of consumer i as

$$\sum_{j=1}^{n} (1 + t_j') X_j^i = L^i$$

The tax system $((t_j), \tau)$ then is equivalent for all consumers to the tax system $((t_j'), 0)$, which does not tax wages. Replacing the former with the latter leaves consumer choices unchanged. Moreover the government collects from consumer i with the former tax system

$$\sum_{j=1}^{n} t_j X_j^i + \tau L^i$$

But using the consumer i's budget constraint

$$L_i = \sum_{j=1}^{n} (1 + t_j') X_j^i$$

this tax revenue can also be written

$$\sum_{j=1}^{n} (t_j + \tau(1 + t_j')) X_j^i = \sum_{j=1}^{n} t_j' X_j^i$$

which is exactly what the government collects from consumer i in the latter tax system. Thus a tax on wages is absolutely equivalent to a uniform tax on goods.

As a consequence only n of the $(n+1)$ rates $((t_j), \tau)$ are determined at the optimum, whatever that is. We may, for instance, fix arbitrarily the rate of the tax on wages. This hardly matters, since we focus here on how taxes are differentiated across goods, and t'_j increases in t_j. We therefore use from now on the t'_j notation, which fixes $\tau = 0$.

We will work on the indirect utility of consumers, which can be written $V_i(q)$, where $q = 1 + t'$ is the vector of consumption prices:

$$V_i(q) = \max_{(X^i, L^i)} U_i(X^i, L^i) \quad \text{under} \quad q \cdot X^i = L^i$$

We are in a second-best situation, since we do not allow for the lump-sum transfers that would implement any Pareto optimum. To model the redistributive objectives of government, we assume that it maximizes a Bergson-Samuelson functional

$$\mathcal{W}(q) = W(V_1(q), \ldots, V_I(q))$$

To fulfill its needs in the most efficient way, the government must maximize $\mathcal{W}(q)$ in q under its budget constraint (remember that $q = 1 + t'$, so choosing the tax rates is equivalent to choosing the consumption prices):

$$\sum_{i=1}^{I} \sum_{j=1}^{n} (q_j - 1) X^i_j(q) = T$$

where the $X^i_j(q)$ are the demands of the various consumers.[47]

Let λ denote the Lagrange multiplier of the budget constraint of government. We have, by differentiating in q_k,

$$\sum_{i=1}^{I} \frac{\partial \mathcal{W}}{\partial V_i} \frac{\partial V_i}{\partial q_k} = -\lambda \sum_{i=1}^{I} \left(X^i_k + \sum_{j=1}^{n} t'_j \frac{\partial X^i_j}{\partial q_k} \right)$$

By Roy's identity,

---

47. We should note here that the indirect utilities $V_i(q)$ are quasi-*convex*, so that even though W is concave, the program we shall solve may not be concave. Diamond-Mirrlees (1971b) prove that the calculations that follow can nevertheless be rigourously justified.

$$\frac{\partial V_i}{\partial q_k} = -\alpha_i X_k^i$$

where α_i is the marginal utility of income of i. We define

$$\beta_i = \frac{\partial \mathcal{W}}{\partial V_i} \alpha_i$$

This new parameter weighs the marginal utility of income of consumer i by his weight in the social welfare function; β_i is called the social marginal utility of income of i, since it is the increase in the value of the Bergson-Samuelson functional when i is given one more unit of income.

We have, by substituting these definitions,

$$\sum_{i=1}^{I} \beta_i X_k^i = \lambda \sum_{i=1}^{I} \left(X_k^i + \sum_{j=1}^{n} t_j' \frac{\partial X_j^i}{\partial q_k} \right)$$

We will now use Slutsky's equation

$$\frac{\partial X_j^i}{\partial q_k} = S_{jk}^i - X_k^i \frac{\partial X_j^i}{\partial R_i}$$

where we defined

$$S_{jk}^i = \left(\frac{\partial X_j^i}{\partial q_k} \right)_{U_i}$$

We get, by rearranging,

$$\sum_{j=1}^{n} t_j' \sum_{i=1}^{I} S_{jk}^i = \frac{\sum_{i=1}^{I} \beta_i X_k^i}{\lambda} - \sum_{i=1}^{I} X_k^i + \sum_{i=1}^{I} X_k^i \sum_{j=1}^{n} t_j' \frac{\partial X_j^i}{\partial R_i}$$

which contains the new parameter

$$b_i = \frac{\beta_i}{\lambda} + \sum_{j=1}^{n} t_j' \frac{\partial X_j^i}{\partial R_i}$$

The first term of b_i is the social marginal utility of income of i, divided by λ, which is the cost of budget resources for the government; the second term is the increase in tax revenue collected on i when his income increases by one unit. The parameter b_i thus measures what is called the net social marginal utility of income of consumer i. It accounts not only for the direct term β_i/λ of social utility (measured in monetary units) but also for the fact that the increase in taxes paid by i allows to reduce tax rates. Of course, b_i is endogenous, just like β_i.

Let us denote the aggregate demand for good k by $X_k = \sum_{i=1}^{I} X_k^i$. Rearranging and using the symmetry of the Slutsky matrix, we finally get

$$\sum_{j=1}^{n} t_j' \sum_{i=1}^{I} S_{kj}^i = -X_k\left(1 - \sum_{i=1}^{I} b_i \frac{X_k^i}{X_k}\right)$$

By definition,

$$\sum_{i=1}^{I} \frac{X_k^i}{X_k} = 1$$

Denote $\bar{b}$ as the average of the b_i's and define the empirical covariance (across consumers) as

$$\theta_k = \text{cov}\left(\frac{b_i}{\bar{b}}, \frac{IX_k^i}{X_k}\right)$$

We can now write

$$-\frac{\sum_{j=1}^{n} t_j' \sum_{i=1}^{I} S_{kj}^i}{X_k} = 1 - \bar{b} - \bar{b}\theta_k$$

which is Ramsey's formula with several consumers, first obtained in this form by Diamond (1975).

The left-hand side of this equation is called the discouragement index of good k. Let indeed the t_j' be small (which must hold if the government collects a low tax revenue T). Then the tax t_j' on good j reduces the consumption of good k by consumer i by $t_j' S_{kj}^i$ at a fixed utility level. The left-hand side is, to a first-order approximation, minus the percentage of decrease of the consumption of good k summed across consumers. Thus it can be interpreted as the relative reduction in the compensated demand for good k induced by the tax system.

As for the right-hand side, it depends negatively on the term θ_k, that is, on the covariance between the net social marginal utility of income and the share of consumer i in the total consumption of good k. With only one consumer, θ_k obviously is zero. It only differs from zero in that consumption structures and the b_i factors differ across agents. For this reason it is called the distributive factor of good k.

Ramsey's formula therefore indicates that the government should discourage less the consumption of these goods that have a positive θ_k, that is, of goods that are heavily consumed by agents with a high net social marginal utility of income. But who are these agents? Coming back to the definition of the b_i's, it is clear that ceteris paribus, the agents with a high $\partial \mathcal{W} / \partial V_i$ also have a high b_i. But these agents, who are privileged by the government in its objective function, are probably also the poorest. This suggests that the tax system should discourage less the consumption of the goods that the poor buy more, since these goods have a positive distributive factor θ_k.

To obtain this formula, we assumed that production exhibited constant returns and moreover had a very simple structure—each good being produced independently from labor alone. It is easy to show that the formula remains valid for any constant returns technology. If returns are decreasing, then firms make profits that (possibly after taxation) are paid to their shareholders. Consumer demands then depend both on consumption prices q and production prices p, which makes the analysis much more complicated (see Munk 1978). Note, however, that these profits are actually rents, and that it is efficient for the government to tax them; if profits in fact are taxed at a 100% rate, then Ramsey's formula again remains valid.

3.1.3   Some Special Cases

First note that if all consumers have the same consumption structure, then all X_k^i / X_k terms are equal to $1/I$ and the covariance of the right-hand side is zero, so the discouragement index is the same for all goods at the optimum.

But the most interesting special case is that studied by Ramsey and Samuelson, where all b_i are identical and equal to some b. This obviously holds if the population can be represented by a single consumer. We will focus this subsection on the study of Ramsey's formula with a representative consumer.

In this case too, all discouragement indexes are equal. This prescription is very different in general from the popular notion that "to avoid distortions," all goods should be taxed at the same rate. Our formula now is

$$-\frac{\sum_{j=1}^{n} t_j' S_{kj}}{X_k} = 1 - b$$

Note that if we move X_k to the right-hand side and sum the equalities across goods, weighted by t', we get

$$-\sum_{j,k=1}^{n} t_j' S_{kj} t_k' = (1-b) \sum_k t_k' X_k$$

The left-hand side is the semi-norm of t' for the semidefinite positive matrix $(-S)$ and therefore it is nonnegative. The right-hand side is the product of tax revenue T with $(1-b)$. Thus $b \le 1$ if the tax is to collect any revenue. In return, we conclude that the discouragement indexes are all nonnegative: the optimal tax system does not encourage the consumption of any good.[48]

At this stage Ramsey's formula still is rather opaque. It nevertheless yields some conclusions. Consider, for instance, the two-good case, $n = 2$. By solving the Ramsey formulas associated with these two goods, and denoting $D = S_{11}S_{22} - S_{12}^2 > 0$ as the determinant of the Slutsky submatrix for the two consumption goods, we find

$$\begin{cases} t_1' = \dfrac{1-b}{D}(S_{12}X_2 - S_{22}X_1) \\[2mm] t_2' = \dfrac{1-b}{D}(S_{21}X_1 - S_{11}X_2) \end{cases}$$

Now the expenditure function is homogeneous of degree one in prices and the Slutsky matrix is its second derivative. Denoting 0 for the good "leisure," Euler's theorem implies that

$$S_{i0} + q_1 S_{i1} + q_2 S_{i2} = 0 \qquad \text{for } i = 1, 2$$

We rewrite these equalities as

$$\begin{cases} S_{12} = -\dfrac{S_{10}}{q_2} - \dfrac{q_1 S_{11}}{q_2} \\[2mm] S_{21} = -\dfrac{S_{20}}{q_1} - \dfrac{q_2 S_{11}}{q_1} \end{cases}$$

Define as usual the compensated elasticities as $\varepsilon_{ij} = S_{ij} q_j / X_i$, whence

---

48. This observation no longer holds in the several-consumer model, where the optimal tax system may in fact encourage the consumptions of some goods.

$$\begin{cases} t'_1 = -\dfrac{1-b}{D}\dfrac{X_1 X_2}{q_2}(\varepsilon_{10} + \varepsilon_{11} + \varepsilon_{22}) \\[2ex] t'_2 = -\dfrac{1-b}{D}\dfrac{X_1 X_2}{q_1}(\varepsilon_{20} + \varepsilon_{11} + \varepsilon_{22}) \end{cases}$$

It follows that

$$t'_1 q_2 - t'_2 q_1 = -\frac{1-b}{D}X_1 X_2(\varepsilon_{10} - \varepsilon_{20})$$

Since $q = 1 + t'$, the left-hand side is just $t'_1 - t'_2$. Thus this equation implies that $t'_1 > t'_2$ if and only if $\varepsilon_{10} < \varepsilon_{20}$, that is, if and only if good 1 is more complementary to leisure than good 2.

To interpret this result, recall that by definition,

$$\varepsilon_{i0} = \left(\frac{\partial \log X_i}{\partial \log w}\right)_U$$

Therefore $\varepsilon_{10} < \varepsilon_{20}$ if an increase in wages induces a larger increase in the consumption of good 2 than in the consumption of good 1 for a fixed utility level. But for a fixed utility level only substitution effects come into play, and a wage increase leads to an increase in labor supply. Thus good 1 must be taxed at a higher rate than good 2 if when the consumer works more, he increases his consumption of good 2 more than that of good 1.

This result was obtained by Corlett-Hague (1953): when preferences are not separable between goods and leisure, the government should deviate from uniform taxation by taxing more heavily the goods that are complementary to leisure (e.g., skis) than the goods that are complementary to labor (e.g., urban transportation). The intuition can be seen by recalling that a uniform taxation is equivalent to a tax on wages, which discourages labor supply. One way to counter this distortion is to discourage the consumption of leisure by taxing more heavily the goods that are complementary to leisure.

Let us now make even more restrictive assumptions: we assume that all compensated cross-elasticities of good k with other goods are zero. Define $\varepsilon_k = -S_{kk}q_k/X_k$ as the direct compensated elasticity of good k. Then we get the inverse elasticities rule:

$$\frac{t'_k}{1 + t'_k} = \frac{1-b}{\varepsilon_k}$$

If these assumptions hold for all goods, then tax rates should be (to a first-order approximation) inversely proportional to demand elasticities;[49] this is the formula from the beginning of this section, except that since returns here are constant, $\varepsilon_S = \infty$. This has been used as a way to justify the so-called sin taxes on tobacco and alcohol, but it is not clear that their demands in fact are price-inelastic.

One may wonder when Ramsey's formula for a representative consumer yields uniform taxation of goods. Deaton (1981) shows that a necessary and sufficient condition is that the utility function be quasi-separable,[50] that is, that the marginal rates of substitution between goods on a given indifference curve be independent of the consumption of leisure. It can be proved that quasi-separability holds if and only if the expenditure function can be written

$$e(u, q, w) = e^*(u, w, b(u, q))$$

It is easy to see that then a wage increase does not change the relative compensated demands of the various goods. Thus Deaton's result generalizes that of Corlett and Hague to the n-good case. This condition clearly is very restrictive.

When the consumers are heterogeneous, then the analysis of the practical consequences of Ramsey's formula becomes very complex. It is in particular impossible to find reasonable conditions for uniform taxation to be optimal.

Note, however, that there may be reasons outside this model that plead for uniform taxation. For instance, uniform taxation can lower

---

49. Contrary to appearances, this formula is perfectly consistent with the Corlett-Hague result. The compensated cross-elasticities indeed are zero if the utility function can be written

$$\sum_{k=1}^{n} u_k(X_k) - BL$$

But then minimizing expenditure yields

$$\forall k, \quad \frac{q_k}{u_k'(X_k)} = \frac{w}{B}$$

It follows that for any good k,

$$u_k'(X_k) = \frac{Bq_k}{w}$$

so that $\varepsilon_{k0} = \varepsilon_k$: the goods that are more complementary to leisure are also those with the less elastic demands.

50. Sometimes the term "implicitly separable" is used. This property should be distinguished from weak separability, which we will encounter in chapter 5.

administration costs, and limit the lobbying by interest groups, since each group attempts to bend the tax system in its favor.

Finally, recall that Ramsey's formula only holds in a world where income is taxed linearly. We will see in chapter 5 that setting this assumption aside has spectacular consequences on the structure of optimal indirect taxation.

3.2   Productive Efficiency

Now consider a production economy where technologies combine several inputs to produce several outputs. If production does not exhibit constant returns, assume also that profits are taxed at a 100% rate. Then Diamond-Mirrlees (1971a) showed that the optimal tax system has another remarkable property: it always maintains the economy on the production possibilities frontier. This is called the productive efficiency property. It implies that there is no reallocation of inputs that would increase the production of every good. More formally, productive efficiency implies that the technical marginal rates of substitution between two given inputs are equal in all productive units that use them. Moreover this holds whether these productive units are firms, households, or the government. A tax on the use of an input cannot vary across sectors without violating this equality and therefore productive efficiency.

That the tax system maintains productive efficiency is a priori rather surprising. We know at least since Lipsey-Lancaster (1956–1957) that in a second-best universe, our usual intuitions may not be valid any more. In particular, two distortions may be better than one distortion, and one might want to "correct" a tax-induced distortion in consumption by a distortion in production. Diamond and Mirrlees have shown that it is in fact not a feature of the optimal tax system.

To prove this result, it is simplest to use a more abstract but also more general approach than in the preceding section. Thus let x_i be the net consumption plan of consumer i, which includes its net consumptions of private goods, of public goods, and its supplies of production factors. If q is the associated price vector, the consumer achieves an indirect utility $V_i(q)$ by maximizing his utility $U_i(x_i)$ under the budget constraint

$$q \cdot x_i \leq 0$$

Once again, this budget constraint assumes that there are no profits redistributed to consumers: if a firm makes profits, they are taxed at a 100% rate. We denote g as the vector of government's net consumptions, assumed to be exogenous. Finally, we assume that firm $j = 1, \ldots, J$ chooses a production plan y_j in its production set Y_j.

First assume that just like in a socialist economy, the government can control the production of each firm, and neglect for now the government's budget constraint. For fixed g, the government tries to set prices q so as to maximize the social welfare

$$\mathscr{W}(q) = W(V_1(q), \ldots, V_n(q))$$

under the scarcity constraint

$$\sum_{i=1}^{n} x_i(q) + g \leq \sum_{j=1}^{J} y_j$$

with $y_j \in Y_j$ for all $j = 1, \ldots, J$.

The proof of the productive efficiency lemma proceeds by contradiction. Thus assume that at the social optimum, production is inefficient: the aggregate production plan $y = \sum_{j=1}^{J} y_j$ lies in the interior of the aggregate production set $Y = \sum_{j=1}^{J} Y_j$. Choose a consumption good k for which all consumers have a positive net demand. Then the indirect utility of any consumer $V_i(q)$ decreases in q_k. By reducing q_k, the government therefore increases social welfare. Under some regularity assumptions the net demands $x_i(q)$ are continuous; since we start from a situation where

$$\sum_{i=1}^{n} x_i(q) + g = y \in \text{Int } Y$$

one can reduce slightly q_k and change the aggregate production plan to respect the scarcity constraint within the bounds of Y. Thus we found a change in the tax system that is feasible and improves social welfare, a contradiction.

In our economies the government of course does not control production. But since at the optimum y must be on the frontier of Y, let p be a vector that is normal to this frontier in Y. Then for every firm j the production plan y_j maximizes profit $p \cdot y_j$ at the production prices p. There thus exists a production price system that decentralizes the production plan y.

Finally, note that the budget constraint of the government automatically holds. Indeed the government must finance

$$p \cdot g = p \cdot \left(\sum_{j=1}^{J} y_j - \sum_{i=1}^{n} x_i \right)$$

But at the optimum of consumer i, $q \cdot x_i = 0$, and thus

$$-p \cdot x_i = (q - p) \cdot x_i = t \cdot x_i$$

where $t = q - p$ is the vector of taxes at the optimum.[51] If we denote $\pi_j = p \cdot y_j$ the before-tax profit of firm j, we therefore get

$$p \cdot g = \sum_{j=1}^{J} \pi_j + t \cdot \sum_{i=1}^{n} x_i$$

which shows that at the optimum the government finances its consumption exactly through the 100% tax on profits and the taxes on consumers. It is in fact a consequence of Walras's law: since all markets are in equilibrium and every agent but one is on its budget constraint, then so must the last agent (the government).

The intuition for this result is simple: if profits are not redistributed, the utilities of consumers and thus social welfare only depend on consumption prices and on the prices consumers get for the inputs they sell. If the government manipulates production prices and the prices paid by firms for inputs, it only adds distortions without correcting the existing ones, and therefore it must reduce the value of the government's objectives.

This theorem in fact has several important consequences for optimal taxation. By definition, productive efficiency excludes using taxes on production factors that are not uniform across firms. For instance, the corporate income tax may be interpreted as a tax on capital that only affects some firms in the private sector and therefore reduces productive efficiency. A similar case can be made against taxes on intermediate goods, which are produced by some

---

51. Note that when no profits are redistributed to consumers, the price systems q and p can be normalized independently. Therefore there exists an infinity of tax systems t that decentralize the optimum. If, for instance, we multiply q (resp. p) by a positive real number λ (resp. μ), then the tax system $t' = \lambda q - \mu p$ leads to exactly the same productions and consumptions than t. Thus comparisons such as $t_k > t_l$ depend on the normalization rule. On the other hand, the comparison of *ad valorem* tax rates $t_k/p_k > t_l/p_l$ does not.

firms and used as inputs by other firms, or against reductions in payroll taxes that are sector-specific. Since productive efficiency concerns all productive units and not only private firms, one can also deduce from the theorem that the government should use the production prices of the private sector as its shadow prices. Finally, consider the world as a whole, and assume that there exists a world government (or perhaps a World Trade Organization) that attempts to maximize global welfare. Then the production efficiency lemma implies that international trade must occur at production prices, that is, without any tariff. International trade indeed can be analyzed as a production technique that transforms exported goods into imported goods.

The production efficiency lemma of course only holds under some assumptions. As we saw above, it can only be generalized to production with decreasing returns if the government can tax profits at a 100 percent rate. Moreover it assumes that there is no limit to the ability of the government to vary tax rates on goods. In fact many goods (e.g., housing, banking, and insurance services) are usually exempt from VAT. In such a situation it may be optimal to violate productive efficiency so as to remedy the impossibility to tax some consumptions. We also implicitly assumed that all production factors can be taxed at different rates. This is rather unrealistic, since few factors are homogeneous. It assumes, for instance, that skilled labor and unskilled labor can be taxed at linear but different rates. Naito (1999) shows that it may in fact be optimal for government to use a shadow price for skilled labor employed in the public production sector that is higher than its market price. Then public firms demand less skilled labor, which reduces its relative wage and thus contributes to redistributing incomes.

References

Boiteux, M. 1956. Sur la gestion des monopoles publics astreints à l'équilibre budgét-aire. *Econometrica* 24: 22–40.

Corlett, W., and D. Hague. 1953. Complementarity and the excess burden of taxation. *Review of Economic Studies* 21: 21–30.

Deaton, A. 1981. Optimal taxes and the structure of preferences. *Econometrica* 49: 1245–60.

Diamond, P. 1975. A many-person Ramsey tax rule. *Journal of Public Economics* 4: 335–42.

Diamond, P., and J. Mirrlees. 1971a. Optimal taxation and public production, I: Production efficiency. *American Economic Review* 61: 8–27.

Diamond, P., and J. Mirrlees. 1971b. Optimal taxation and public production, II: Tax rules. *American Economic Review* 61: 261–78.

Lipsey, R., and K. Lancaster. 1956–1957. The general theory of second best. *Review of Economic Studies* 24: 11–32.

Munk, K. 1978. Optimal taxation and pure profit. *Scandinavian Journal of Economics* 80: 1–19.

Naito, H. 1999. Re-examination of uniform commodity taxes under a nonlinear income tax system and its implication for production efficiency. *Journal of Public Economics* 71: 165–188.

Ramsey, F. 1927. A contribution to the theory of taxation. *Economic Journal* 37: 47–61.

Salanié, B. 2000. *The Microeconomics of Market Failures*. MIT Press.

Samuelson, P. 1986. Theory of optimal taxation. *Journal of Public Economics* 30: 137–43.

4   Direct Taxation

Chapter 3 characterized optimal indirect taxation when the tax on wages is proportional. In practice, most developed countries use a graduated income tax. Even when a "flat tax" with a single tax rate is proposed (as in the United States), it usually comprises a personal exemption so that the tax is progressive.[52] The shape of the income tax schedule is a key element of the democratic debate. It clearly cannot escape value judgments, but economists nevertheless can contribute to the debate. Note that the personal income tax is not the only tax that depends on income. Thus in this chapter direct taxation in fact comprises all taxation that depends on primary income, which includes payroll taxes such as social contributions but also all means-tested benefits.

The study of optimal direct taxation must take into account disincentive effects on labor supply. This has been obvious for some time, but only since Mirrlees (1971) do we have a model that allows us to discuss the trade-off between equity (the search for a redistribution that implements social views) and efficiency (minimizing distortions induced by the tax system).

4.1   The Emergence of the Model

The literature on optimal direct taxation assumes that consumer-workers are born with heterogeneous, innate earning capacities w. We may identify w to human capital, or perhaps to productivity[53] or to the wage that the individual can obtain on the labor market. This last interpretation nevertheless neglects some general equilibrium

---

52. We call a tax progressive when its average rate increases with the taxable basis.
53. For simplicity, I will use that term in this chapter.

considerations, to which we will return later. We also usually sup-
pose that all consumers have the same utility function $U(C, L)$, defined over a single consumption good[54] C and a labor supply L. This
simplifying assumption in fact plays an important role, since it sets
aside all individual differences in preferences, and thus all considerations that have to do with horizontal equity.

The definition of the proper redistributive objectives of government has been debated for quite some time. Some classical authors
argued for a tax that would be proportional to the ability to pay;
others preferred a tax that would equalize the "sacrifices" of taxpayers. The latter camp was split between those who favored equal
sacrifice (the same reduction in utility for all) and those who preferred equiproportional sacrifice (where percentages of utility reductions are equalized across taxpayers).[55]

Nowadays we model social preferences in this field by endowing
the government with an additive Bergson-Samuelson functional:

$$W = \int \Psi(\mathcal{U}(w)) \, dF(w)$$

where $\mathcal{U}(w)$ is the after-tax utility of consumer w, F is the cumulative
distribution function of w in the population, and Ψ is an increasing
and concave function that weights the utilities of the agents according to redistributive objectives. As an example, in simulations the
function

$$\Psi(u) = \frac{u^\rho}{\rho}$$

is often used, where ρ is a parameter smaller than one that indexes
the social aversion to inequality (and $\Psi(u) = \log u$ for $\rho = 0$). When
$\rho = -\infty$, the dominant term in the integral that defines W is that
which yields the lowest $\mathcal{U}(w)$. We call the resulting social preferences Rawlsian: the government aims at maximizing the utility of
the least favored member of society.[56] The $\rho = 1$ case represents

---

54. Chapter 5 reintroduces a multiplicity of consumption goods.
55. Around 1900 the marginalists often applied "Bernoulli's law," that is, a utility of
income given by $U(x) = \log(x)$ whereby all agents derive an identical increment of
utility from proportional income increases. So it is easy to say that the equal sacrifice
principle leads to a proportional tax, while equiproportional sacrifice argues for a
progressive tax.
56. In deference to John Rawls, whose *Theory of Justice*, published in 1971, is the most
important writing in this field.

(unweighted) utilitarian preferences: the government simply maximizes the integral of utilities over the population.[57]

First assume that labor supply is perfectly inelastic (so that we can neglect the dependence of utility on L) and that individual w earns before-tax income $Y(w)$. All preferences on income are identical and are given by a function U. The government aims at financing public good expenditures R.[58] Thus, if government collects from individual w a tax revenue $T(w)$, then it must be that

$$\int T(w)\,dF(w) = R$$

The individual indexed by w then reaches utility

$$\mathscr{U}(w) = U(Y(w) - T(w))$$

The optimal income tax is obtained by maximizing

$$W = \int \Psi(\mathscr{U}(w))\,dF(w)$$

under the governement's budget constraint. If λ is the multiplier associated to that constraint, we get immediately

$$\forall w, \quad \Psi'(\mathscr{U}(w))U'(Y(w) - T(w)) = \lambda$$

This is what Edgeworth (1897) called the principle of equimarginal sacrifice. If $\Psi \circ \mathscr{U}$ is strictly concave, then we obtain Edgeworth's conclusion:

The solution of this problem in the abstract is that the richer should be taxed for the benefit of the poorer up to the point where complete equality of fortunes is attained.

Therefore government should collect taxes so as to equalize all after-tax incomes $(Y(w) - T(w))$. In fact Edgeworth only considered the utilitarian case where $\Psi(u) = u$. Even in that case the result holds if U is strictly concave, which can be justified by the standard assumption that the marginal utility of income is decreasing. This may seem surprising; after all, utilitarianism is in general not viewed as

---

57. See Salanié (2000, ch. 1) for a brief discussion of the theories of justice that underlie these representations.
58. In all of this chapter we neglect the dependence of utility on the production of the public good, which is held fixed.

a very redistributive social philosophy.[59] Nevertheless, it rests on several crucial assumptions, the most important of which is the perfect inelasticity of labor supply.

It seems quite natural that if the agents do not react to taxation, this should transfer income from the agents who have a lower marginal utility of income (the rich) to those who have a high marginal utility of income (the poor). And there is no reason for this process to stop until marginal utilities of income are equalized. In the real world the reactions of the workers who are taxed counter this process of equalization: taxation changes the primary incomes $Y(w)$. A simple way to take this into account seems to be to write primary incomes as

$$Y(w) = wL(w)$$

The simplest interpretation is that individual w has a fixed productivity w.[60] The labor market is assumed to be competitive, so that each individual is paid his productivity level. Then everyone chooses their labor supply so as to maximize after-tax utility

$$L(w) = \arg \max_{L} U(wL - T(w), L)$$

At this stage the model is still not very realistic. Assume, for instance, as we will do later, that utility takes the quasi-linear form

$$U(C, L) = C - v(L)$$

Then it is easy to see that the tax has no influence on labor supply $L(w)$ (with a general utility function, the tax would have an income effect on labor supply, just as any lump-sum transfer). To reintroduce the effect of the income tax on behavior, we must take into account an essential limit to the ability of the government. The government indeed cannot observe the productivities of the agents; it is very easy for an agent who has a high productivity w to claim to have a lower productivity so as to pay a lower tax. The government can only tax primary income $Y(w) = wL(w)$, so the tax must take the form

$$T(w) = T(Y(w))$$

59. We will see later in analyzing Mirrlees's model that it confirms this opinion.
60. This implicitly assumes that the production function exhibits an infinite elasticity of substitution between skills. Otherwise, the productivity of each skill depends on how it is combined with other skills. We will return to this point later.

This apparently innocuous remark in fact has very important consequences. As Mirrlees (1971) writes:

> As a result of using men's economic performance as evidence of their economic potentialities, complete equality of social marginal utilities of income ceases to be desirable, for the tax system that would bring about this result would completely discourage all unpleasant work.

Note here that if the government could observe both primary income Y and labor supply L, it could infer the value of the productivity $w = Y/L$. Thus we must assume that the government cannot observe L. This is arguably too strong if L represents hours of work: one could imagine that each employer must be made to report the hours worked by each employee to the tax authority. It is more plausible if L also has unobservable components such as effort.

Under this observability constraint, it is clear that even with a quasi-linear utility function, the tax influences labor supply, since the program of individual w becomes

$$L(w) = \arg \max_{L}(wL - T(wL) - v(L))$$

A confiscatory taxation then reduces production and thus the size of the social pie. Classical authors were aware of that risk, as Edgeworth wrote:

> ... the first approximation to the solution of the problem is obtained by minimising the total sacrifice, subject to the condition that production is not much diminished.

However, Edgeworth and his contemporaries did not know how to model the trade-off between efficiency and equity. The great merit of Mirrlees is that he invented a model that yields operational results.

4.2   Mirrlees's Model

The preceding discussion leads us to the model introduced in the literature by Mirrlees (1971).[61] The government's problem is to choose the income tax schedule $T(.)$ so as to maximize

$$W = \int_{0}^{\infty} \Psi(\mathscr{U}(w))\, dF(w)$$

---

61. Some elements of this model were already featured in Vickrey (1945, sec. III).

where

$$\mathscr{U}(w) = U(wL(w) - T(wL(w)), L(w))$$

and $L(w)$ maximizes over L

$$U(wL - T(wL), L)$$

all of this under the government's budget constraint

$$\int_0^\infty T(wL(w))\, dF(w) \geq R$$

At this level of generality, the problem is very difficult: Mirrlees's paper has as many as 141 numbered equations. The optimal tax can be characterized, but the resulting formulas are rather opaque. We will begin by solving in a simple way an interesting special case.

4.2.1   The Rawlsian Case

Let us now assume that the government's preferences are Rawlsian. First note that $\mathscr{U}(w)$ always is an increasing function; actually

$$\mathscr{U}(w) = \max_L U(wL - T(wL), L)$$

Applying the envelope theorem leads to

$$\mathscr{U}'(w) = (1 - T')LU'_C \geq 0$$

given $T' \leq 1$, which must obviously hold for the optimal tax.[62] Thus the least favored individual is the one with the lowest w, say $\underline{w}$. If his productivity is low enough, then the optimal tax will discourage him from working (it is obviously true if $\underline{w} = 0$). Then he will only live off transfers $-T(\underline{w})$, and a Rawlsian government will seek to make these transfers as large as possible. This implies maximizing tax revenue from individuals who actually work. More generally, the optimal tax schedule must maximize tax revenue under two constraints: the incentive constraint and the constraint that the utility of the least favored individual should be equal to the value of the government's social objective function.[63] Piketty (1998) showed that under this ob-

---

62. No individual will choose his labor supply to locate at a point where $T' > 1$. Otherwise, he could increase his utility by reducing his labor supply. If $T' = 1$ as in the case of a guaranteed minimum income, the only rational choice is $L = 0$.

63. Any schedule that does not solve this program can be replaced with one that is socially preferred.

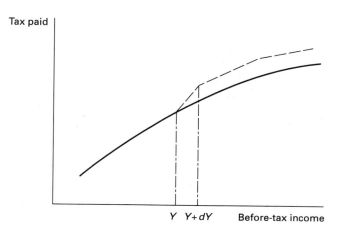

Figure 4.1
Marginal change in the tax schedule

jective of maximizing tax revenue, it is very easy to characterize the optimal tax if one moreover assumes that there is no income effect on labor supply.

Let us start from the optimal income tax and increase the marginal tax rate by an infinitesimal amount dT' on a small interval $[Y, Y + dY]$, as illustrated on figure 4.1. Two effects should be distinguished. First note that to the first order, the tax paid by every individual whose primary income is larger than Y increases by $dT'dY$.[64] Let w_Y denote the productivity level that corresponds to the primary income Y. Since these individuals are $(1 - F(w_Y))$ in number, tax revenue increases by

$$dT'dY(1 - F(w_Y)) \qquad\qquad (1)$$

On the other hand, those individuals whose primary income was between Y and $(Y + dY)$ face a higher marginal tax rate. Their net wage indeed decreases from $w_Y(1 - T')$ to $w_Y(1 - T' - dT')$, which is a relative reduction of $dT'/(1 - T')$. By the definition of the elasticity of labor supply ε_L, their labor supply decreases by $L\varepsilon_L dT'/(1 - T')$ and for each such individual, tax revenue goes down by

$$T'Y\varepsilon_L \frac{dT'}{1 - T'}$$

---

64. Since we excluded income effects, these individuals do not change their labor supply.

Let f denote the probability distribution function of w; these people number $f(w_Y)\,dw_Y$. Moreover

$$\frac{dY}{dw_Y} = \frac{d(wL)}{dw} = L(1 + \varepsilon_L)$$

so the individuals affected by the disincentive are

$$f(w_Y)\frac{dY}{L(1 + \varepsilon_L)}$$

Then total tax revenue decreases by

$$\frac{\varepsilon_L}{1 + \varepsilon_L}T'w_Y\frac{dT'}{1 - T'} + f(w_Y)\,dY \tag{2}$$

But since we started from the optimal tax, the effects (1) and (2) must exactly cancel out, so

$$\frac{T'(Y)}{1 - T'(Y)} = \left(1 + \frac{1}{\varepsilon_L}\right)\frac{1 - F(w_Y)}{w_Y f(w_Y)}$$

This formula is more complex than it seems, since w_Y and ε_L both depend on the tax schedule. However, it clearly exhibits two of the three main determinants of the optimal tax. The first one, of course, is the elasticity of labor supply: as could be expected, the larger the elasticity is, the lower are the optimal marginal tax rates. The second factor was more difficult to anticipate. It depends on the distribution of productivities in the population and shows that the optimal marginal tax rate is higher when w is lower in the distribution of productivities (since the $(1 - F(w))/w$ term is decreasing in w), and when the concentration of individuals around the productivity under examination is smaller.[65]

Piketty's argument makes it clear why we find this second term. When we increase the marginal tax rate at productivity level w, we collect more tax on more productive individuals, who are $(1 - F(w))$ in number; on the other hand, such a rate increase has a disincentive effect on the individuals whose productivity is close to w. The number of these individuals is proportional to $f(w)$, and the disincentive effect is more detrimental, for a given elasticity of labor supply, when they are more productive. We will see later that the shape

---

65. Note that $f(w)/(1 - F(w))$ is what statisticians call the hazard function of the distribution F.

of this term in fact largely determines the shape of the optimal tax schedule.

4.2.2 The General Approach

Let us come back to the general case and see how far we can carry the analysis. Unfortunately, it is rather hard to make progress in the analysis of the optimal tax schedule without making specific assumptions. Readers who are more interested in the practical applications of theory can skip this subsection without much loss.

The tax schedule defines a relationhip $C = Y - T(Y)$ between the consumption of the taxpayer and his before-tax income. $Y = wL$. It is therefore useful to define a new utility function by

$$u(C, Y, w) = U\left(C, \frac{Y}{w}\right)$$

Note that u is increasing in C and w and decreasing in Y. The revelation principle (e.g., see Salanié 1997, ch. 2) implies that the government cannot do better than by choosing a direct revealing mechanism, that is, a pair of functions $(C(w), Y(w))$ such that each taxpayer finds it best to announce his own productivity:

$$\forall w, \ w', \quad u(C(w), Y(w), w) \geq u(C(w'), Y(w'), w)$$

This double infinity of incentive constraints obviously is not easy to handle. However, we will see below how it can be simplified by imposing a very weak condition of the preferences of taxpayers. We assume from now on that the marginal rate of substitution between consumption and before-tax income is smaller for more productive individuals:

$$\left(\frac{\partial C}{\partial Y}\right)_u = \frac{u'_Y}{u'_C} \quad \text{decreases in } w$$

This condition is sometimes called *agent monotonicity*; it corresponds to the Spence-Mirrlees condition (*single crossing condition*) in contract theory (see Salanié 1997, ch. 2). Assume, for instance, that preferences are quasi-linear,

$$U(C, L) = C - v(L)$$

Then $u(C, Y, w) = C - v(Y/w)$ and

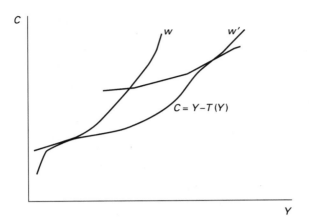

Figure 4.2
Spence-Mirrlees condition

$$\left(\frac{\partial C}{\partial Y}\right)_{u} = \frac{1}{w}v'\left(\frac{Y}{w}\right)$$

which decreases in w if and only if $Lv'(L)$ increases in L. This last condition is easily seen to be equivalent to the elasticity of labor supply being larger than -1. Since all empirical estimates are much larger than that, the Spence-Mirrlees condition indeed is rather weak.

Figure 4.2 illustrates why this condition is so useful. We pictured two indifference curves for productivities $w < w'$ in the (Y, C) plane, along with the tax schedule $C = Y - T(Y)$. Under the Spence-Mirrlees condition the indifference curve of w by definition is steeper than that of w' at the point where they cross. It is easy to see on the figure that this implies $C(w) < C(w')$ and $Y(w) < Y(w')$: more productive agents have higher consumption and before-tax income.

To prove it more rigorously, let us define the utility of taxpayer w when he claims to have productivity w':

$$V(w', w) = u(C(w'), Y(w'), w)$$

For the mechanism to be revealing, V must be maximal in $w' = w$. Assume that all functions are differentiable and that income Y is positive. Then we have the first-order necessary condition

$$\frac{\partial V}{\partial w'}(w, w) = 0 \qquad\qquad\qquad\qquad\qquad \text{(NC1)}$$

and the second-order necessary condition

$$\frac{\partial^2 V}{\partial w'^2}(w, w) \leq 0 \qquad\qquad\qquad\qquad (NC2)$$

Differentiating (NC1) gives us

$$\frac{\partial^2 V}{\partial w'^2} + \frac{\partial^2 V}{\partial w' \partial w} = 0$$

so (NC2) can be rewritten as

$$\frac{\partial^2 V}{\partial w' \partial w} \geq 0$$

We compute easily

$$\frac{\partial V}{\partial w'} = u'_C C' + u'_Y Y'$$

and

$$\frac{\partial^2 V}{\partial w' \partial w} = u''_{Cw} C' + u''_{Yw} Y'$$

Condition (NC1) then makes it possible to write

$$C' = -\frac{u'_Y}{u'_C} Y'$$

and (NC2) becomes

$$\left(-u''_{Cw} \frac{u'_Y}{u'_C} + u''_{Yw} \right) Y' \geq 0$$

But the Spence-Mirrlees condition implies, by differentiating the marginal rate of substitution in w, that

$$-\frac{u''_{Yw}}{u'_C} + \frac{u''_{Cw} u'_Y}{(u'_C)^2} \leq 0$$

so (NC2) just says that $Y' \geq 0$. The Spence-Mirrlees condition thus does imply that income increases with productivity, and since

$$C' = -\frac{u'_Y}{u'_C} Y'$$

consumption also increases with productivity.

The Spence-Mirrlees condition in fact allows us to reduce the incentive constraints to a much more manageable form. To see this, write

$$\frac{\partial V}{\partial w'}(w', w) = u_C'(C(w'), Y(w'), w)C'(w') + u_Y'(C(w'), Y(w'), w)Y'(w')$$

We also have

$$0 = \frac{\partial V}{\partial w'}(w', w')$$

$$= u_C'(C(w'), Y(w'), w')C'(w') + u_Y'(C(w'), Y(w'), w')Y'(w')$$

from which we get

$$\frac{\partial V}{\partial w'}(w', w) = Y'(w')u_C'(C(w'), Y(w'), w)\Delta$$

where

$$\Delta = \frac{u_Y'}{u_C'}(C(w'), Y(w'), w) - \frac{u_Y'}{u_C'}(C(w'), Y(w'), w')$$

has the sign of $(w - w')$, by the Spence-Mirrlees condition. Since Y' and u_C' are both positive, we deduce that

$$\frac{\partial V}{\partial w'}(w', w) \text{ has the sign of } (w - w')$$

so $V(w', w)$ indeed is maximal in $w' = w$.

To sum up these rather abstract developments, the Spence-Mirrlees condition, which is very weak, implies that more productive agents earn more and consume more. On a technical plane, it allows us to sum up the incentive constraints in the first-order necessary condition

$$\forall w, \quad u_C'(C(w), Y(w), w)C'(w) + u_Y'(C(w), Y(w), w)Y'(w) = 0 \qquad \text{(C1)}$$

and the second-order condition

$$\forall w, \quad Y'(w) \geq 0 \qquad \text{(C2)}$$

The problem to be solved then is to find two functions C and Y that maximize the objective funtion

$$\int_0^\infty \Psi(u(C(w), Y(w), w)) \, dF(w)$$

under the incentive constraints (C1) and (C2) and the government's budget constraint

$$\int_0^\infty (Y(w) - C(w))\, dF(w) \geq R$$

This problem can be treated in its general form (e.g., see Ebert 1992). It is still rather complex, mostly because constraint (C2) may be binding on some intervals at the optimum.[66] With a lot of work, one could prove rather weak properties of the optimal tax schedule. Rather than to pursue this approach, we will now adopt a more heuristic approach based on assuming quasi-linear utility functions. This will allow us to discuss the shape of the optimal tax schedule more precisely.

4.2.3   The Quasi-linear Case

We will focus on the special case where the utility function of taxpayers is quasi-linear:

$$U(C, L) = C - v(L)$$

This assumption is rather restrictive, of course, since it sets aside income effects on labor supply and it also means that the marginal utility of income is constant. However, it will allow us to come to a very simple formula for the optimal tax. To do so, we will skip some mathematical difficulties.

The Rawlsian case helped us derive two of the three determinants of the optimal tax schedule. On the other hand, focusing on the maximization of tax revenue meant that we forgot about redistribution from the rich to the middle class. We will now see that taking into account more general redistributive objectives adds a third term in the formula that determines the optimal marginal tax rate.

The computations at this stage become a bit more complex. To solve the government's problem, we begin by eliminating the tax schedule. First note that

$$\mathcal{U}(w) = \max_{L \geq 0}(wL - T(wL) - v(L)) = wL(w) - T(wL(w)) - v(L(w))$$

so the government's budget constraint can be written

---

66. Such intervals correspond to discontinuities of the marginal tax rate $T'(Y)$, just as in the transition between two brackets of the actual income tax schedule; then a group of taxpayers chooses the same point (Y, C). This is called *bunching*.

$$\int_0^\infty (wL(w) - \mathcal{U}(w) - v(L(w)))\, dF(w) \geq R$$

Assume that the tax schedule is continuously differentiable. Then by the envelope theorem we have

$$\mathcal{U}'(w) = (1 - T'(wL(w))L(w)$$

If moreover $L(w) > 0$, then the first-order condition of the taxpayer's program is

$$w(1 - T'(wL(w))) = v'(L(w))$$

so that[67]

$$\mathcal{U}'(w) = \frac{L(w)v'(L(w))}{w}$$

Of course, the first-order condition is not enough to characterize the solution of the taxpayer's program. However, we will assume that it is sufficient, which amounts to neglecting the constraint $Y'(w) \geq 0$ in the general approach.

Under these assumptions the government's problem amounts to choosing functions $\mathcal{U}$ and L so as to maximize

$$\int_0^\infty \Psi(\mathcal{U}(w)) f(w)\, dw$$

under the budget constraint

$$\int_0^\infty (wL(w) - \mathcal{U}(w) - v(L(w))) f(w)\, dw = R$$

and the differential constraint

$$\mathcal{U}'(w) = \frac{L(w)v'(L(w))}{w}$$

To solve this problem, we use Pontryagin's maximum principle.[68] We choose $\mathcal{U}(w)$ as a state variable $L(w)$ as a control variable. Denoting λ the multiplier associated to the budget constraint and $\mu(w)$ the multiplier attached to the differential constraint, the Hamiltonian can be written

---

67. Note that this formula also trivially holds if $L(w) = 0$.
68. This is briefly described in appendix B.

$$\mathcal{H} = \Psi(\mathcal{U})f + \lambda(wL - \mathcal{U} - v(L))f + \mu\frac{Lv'(L)}{w}$$

Pontryagin's maximum principle states the following:

- $L(w)$ maximizes $\mathcal{H}$ in L so that

$$\lambda(w - v')f + \mu\frac{v' + Lv''}{w} \leq 0$$

with an equality if $L(w) > 0$
- the derivative of μ is given by

$$\mu' = -\frac{\partial\mathcal{H}}{\partial\mathcal{U}}$$

whence

$$\mu' = (\lambda - \Psi'(\mathcal{U}))f$$

- μ verifies the two transversality constraints

$$\mu(0) = \lim_{w\to\infty} \mu(w) = 0$$

Let us first analyze the conditions on μ. Integrating the definition of μ' between w and infinity, and using the transversality condition at infinity, we get

$$\mu(w) = \int_w^\infty (\Psi'(\mathcal{U}(t)) - \lambda)f(t)\,dt$$

Now use the transversality condition in zero; this yields an expression for the multiplier associated to the budget constraint[69]

$$\lambda = \int_0^\infty \Psi'(\mathcal{U}(t))f(t)\,dt \tag{L}$$

For simplicity, define the function D by

$$D(w) = \frac{1}{1 - F(w)}\int_w^\infty \Psi'(\mathcal{U}(t))f(t)\,dt$$

This function by definition is the average value of $\Psi'(\mathcal{U})$ on the

---

69. Economic reasoning could have given us that equation: a uniform tax decrease of one dollar on each taxpayer increases the value of the social objective function by the right-hand side of (L), and its cost, by definition, equals λ.

interval $[w, +\infty[$. But Ψ' is the marginal weight given to utility in the social objective, and given redistributive objectives, it must be decreasing. Thus the function $D(w)$ is also decreasing. Using its definition, we finally get $\lambda = D(0)$ and

$$\mu(w) = (1 - F(w))(D(w) - D(0))$$

which cannot be positive.

Now choose some w such that $L(w) > 0$. Then we have the equation

$$\lambda(w - v')f + \mu \frac{v' + Lv''}{w} = 0$$

Note that since

$$w(1 - T') = v'$$

we have $w - v' = wT'$. Moreover let the taxpayer face a net wage w_n. His labor supply is given by

$$v'(L) = w_n$$

so its elasticity is

$$\varepsilon_L = \frac{\partial \log L}{\partial \log w_n} = \frac{w_n}{Lv''}$$

Here the net marginal wage is $w_n = w(1 - T')$, and thus we get

$$\varepsilon_L = \frac{w(1 - T')}{Lv''}$$

whence

$$v' + Lv'' = w(1 - T')\left(1 + \frac{1}{\varepsilon_L}\right)$$

We finally deduce that

$$D(0)wT'f = (1 - F)(D(0) - D(w))(1 - T')\left(1 + \frac{1}{\varepsilon_L}\right)$$

By rearranging, we obtain

$$\frac{T'(Y)}{1 - T'(Y)} = \left(1 + \frac{1}{\varepsilon_L(w_Y)}\right)\frac{1 - F(w_Y)}{w_Y f(w_Y)}\left(1 - \frac{D(w_Y)}{D(0)}\right) \qquad \text{(F)}$$

at every point where the taxpayer works ($Y > 0$), and with w_Y defined by the equality $Y = Y(w_Y)$.

This formula calls for a first, technical remark. Using $w(1 - T') = v'$, we get

$$\frac{T'(Y)}{1 - T'(Y)} = \frac{1}{1 - T'(Y)} - 1 = \frac{w_Y}{v'(Y/w_Y)} - 1$$

which is an increasing function of w_Y and a decreasing function of Y. Thus it is quite possible that formula (F) leads to w_Y being decreasing in Y, which violates the second-order condition (C2) and invalidates all our computations. It never is the case when the right-hand side of the formula is decreasing in w_Y, but since the third term is increasing, this is by no means certain.[70] If this problem occurs in Y, then the optimal marginal tax rate must be discontinuous in Y.

Note that this formula differs from that obtained in the Rawlsian case only because of the new, third term

$$1 - \frac{D(w_Y)}{D(0)}$$

which reflects the profile of redistributive objectives over the population. Since $D(w)$ is decreasing, this term is increasing: if the government wishes to redistribute between high incomes and middle incomes, it should raise the marginal tax rate on high incomes.

In general, $D(w)$ is a rather complicated function. It simplifies if we adopt "weighted utilitarianism" by choosing weights $a(w)$ that decrease in w and by replacing $\Psi(\mathscr{U})(w)$ with $a(w)\mathscr{U}(w)$, as is often done in simulations of optimal schedules. Then

$$D(w) = \frac{\int_w^\infty a(t)\, dF(t)}{1 - F(w)}$$

so $D(w)$ is simply the average value of a over the interval $[w, +\infty[$. This shows that in the special case of classical utilitarianism where $a(w)$ is constant, so is $D(w)$ and the marginal tax rates are uniformly zero: the optimal income tax consists of having all taxpayers pay the same amount. This is quite different from Edgeworth's result.

---

70. It is easy to see that with Rawlsian preferences and a nondecreasing elasticity of labor supply, the second-order condition holds if and only if $(1 - F(w))/wf(w)$ is nonincreasing in w, which is empirically plausible given the observed distribution of income.

The reason is simple: with constant $a(w)$ and quasi-linear preferences, taxes only enter the social objective function through

$$\int_0^\infty T(wL(w))\, dF(w) = R$$

and the government can achieve the first best by using only lump-sum taxes (which must be uniform since taxpayers are observationally equivalent).

The formula (F) thus obtained allows us to prove very simply some properties that are quite general. First note that the right-hand side is always nonnegative, so $0 \le T' < 1$ wherever $L > 0$. Now denote $\underline{w}$ the lower bound of the support of f. It is easy to see that $D(\underline{w}) = D(0)$, so the marginal tax rate is zero for the least productive agent if that agent works at the optimum.[71] Finally, the marginal tax rate has a somewhat surprising property. Assume that the maximal productivity is finite, at $\overline{w}$; then the second term and therefore the marginal tax rate are also zero in $\overline{w}$. The optimal tax schedule thus cannot be uniformly progressive: its average rate T/Y must decrease above some income level. This is actually easy to understand: it is useless to have a positive marginal rate "at the top" because there is no one above from whom the extra tax revenue can be collected, and any positive marginal tax rate creates distortions. We should not, however, focus on this property. First, simulations show that the optimal marginal rate can be high even rather far to the right in income distribution. Second, given the large dispersion of high incomes, it may not be appropriate to model them with a finite $\overline{w}$. If the income distribution extends to infinity, then there is no reason why the marginal rate should tend to zero at infinity, as we will see later.

4.3   Generalizations

Even in the quasi-linear setup our analysis of Mirrlees's model neglected several important points. For instance, we focused on tax-payers who choose to work. In fact, if

$$w(1 - T'(0)) < v'(0)$$

---

71. This would not hold if some low-productivity agents found it best not to work. Also note that in the Rawlsian case, the function $D(w)$ is zero for all $w > \underline{w}$; it is not continuous in $\underline{w}$, which explains why the marginal tax rate is not zero in $\underline{w}$.

then the individual with productivity w prefers not to work.[72] This may happen for low-productivity taxpayers if the marginal rates they face are too high. Since marginal rates for low-skilled agents are rather high in many developed countries, it would be useful to integrate this case in the analysis. This point is related to one of the weaknesses of Mirrlees's model: its static character. Productivity (or more generally employability) of an individual is not constant over time. More important, it is well established that low-skilled agents who are excluded from work for some time see their productivity deteriorate over time. By neglecting these dynamic aspects, the model underestimates the negative effects of high marginal rates on the low-skilled.

Even if we allow for the income tax to discourage some people from working, the model does not allow for any other source of unemployment. In continental Europe, for instance, the minimum wage may interact with taxation to create unemployment, as we saw earlier. This type of distortion (and still others) should be added to the model to make it more realistic.

Another remark is in order here. One often hears that high taxes may cause some of the more productive workers to leave the country. If one wants to prevent this flight of human capital, one should take into account a participation constraint that says that the utility $\mathscr{U}(w)$ cannot fall below some exogenous threshhold $\underline{U}(w)$ that is related to the aftertax income that the worker can get into a foreign country. In a similar way (but at the other end of the income distribution), high marginal rates on the low-skilled may tempt them to switch to underground work. Taking into account the first (resp. second) factor should force the average tax rate (resp. marginal tax rate) down at the bottom (resp. the top) of the distribution.

We mostly focused on the case where preferences are quasi-linear. This excludes income effects on labor supply, while it is clear there are such effects. It is possible to study the form of the optimal tax schedule with a general utility function, but it is hard to interpret the results (e.g., see Saez 2001). These results are nevertheless useful in simulations, as we will see later.

The exogeneity of wages w is another limit of the model. It can be justified by assuming that the production function has an infinite elasticity of substitution between all productivities w:

---

72. We might of course assume that $v'(0) = 0$ to eliminate this possibility. It is true by construction when labor supply has constant elasticity $c > 0$, since then $v'(L) = BL^{1/c}$.

$$Q = \int_0^\infty wL(w)\, dF(w)$$

Then cost minimization does imply that each individual should be paid his productivity w. When the elasticity of substitution is finite, things are more complicated: equilibrium wages depend on what combination of productivities is used, and that in turn depends on labor supplies and therefore on the tax schedule. It is unfortunately quite difficult to specify a simple production function that models the limits to factor substitution with an infinite number of factors. One could think, for instance, of a CES production function with constant elasticity of substitution σ:

$$Q^{(\sigma-1)/\sigma} = \int_0^\infty (wL(w))^{(\sigma-1)/\sigma}\, dF(w)$$

but such a formula implicitly assumes that very low skills are just as substitutable to high skills than to midlevel skills, which seems doubtful.

To examine this issue, we will therefore focus on a two-type model. There are n_1 individuals of type 1 (with low productivity) and n_2 individuals of type 2 (with high productivity). The production function has constant returns

$$Q = F(n_1 L_1, n_2 L_2)$$

We can rewrite this as

$$Q = n_1 L_1 f(l)$$

where

$$l = \frac{n_2 L_2}{n_1 L_1}$$

and the function f is increasing and concave. For simplicity, we again assume quasi-linear preferences: if type i is paid a wage rate w_i and pays a tax T_i, his utility is

$$U_i = w_i L_i - T_i - v(L_i)$$

The objective of the government is to maximize

$$n_1 U_1 + \mu n_2 U_2$$

where $0 < \mu < 1$ accounts for redistributive objectives by reducing the weight given to the utility of the more productive type. The government may choose a tax schedule $T(Y)$ and let the agents decide on their labor supply. It may also rely on the revelation principle and use a direct revealing mechanism, that is, two pairs (T_1, Y_1) and (T_2, Y_2) such that type 1 prefers the first pair and type 2 prefers the second pair. The government must take into account several constraints:

• its budget constraint

$$n_1 T_1 + n_2 T_2 = R$$

• the incentive constraints that state that each type chooses the pair (T_i, Y_i) that is destined for him. One could prove that if redistributive objectives are strong enough, only one of the two constraints is binding at the optimum: that relative to type 2, or

$$Y_2 - T_2 - v\left(\frac{Y_2}{w_2}\right) = Y_1 - T_1 - v\left(\frac{Y_1}{w_2}\right)$$

The intuition is very simple: given a tax that increases in income, the difficulty is to prevent the more productive types from claiming to be less productive (by working Y_1/w_2 hours) so as to pay less tax.

• the equalities between marginal productivities and wages, or

$$\begin{cases} w_1 = f(l) - lf'(l) \\ w_2 = f'(l) \end{cases}$$

To solve this problem, it is easier to define the auxiliary variables $L_i = Y_i/w_i$, which are just the labor supplies of each type at the optimum of the program. First we eliminate T_1 and T_2 by using the government's budget constraint and the incentive constraint of type 2. We easily obtain

$$\begin{cases} (n_1 + n_2)T_1 = R - n_2\left\{ w_2 L_2 - w_1 L_1 - \left[v(L_2) - v\left(\frac{L_1 w_1}{w_2}\right)\right]\right\} \\ (n_1 + n_2)T_2 = R + n_1\left\{ w_2 L_2 - w_1 L_1 - \left[v(L_2) - v\left(\frac{L_1 w_1}{w_2}\right)\right]\right\} \end{cases}$$

Then we can rewrite the objective function (up to a constant term) as

$$n_1[w_1L_1 - v(L_1)] + n_2\mu[w_2L_2 - v(L_2)]$$

$$+ \frac{n_1n_2(1-\mu)}{n_1+n_2}\left\{w_2L_2 - w_1L_1 - \left[v(L_2) - v\left(\frac{L_1w_1}{w_2}\right)\right]\right\}$$

This formula depends on L_1 and L_2 both directly and indirectly (through the definitions of w_1 and w_2). First assume that both skill levels are infinitely substitutable, as in Mirrlees's model. Then $f(l) = a + bl$ and wages are fixed at $w_1 = a$ and $w_2 = b$. Maximizing the objective in L_1 and L_2 yields easily

$$\begin{cases} v'(L_1) = w_1\left\{1 - \frac{n_2(1-\mu)}{n_1+n_2}\left[1 - \frac{1}{w_2}v'\left(\frac{L_1w_1}{w_2}\right)\right]\right\} \\ v'(L_2) = w_2 \end{cases} \tag{G}$$

Note that the incentive constraints imply as usual that $Y_1 < Y_2$, or $L_1w_1/w_2 < L_2$ and therefore

$$v'(L_1w_1/w_2) < v'(L_2) = w_2$$

It follows by substituting in (G) that $v'(L_1) < w_1$.

To interpret these formulas, recall that when type i faces a marginal tax rate T_i', his labor supply is given by

$$w_i(1 - T_i') = v'(L_i)$$

It follows immediately that

$$\begin{cases} T_1' > 0 \\ T_2' = 0 \end{cases}$$

Once again, the marginal tax rate is zero "at the top": the optimal tax should not affect the incentives to work of the most productive agents. On the other hand, the marginal tax rate on the less productive agents is positive; it depends both on redistributive objectives (through μ), on before-tax inequality (through the ratio of wages) and on the distribution of productivities (through n_1 and n_2).

Now return to the general case. When differentiating the objective in L_1 and L_2, we must now take into account how wages depend on labor supplies, that is,

$$\begin{cases} \dfrac{\partial w_1}{\partial L_1} = \dfrac{l^2}{L_1} f''(l) \\[2mm] \dfrac{\partial w_1}{\partial L_2} = -\dfrac{l^2}{L_2} f''(l) \\[2mm] \dfrac{\partial w_2}{\partial L_1} = -\dfrac{l}{L_1} f''(l) \\[2mm] \dfrac{\partial w_2}{\partial L_2} = \dfrac{l}{L_2} f''(l) \end{cases}$$

Since $f''(l) \le 0$, these derivatives imply that when the employment of the more productive increases, their wage rate decreases and that of the less productive increases (with opposite effects when the employment of the less productive increases).

Focus on the total derivative of the objective in L_2. The direct derivative can be written $A(w_2 - v'(L_2))$, where A is a positive coefficient. We must add the indirect derivative (which goes through w_1 and w_2), that is,

$$n_1 \frac{\partial w_1}{\partial L_2} L_1 + \mu n_2 \frac{\partial w_2}{\partial L_2} L_2 + \frac{n_1 n_2}{n_1 + n_2} (1 - \mu)$$

$$\times \left[\frac{\partial w_2}{\partial L_2} L_2 - \frac{\partial w_1}{\partial L_2} L_1 + L_1 v' \left(\frac{L_1 w_1}{w_2} \right) \frac{\partial (w_1/w_2)}{\partial L_2} \right]$$

This term simplifies into

$$\frac{n_1 + n_2 \mu}{n_1 + n_2} \left(\frac{\partial w_1}{\partial L_2} L_1 n_1 + \frac{\partial w_2}{\partial L_2} L_2 n_2 \right) + \frac{n_1 n_2}{n_1 + n_2} (1 - \mu) L_1 v' \left(\frac{L_1 w_1}{w_2} \right) \frac{\partial (w_1/w_2)}{\partial L_2}$$

But the term

$$\frac{\partial w_1}{\partial L_2} L_1 n_1 + \frac{\partial w_2}{\partial L_2} L_2 n_2 = -l^2 f''(l) \frac{L_1 n_1}{L_2} + l f''(l) n_2$$

is zero. Moreover the concavity of f implies that w_1 (resp. w_2) is an increasing (resp. decreasing) function of l and therefore of L_2. It follows that

$$\frac{\partial (w_1/w_2)}{\partial L_2} > 0$$

and thus that (since $\mu < 1$) the indirect derivative is positive. Thus

$(w_2 - v(L_2'))$ must be zero at the optimum, or equivalently, T_2' must be negative.

This result was proved by Stiglitz (1982). It should not be interpreted too narrowly: with negative marginal tax rates, taxpayers would be tempted to overestimate their income, which would be difficult to prevent. The message to remember is that in taking into account general equilibrium effects on wage determination, government should be induced to lower the marginal tax rate on the more productive individuals. By doing so, the government increases their labor supply; by increasing their use in production, this reduces the before-tax wage differential and thus relaxes the incentive constraint. Because of general equilibrium effects, taxation acts both on primary incomes and on disposable incomes, whereas only the latter effect was present in Mirrlees's model.

Finally, note that Mirrlees's model assumes that taxpayers are perfectly informed of their productivity before deciding on their labor supply. This is a natural assumption if one identifies L to labor supply; it is less tenable if L comprises effort, in which case the way the labor market values effort may not be known to the agent. In such a situation Varian (1980) and Eaton-Rosen (1980) showed that the tax acts as an insurance device. The argument is exactly the same as that of Domar and Musgrave mentioned in chapter 2: by taxing part of the income fluctuations of taxpayers, the government insures them against their productivity risk. Assume, for instance, that all taxpayers are identical, with productivity W; then the optimal tax when W is known by the taxpayers is simply a uniform lump-sum tax. On the other hand, if W is random and independent across agents, then the optimal tax has a positive marginal rate that allows the government to mutualize the risk represented by W.

The most interesting situation is clearly that when agents differ ex ante and where their productivity is random. This model was studied by Mirrlees (1990). Mirrlees assumes that the ex post productivity of the agent with innate productivity w is wm, where m is a random variable with unit expectation distributed identically and independently across agents. Mirrlees studies the optimal linear (affine) tax

$$T(Y) = -G + tY$$

Given such a tax, taxpayer w chooses his labor supply $L(G, (1 - t)w)$ so as to maximize

$$E_m U(G + (1 - t)wmL, L)$$

where E_m is the expectation over the variable m.

Let $v(G, (1 - t)w)$ denote the value of this program. If the government has utilitarist preferences, it will maximize in G and t

$$E_w v(G, (1 - t)w)$$

where E_w is the expectation over the variable w, under the budget constraint

$$-G + tE_w(wL(G, (1 - t)w)) = R$$

Mirrlees proved that to the first order in R, the optimal marginal rate is

$$t = AVw + BVm$$

where A and B are two positive coefficients that depend on the preferences U, and Vz denotes the variance of the random variable z. This formula calls for several remarks. First, the optimal marginal rates increases with inequality, as it is measured by the variances of the distributions of productivities. Second, we find again that the marginal rate is positive even if all agents are ex ante identical ($Vw = 0$). Adding uncertainty always increases the marginal rate. On the other hand, one can show that $A > B$ if the elasticity of labor supply ε_L is positive; then for a given level of ex post inequality ($Vm + Vw$), the optimal marginal rate is higher when the ex ante inequality Vw is greater.

4.4   Simulations

The shape of the schedule of the optimal income tax clearly is a central issue in this literature. Starting with Smith, the classical authors thought that the tax should have a single rate, but with a personal exemption equal to the subsistence wage. This exemption thus conferred some progressivity to the tax.[73] The concept of a schedule with increasing marginal rates came to the fore only slowly.[74] Nowadays, all developed countries use this type of schedule—even

---

73. Remember that the tax is called progressive when its average rate (not necessarily its marginal rate) increases with income.
74. It was the second point of the platform of the *Communist Party Manifesto* written by Marx and Engels in 1848—the first point being the abolition of landownership.

though some economists would prefer a *flat tax* with a single rate above a personal exemption.

One of the objectives of Mirrlees was to measure the progressivity of the optimal tax schedule. To do so, he calibrated social preferences, the elasticity of labor supply and the distribution of productivities in a "reasonable" way. He then computed the optimal schedule. To his surprise, he found that this hardly differed from an affine function, that is from a negative tax

$$T(Y) = -G + tY$$

whose marginal rate is independent of income.[75] Many authors have done their own simulations and proved that Mirrlees's results were not very robust. However, their own results are so variable that it seems difficult to draw general conclusions without resorting to empirical estimation of the parameters of the model.

More recently the breakdown of the determinants of the marginal rates into its three factors, as obtained in section 4.2.3, was used by Diamond (1998) to argue that the tax must be progressive above some productivity level. In the absence of precise information on the variation of the elasticity of labor supply with productivity, Diamond assumes that it is constant—which corresponds to a function v of the form

$$v(L) = AL^{1+(1/\varepsilon_L)}$$

In this case the first term of the formula that gives marginal rates is constant. Now assume that above some productivity w_0, the distribution of productivities is well approximated by a Pareto distribution,[76] with a probability distribution function

$$f(w) = \frac{B}{w^{1+a}}$$

Then it is easy to check that the second term

$$\frac{1 - F(w)}{wf(w)}$$

is also constant above w_0. Thus the shape of marginal tax rates in

---

75. It is still progressive if $G > 0$.
76. The Pareto distribution is in fact often used in the empirical literature to parameterize the distribution of income.

this region is entirely dictated by the third term, which we know is increasing. Thus marginal tax rates must be increasing for sufficiently high incomes.[77]

This argument obviously is not final. For twenty years after Mirrlees's paper was published, simulations of the optimal tax schedule relied on often vague calibrations of the distribution F. Today it seems clear that it is preferrable to use individual data to estimate this distribution. This is in fact a complicated matter. First, we only have data on wages, which depend on productivities but also on labor supply behavior as induced by the current tax system. To infer productivities from wages, we must "invert" the existing tax system. Second, this inversion is problematic for the unemployed and the inactive, who by definition do not earn wages and are very numerous at the bottom of the distribution. Third, the taxable unit often is the household rather than the individual. As we know, it is difficult to estimate the elasticity of labor supply for an individual, but the task appears daunting, both conceptually and in practice, when we deal with a household.

These reservations notwithstanding, it seems (e.g., based on work on US data by Saez 2001) that the term

$$\frac{1 - F(w)}{wf(w)}$$

is decreasing until fairly high productivity levels. This suggests that with Rawlsian preferences and a constant elasticity of labor supply, marginal rates should be decreasing for low to middle incomes. Of course, this tendency could be countered by strong redistributive objectives. It is only for high productivities that the distribution F seems to be well approximated by a Pareto distribution, so that Diamond's argument applies. Saez (2001) simulates on US data a marginal rate curve that slopes upwards starting at around 75,000 dollars/year, which is rather high. Thus marginal rates should be decreasing for most taxpayers.

Another lesson from recent simulations is that the optimal marginal rates are very high at the bottom of the distribution: these individuals are not very many, and since their productivity is low, it

---

77. Note, however, that with Rawlsian preferences, the third term is constant; margianl rates can only be increasing for high incomes if the government is concerned with redistributing income from high earners to the middle class.

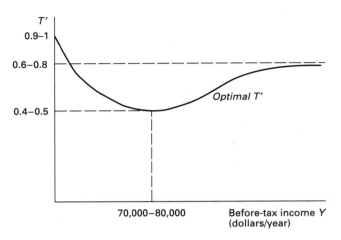

Figure 4.3
Optimal marginal tax rates

is no great loss if they work little. To sum up, one may represent (in a purely illustrative way) what the optimal tax schedule may look like on figure 4.3. It clearly makes little sense to compare the optimal marginal rates with the rates on existing tax schedules. On the other hand, the figure suggests that to the best of our knowledge,

• the optimal marginal rates at the bottom of the distribution are very high, but are nevertheless lower than in several existing tax systems, where guaranteed minimum income systems induce a 100% marginal rate

• in existing tax systems, marginal tax rates slope up much earlier than is shown in figure 4.3.

The asymptotic marginal tax rate (the marginal tax rate that applies to the highest incomes) is even more controversial. Let us go back to the situation studied by Diamond where preferences are quasi-linear and the distribution F is a Pareto distribution with parameter a. Denote by g the social weight of the richest individuals, defined by

$$g = \frac{\Psi'(\infty)}{E\Psi'}$$

Then it is easy to see that $g = D(\infty)/D(0)$. An immediate computation gives

Table 4.1
Asymptotic marginal rates

ε_L	$T'(\infty)$
0	1
0.1	0.73
0.25	0.55
0.5	0.43
0.75	0.37
1	0.33

$$T'(\infty) = \frac{(1 + \varepsilon_L)(1 - g)}{a\varepsilon_L + (1 + \varepsilon_L)(1 - g)}$$

Given the data, $a = 2$ seems to be a reasonable value for the Pareto parameter.[78] Assume, for instance, that $g = 0.5$. Then table 4.1 gives the value of the asymptotic marginal rate for several "reasonable" values of the elasticity of labor supply. For the purpose of comparison, the existing asymptotic marginal rate is about 50 percent in the United States and 70 percent in a high-tax country like France.

The clear lesson from table 4.1 is that the optimal asymptotic marginal rate varies a lot with the elasticity of labor supply.[79] What do we know about ε_L? As we saw in chapter 2, there is a very large literature on the estimation of labor supply behavior. This literature usually presents nonnegligible estimates of the income effect, but Saez (2001) proves that if ε_L now denotes the uncompensated elasticity of labor supply and r the (normally negative) income effect, then the optimal asymptotic marginal rate is

$$T'(\infty) = \frac{(1 + \varepsilon_L)(1 - g)}{a(\varepsilon_L - r) + (1 + \varepsilon_L)(1 - g + r)}$$

In principle, we just have to insert in this formula the consensus estimates for ε_L and r. Unfortunately, there is no such consensus at this time, even for high incomes. This implies that it is difficult to answer some politically charged questions. Consider, for instance, the highest point of the Laffer curve, which is the asymptotic marginal rate t^* that maximizes tax revenue on the high earners. It is

78. In this subsection we denote a the parameter of the Pareto distribution of productivities, and not that of the income distribution as in Saez (2001).
79. It also varies with g, but g is even more difficult to estimate than ε_L.

obtained for $g = 0$ (when preferences are Rawlsian). With our calibration and without an income effect, this gives

$$t^* = \frac{1 + \varepsilon_L}{1 + 3\varepsilon_L}$$

Take a high-tax country like France. This formula means that France has gone beyond the top of the Laffer curve if and only if ε_L is larger than 0.27, which may or may not be true.

To answer this type of question, some economists have tried to use directly the natural experiments created by tax reforms. We already mentioned in chapter 2 the study by Eissa (1995), which analyzes the effect of the 1986 Tax Reform Act in the United States on labor supply of women married to high earners.[80] One shortcoming of this line of work is that it assimilates ε_L to the elasticity of labor supply, whereas as we noted earlier, L may also measure the more evasive effort of the worker. Feldstein (1995) initiated another group of studies that aims at measuring directly the elasticity of taxable income. He uses data on tax statements to compare the variation in taxable income of two groups following TRA86. The first group contains households that were in the highest tax bracket in 1985; the second group contains households that were in the preceding tax bracket. TRA86 reduced the marginal rate T' (or equivalently, increased the "retention rate" $1 - T'$) much more for the first group than for the second group. By taking the ratio of the difference in the increases in taxable income for the two groups divided by the difference in the increases in the retention rates, Feldstein gets an implicit elasticity of taxable income of about one, which is rather high.

Feldstein's study has been criticized for relying on a "difference of difference" estimator that implicitly assumes that in the absence of any tax reform, the taxable incomes of both groups would have increased at the same rate. In fact, there was a trend toward increasing inequality in the United States at the time of TRA86, which may bias Feldstein's estimate upward. Other authors have obtained estimates closer to 0.5, which is still fairly high. Moreover estimates linked to other tax reforms are usually lower.

---

80. Recall that Eissa estimates that the labor supply elasticity of this subpopulation is about 0.8.

References

Diamond, P. 1998. Optimal income taxation: An example with a U-shaped pattern of optimal marginal tax rates. *American Economic Review* 88: 83–95.

Eaton, J., and H. Rosen. 1980. Optimal redistributive taxation and uncertainty. *Quarterly Journal of Economics* 95: 357–64.

Ebert, U. 1992. A reexamination of the optimal nonlinear income tax. *Journal of Public Economics* 49: 47–73.

Edgeworth, F. 1897. The pure theory of taxation, III. *Economic Journal* 7: 550–71.

Eissa, N. 1995. Taxation and labour supply of married women: The Tax Reform Act of 1986 as a natural experiment. NBER Working Paper 5023.

Feldstein, M. 1995. The effect of marginal tax rates on taxable income: A panel study of the 1986 Tax Reform Act. *Journal of Political Economy* 103: 551–72.

Mirrlees, J. 1971. An exploration in the theory of optimal income taxation. *Review of Economic Studies* 38: 175–208.

Mirrlees, J. 1990. Taxing uncertain incomes. *Oxford Economic Papers* 42: 34–45.

Piketty, T. 1997. La redistribution fiscale face au chômage. *Revue Française d'Économie*. 12: 157–201.

Saez, E. 2001. Using elasticities to derive optimal tax rates. *Review of Economic Studies* 68: 205–29.

Salanié, B. 1997. *The Economics of Contracts*. MIT Press.

Salanié, B. 2000. *The Microeconomics of Market Failures*. MIT Press.

Stiglitz, J. 1982. Self-selection and Pareto efficient taxation. *Journal of Public Economics* 17: 213–40.

Varian, H. 1980. Redistributive taxation as social insurance. *Journal of Public Economics* 14: 49–68.

Vickrey, W. 1945. Measuring marginal utility by reactions to risk. *Econometrica* 13: 319–33.

5 Mixed Taxation

We characterized optimal indirect taxation in chapter 3 when the tax on wages is proportional. We saw there that in the simplest case (a representative consumer, zero cross-elasticities of demand), the tax rates on the various goods are inversely proportional to the compensated elasticities of their demand functions. We will see in this chapter that with an optimal direct tax (which in general is non-linear), this result breaks down completely: in this and some other cases, indirect taxation in fact becomes superfluous.

Before presenting and discussing this result, note that it goes against the grain of traditional analyses. These assigned to direct and indirect taxation two distinct roles: redistribution for direct taxation, and efficiency for indirect taxation, which was understood to cause less distortions in the economy. A more elaborate analysis shows that at least approximately, direct taxation can in fact play these two roles.

First note that assigning to the individuals heterogenous wage rates does not change the analysis of chapter 3. The wage rate w (which was normalized to one) in fact played no role there. The reader may check that transforming w into fixed w_i's (which may or may not be known to the government) does not modify Ramsey's formula.

5.1 The Negative Income Tax

Let us start by introducing a negative income tax in the economy. Instead of paying a tax on wages $\tau w_i L^i$, consumer i now pays $(\tau w_i L^i - G)$, where G is a uniform transfer whose value must be determined at the optimum. Let us stay with the normalization $\tau = 0$, which corresponds to parameterizing the indirect tax rates as t'_j. The government's budget constraint then becomes

$$\sum_{i=1}^{I}\sum_{j=1}^{n} t_j' X_j^i(q, G) = T + IG$$

An increase in the uniform transfer dG increases the left-hand side by

$$\sum_{i=1}^{I}\sum_{j=1}^{n} t_j' \frac{\partial X_j^i}{\partial R_i} dG$$

and increases the right-hand side by IdG. The net cost for the social objective is obtained by weighting the difference of these two effects by the multiplier of the government's budget constraint λ so that it is

$$\lambda\left(I - \sum_{i=1}^{I}\sum_{j=1}^{n} t_j' \frac{\partial X_j^i}{\partial R_i}\right) dG$$

On the other hand, this variation dG increases utilities and thus the social objective increases by

$$\sum_{i=1}^{I} \frac{\partial W}{\partial V_i} \frac{\partial V_i}{\partial R_i} dG = \sum_{i=1}^{I} \beta_i \, dG$$

At the optimum these two terms must be equal, so

$$\sum_{i=1}^{I} \beta_i = \lambda\left(I - \sum_{i=1}^{I}\sum_{j=1}^{n} t_j' \frac{\partial X_j^i}{\partial R_i}\right)$$

which we can rewrite as

$$\sum_{i=1}^{I}\left(\frac{\beta_i}{\lambda} + \sum_{j=1}^{n} t_j' \frac{\partial X_j^i}{\partial R_i}\right) = I$$

But we can see in the left-hand side what we called the net social marginal utility of income b_i. Therefore this equality just says that the average of the b_i's is one:

$$\bar{b} = 1$$

Given this equality, Ramsey's formula becomes

$$-\frac{\sum_{j=1}^{n} t_j' \sum_{i=1}^{I} S_{kj}^i}{X_k} = -\theta_k$$

Recall that θ_k is the distributive factor of good k, that is, the co-variance between the b_i's and the consumptions of good k. Therefore the optimal discouragement index is positive for luxuries and negative for necessities. Indirect taxation should encourage the consumptions of the poorest individuals and discourage the consumptions of the richest. Although simple, this is not quite the standard interpretation of Ramsey's formula.

If the consumers can be aggregated into a representative consumer, then θ_k is zero for each good k and the discouragement indexes are all zero, which implies that all tax rates t'_j must be zero! But since we already fixed τ at zero, how does the government collect revenue? The answer is simple: it should fix the value of G at $-T/I$ and finance itself only with a uniform tax equal to $-G$. This result in fact is rather obvious: we know that lump-sum taxation leads to a first-best optimum, and lump-sum taxation is quite feasible in a world where all consumers are identical. Still, the usefulness of the "inverse elasticities rule" is badly shaken once a negative income tax is possible. But it is not clear why it should not be possible; so this is a first, rather destructive attack on Ramsey's model.[81]

5.2   Is Indirect Taxation Useful?

We have just seen that introducing a negative income tax makes indirect taxation superfluous when all consumers are identical. However, it appears to still be useful when consumers differ. We will now see that even this is not warranted. Let us go back to Mirrlees's model and introduce indirect taxes. To keep maximum generality, we give the utility function the general form $U(X, L, w)$. Thus individual preferences may a priori differ arbitrarily (through w) and exhibit all sorts of income effects and cross-elasticities between each good X_k and labor.

As in chapter 3 we normalize producer prices to one, which implicitly assumes that production has constant returns. With a direct tax $T(.)$ and indirect taxes t_j, consumer w's budget constraint is

$$\sum_{j=1}^{n}(1 + t_j)X_j(w) = wL(w) - T(wL(w))$$

---

81. Even in this representative agent model, it may be useful to create taxes on some goods if prices are constrained, as shown by Bénard and Chiappori (1989). Thus, if rents are controlled, it may be useful to subsidize substitutes to housing (like hotel rooms) and to tax complements (such as furniture).

and the total tax revenue on this consumer is

$$\sum_{j=1}^{n} t_j X_j(w) + T(wL(w)) = wL(w) - \sum_{j=1}^{n} X_j(w)$$

The government's budget constraint then can be written

$$\int_0^\infty \left(wL(w) - \sum_{j=1}^{n} X_j(w) \right) dF(w) = R$$

There is a slight change here from Mirrlees's model. Since we have more general utility functions, we must recompute the derivative of the utility function in w. Let v be the multiplier of consumer w's budget constraint in his maximization program. The first-order condition in L of this program is

$$U_L' = -vw(1 - T')$$

while the envelope theorem implies that

$$\mathscr{U}'(w) = \frac{\partial U}{\partial w} + vL(1 - T')$$

Thus we get

$$\mathscr{U}'(w) = -\frac{LU_L'}{w} + \frac{\partial U}{\partial w}$$

Since once again we rewrote the constraints so as to eliminate the tax schedule, the government's problem is simply to choose a state variable $\mathscr{U}$ and control variables that maximize the social objective function

$$\int_0^\infty \Psi(\mathscr{U}(w)) dF(w)$$

under the government's budget constraint and the differential equation on $\mathscr{U}$.

The choice of control variables is a bit subtle. In our study of Mirrlees's model we chose L as our control variable. It would seem logical here to choose L and the consumptions X. But $\mathscr{U}$, X, and L are linked by

$$U(X(w), L(w), w) = \mathscr{U}(w)$$

Thus we may only choose $(n - 1)$ consumptions as control variables.

We choose $(X_2, \ldots, X_n)$, with X_1 determined as an implicit function of $(X_2, \ldots, X_n, L, \mathcal{U})$ by the definition of utilities above.

Let us write the Hamiltonian as usual by assigning a multiplier λ to the government's budget constraint and a multiplier $\mu(w)$ to the differential equation:

$$\mathcal{H} = \left(\Psi(\mathcal{U}) + \lambda \left(wL - \sum_{j=1}^{n} X_j \right) \right) f + \mu \left(-\frac{LU'_L}{w} + \frac{\partial U}{\partial w} \right)$$

Choose some good $k = 2, \ldots, n$. Since X_k is a control variable, its value must maximize the Hamiltonian. The X_k term enters $\mathcal{H}$ directly (in $\sum_{j=1}^{n} X_j$, in U and U'_L) and indirectly (through X_1 in these three same terms). It follows that

$$\lambda f \left(1 + \left(\frac{\partial X_1}{\partial X_k} \right)_U \right)$$

$$= -\mu \left(-\frac{L}{w} \left(U''_{L1} \left(\frac{\partial X_1}{\partial X_k} \right)_U + U''_{Lk} \right) + U''_{w1} \left(\frac{\partial X_1}{\partial X_k} \right)_U + U''_{wk} \right) \qquad (1)$$

This equation seems very complicated, but it can be simplified by replacing the marginal rate of substitution of X_1 for X_k with its value, that is by the ratio of marginal utilities, which is equal to the ratio of consumer prices at the optimum of the consumer's program:

$$\left(\frac{\partial X_1}{\partial X_k} \right)_U = -\frac{U'_k}{U'_1} = -\frac{1 + t_k}{1 + t_1}$$

Now use the first equality in the right-hand side of (1) and the second equality in the left-hand side. This yields

$$\lambda f \left(1 - \frac{1 + t_k}{1 + t_1} \right) = -\mu \left(-\frac{L}{w} \left(-U''_{L1} \frac{U'_k}{U'_1} + U''_{Lk} \right) - U''_{w1} \frac{U'_k}{U'_1} + U''_{wk} \right) \qquad (2)$$

which shows how indirect taxes should be differentiated at the optimum. We can simplify the right-hand side further by noting that if y is any variable, then

$$\frac{\partial \log(U'_k / U'_1)}{\partial y} = \frac{U''_{ky}}{U'_k} - \frac{U''_{1y}}{U'_1}$$

Let us apply this formula with $y = L$ and $y = w$ and then substitute equation (2); this becomes

$$\lambda f\left(1 - \frac{1+t_k}{1+t_1}\right) = -\mu U_k'\left(-\frac{L}{w}\frac{\partial \log(U_k'/U_1')}{\partial L} + \frac{\partial \log(U_k'/U_1')}{\partial w}\right) \tag{3}$$

If tax rates on goods are differentiated at the optimum, it must be that the marginal rates of substitution between goods vary across consumers (through w) or as a function of labor supply (through the derivative in L). The multiplier of the government's budget constraint λ is clearly positive. We saw in chapter 4 that the multiplier μ was negative; we will assume that it is also negative here. The marginal rate of substitution U_k'/U_1' can be interpreted as the propensity to trade good 1 for good k. We can therefore deduce from (3) that good k should be taxed at a higher rate than good 1 if the propensity to trade good 1 for good k decreases in L or increases in w.

In more economic terms, government should tax more heavily goods that are more complementary to leisure or that weigh more heavily in the preferences of the more productive agents. These two points already arose in chapter 3, but the intuition here is a bit different. Government would like to tax directly differences in productivities. Since these are unobservable, it will tax more heavily goods whose consumption signals a high productivity. This is clearly the case for purchases of goods that the more productive prefer. Moreover taxing more heavily goods that are more complementary to leisure makes work more attractive and thus relaxes the incentive constraint on the more productive agents.

Assume now that the utility functions of all consumers can be written

$$U(X, L, w) = \tilde{U}(h(X), L, w) \tag{4}$$

where $h(X)$ is a scalar function (an "aggregator")[82] so that the utility function is weakly separable.

Then the marginal rates of substitution between goods are

$$\frac{U_k'}{U_1'} = \frac{\partial \tilde{U}(h_k')/\partial h}{\partial \tilde{U}(h_1')/\partial h} = \frac{h_k'}{h_1'}$$

and are thus independent of L and w. We deduce immediately from equation (3) that taxes on the various goods must have a uniform

---

82. This generalizes, inter alia, the quasi-linear case studied in chapter 4, since the disutility of labor can now depend on productivity:

$$U(X, L, w) = h(X) - v(L, w)$$

rate (e.g., contrary to VAT). This rate may even be chosen to be zero, as we know that a uniform tax on goods is equivalent in this model to a proportional tax on wages, which can be absorbed in the schedule of the optimal direct tax $T(.)$. Nevertheless, there is no reason in this model why a zero tax should be preferred to any other uniform tax on goods.

Thus, whatever the social objectives (the function Ψ), indirect taxation is superfluous if the direct tax is chosen optimally and the utility function take the form given in (4). This surprising result is due to Atkinson-Stiglitz (1976). It deals a severe blow to the traditional analyses of the respective roles of direct and indirect taxation.

5.3   Criticisms

One may wonder a priori whether the Atkinson-Stiglitz result depends on the fact that we allowed for an arbitrary nonlinear income tax and only for linear indirect taxes. It is easy to see that this is not true; the argument indeed only relies on marginal rates. If the tax on good k were $T_k(X_k)$, we would just need to replace t_k with T_k' and t_1 with T_1' in formula (3). If utility functions are weakly separable as in (4), then the marginal rates of all indirect taxes must be equal at the optimum—and one can choose them equal to zero. On the other hand, restricting the form of the income tax schedule would, of course, reintroduce a role for nonuniform indirect taxation.

By fixing the producer prices at one, we implicitly assumed that production exhibits constant returns. One could, however, check that without this constraint, the Atkinson-Stiglitz result still holds if government can tax profits in an arbitrary way. This argument is perfectly analogous to one we already discussed in chapter 3.

It may be more interesting to elucidate the mechanism that underlies the result. It is in fact rather obvious. Note that in this model the only heterogeneity between individuals comes from their productivities. Given utility functions that satisfy (4), these differences in productivities only show up in their incomes, and not in their relative demands for goods. Then the "targeting principle" familiar to economists suggests that only incomes should be taxed (of course, a uniform taxation on goods is only another way to tax incomes).

A contrario, the result does not hold if there are several dimensions of heterogeneity or if (4) is too restrictive. To illustrate the first possibility, assume that agents also differ through their inherited wealth, and that the tax on bequests only partially corrects for this inequality. Then taxing luxuries (which by definition are more often bought by the rich) is one way to attack this second source of heterogeneity (see Cremer-Pestieau-Rochet 2001).

The second possibility is illustrated by some microeconometric studies such as that of Browning-Meghir (1991), which rejects (4). First, marginal rates of substitution among goods certainly depend on hours of work. We already saw in chapter 3 that some goods are complementary to leisure (skis) and others are complementary to work (urban transportation). Christiansen (1984) shows, as one might expect, that social objectives can be improved by substituting at the margin (for a given tax revenue) taxes on skis and subsidies to urban transportation for a cut in the income tax. More precisely, consider the conditional demand functions as introduced by Pollak (1969). They are the solution $X(q, R, L)$ of the program

$$\max_{X} U(X, L) \quad \text{given} \quad q \cdot X \leq R$$

If U is weakly separable, these conditional demands are independent of L. Christiansen shows that one should introduce a small tax $dt_j > 0$ on good j (and cut the income tax accordingly) if and only if $X_j(q, R, L)$ decreases in L.

We assumed so far that agents were perfectly informed of their productivity. Otherwise, one should distinguish goods that are consumed before uncertainty is revealed from those that are consumed afterward (see Cremer-Gahvari 1995). As we saw in chapter 4, taxes reduce the risk agents bear, but this insurance has no value for goods that are consumed before uncertainty is revealed. This suggests that goods such as housing services should be taxed relatively lightly, since households start consuming them early in their life cycle.

One can also not exclude that agents who were lucky enough to be born with a high productivity have particular tastes. If there is a positive correlation between the taste for fine wines and productivity, then fine wines should be taxed relatively heavily (God forbid!). Of course, it is hard to say whether such deviations from (4) induce a first- or second-order departure from the Atkinson-Stiglitz result.

Naito (1999) recently showed that if the productive sector consists of several sectors that use different skill levels in varying proportion, then it may be optimal to have nonuniform taxes on goods, whatever the preferences. Assume, for instance, that there are only two levels of skills, unskilled labor and skilled labor, as in the Stiglitz (1982) model we studied in chapter 4. There are two productive sectors that produce the two consumption goods from both types of labor alone. We know from our discussion of Harberger's model in chapter 1 that in such a case, an infinitesimal tax on the consumption good that is produced by the most skill-intensive sector reduces the relative wage of skilled labor and thus the wage differential. As in Stiglitz's model this relaxes the incentive constraint and therefore improves the social objective. This first-order gain should be compared with the usual second-order loss (see the discussion of social welfare losses in chapter 2). Thus government should substitute at the margin a tax on the most skilled-intensive good to the income tax, so as to reduce ex ante inequality.

To conclude this discussion of the Atkinson-Stiglitz result, it may be useful to emphasize that the result was obtained in a theorist's world. In the real world the administrative costs of taxes and the risk of evasion are important determinants of the choice among taxes. In this regard, VAT has some real advantages. In most countries it is collected by the "subtraction method," whereby firms declare their purchases from other firms in order to deduct them from their own sales. This has low administrative costs and makes evasion easy to detect. On the other hand, the income tax has high collection costs and is much easier to evade. Thus it may be better to collect at least part of the tax revenue by VAT (in any case, uniform VAT still does not violate the Atkinson-Stiglitz result).[83] Thus many developing countries have created an income tax, but their weak tax authorities find it hard to collect the tax. These countries must therefore de facto rely in a large part on indirect taxation to finance public expenditures.

References

Atkinson, A., and J. Stiglitz. 1976. The design of tax structure: Direct versus indirect taxation. *Journal of Public Economics* 6: 55–75.

Bénard, J., and P.-A. Chiappori. 1989. Second-best optimum under Morishima separability and exogenous price constraints. *European Economic Review* 33: 1313–28.

Boadway, R., M. Marchand, and P. Pestieau. 1994. Towards a theory of the direct-indirect tax mix. *Journal of Public Economics* 55: 71–88.

---

83. Boadway-Marchand-Pestieau (1994) discuss this argument in more detail.

Browning, M., and C. Meghir. 1991. The effects of male and female labour supply on commodity demands. *Econometrica* 59: 925–51.

Christiansen, V. 1984. Which commodity taxes should supplement the income tax? *Journal of Public Economics* 24: 195–220.

Cremer, H., and F. Gahvari. 1995. Uncertainty and optimal taxation: In defense of commodity taxes. *Journal of Public Economics* 56: 291–310.

Cremer, H., P. Pestieau, and J.-C. Rochet. 2001. Direct versus indirect taxation: The design of the tax structure revisited. *International Economic Review* 42: 781–800.

Naito, H. 1999. Re-examination of uniform commodity taxes under a nonlinear income tax system and its implication for production efficiency. *Journal of Public Economics* 71: 165–88.

Pollak, R. 1969. Conditional demand functions and consumption theory. *Quarterly Journal of Economics* 83: 70–78.

6   The Taxation of Capital

Our discussion of optimal direct taxation in chapter 4 focused on labor income. But labor income only comprises about two-thirds of GDP, while one-third goes to capital. Taxation of capital therefore deserves its own analysis. It is a very vast subject, since many things go under the name of capital. The common element to all of these is that capital is accumulated savings, whether it be physical capital (machines and buildings used for production, but also housing held by families) or financial capital (bank and financial assets, e.g., bonds and shares). Thus taxation of capital in fact involves two sorts of taxes:

• taxes on the stock of capital like the wealth tax, the tax on bequests, property taxes

• taxes on the income from savings, such as the corporate income tax,[84] taxation of interest and dividends, and the taxation of capital gains.[85]

The economic analysis of these two cases in fact is very similar, since capital stocks stem from accumulated savings. Thus the distinction will play no role in this chapter.

As in the last three chapters, the standpoint adopted here is that of optimal taxation. Thus our main concern here is with the optimal level of capital taxation. However, we will also return to the incidence of capital taxation. In the whole chapter we neglect considerations linked to risk. This makes the analysis much less realistic but also much more tractable. The reader should remember on this topic the discussion of the Domar-Musgrave effect in chapter 2.

---

84. Although the question of what the corporate income tax actually taxes is controversial.

85. The stock-flow distinction is not very clear when it comes to capital gains; however, they are usually taxed as income.

In many European countries the press and some politicians complain that the taxation rate of capital goes down while taxation of labor income seems to increase inexorably. This is deemed unfair, since a common (but simplistic) theory of incidence suggests that workers pay the tax on labor income and capitalists pay the tax on capital. This is also thought to encourage substitution of capital for labor, thus reducing labor demand. Therefore the relative decline of the taxation of capital would be partly responsible for high unemployment and low wages.

As often in the theory of taxation, theoretical results are quite remote from popular discourse. We will see in this chapter that at least to a first approximation, there is no strong reason to tax capital at all: the optimal tax rate on capital is zero! This a priori surprising result actually is an old theme in economic literature. It is linked to the optimality of a consumption tax, to which we will return in chapter 9. As is easily seen by writing the intertemporal budget constraint of a worker-consumer who receives and leaves no bequest,

$$\sum_{t=1}^{T} \frac{C_t}{(1+r)^t} = \sum_{t=1}^{T} \frac{w_t L_t}{(1+r)^t}$$

a tax on consumption is equivalent to a tax that bears on labor income only, to the exclusion of income from savings.

As early as the seventeenth century Hobbes had stated a moral argument for the consumption tax:

Equality of imposition consisteth rather in the equality of that which is consumed, than of the riches of the person who consumes the same. For what reason is there, that he which laboureth much, and sparing the fruits of his labour, consumeth little should be more charged, than he that living idly, getteth little and spendeth all he gets; seeing the one has no more protection from the Common-wealth, than the other.—Thomas Hobbes, *Leviathan* (1651)

Consider Mrs. Thrifty and Mr. Bigspender. They receive (and spend) the same discounted labor income over their life cycles, but Mrs. Thrifty saves for her retirement while Mr. Bigspensder spends his income within each period. They both by construction pay the same tax on labor income. But the actual income tax also taxes income from savings. Thus Mrs. Thrifty pays more income tax, since she is taxed at retirement time on the income she draws from her accumulated savings. Only a consumption tax could tax Mr. Bigspender and Mrs. Thrifty equally.

Moral arguments needn't carry much weight in economics, but the above example suggests a more technical argument linked to the double taxation of savings. This argument was stated in its classical form by John Stuart Mill:

If, indeed, reliance could be placed on the conscience of the contributors, or sufficient security taken for the correctness of their statements by collateral precautions, the proper mode of assessing an income tax would be to tax only that part of income devoted to expenditure, exempting that which is saved. For when saved and invested (and all savings, speaking generally, are invested), it thenceforth pays income tax on the interest and profits which it brings, notwithstanding that it has already been taxed on the principal. Unless therefore savings are exempted from income tax, the contributors are twice taxed on what they save and only once on what they spend.... The difference thus created to the disadvantadge of prudence and economy is not only impolitic but unjust.—John Stuart Mill, *Principles of Political Economy* (1848)

Our task now is to evaluate the real strength of this argument. Double taxation of income saved certainly introduces a new distortion in the economy. But is it "impolitic" in a second-best world? After all, taxing labor income also introduces a distortion by reducing labor supply. It might be that introducing a distortion on the supply of capital helps correct for the first distortion, thus improving welfare. The whole second-best literature shows that counting distortions is not the right way to do welfare analysis. We must therefore study taxation of capital more rigorously.

6.1   Applying Classical Results

As we saw in chapter 2, the effect of taxation of income from savings is to increase the price of future consumption relative to that of current consumption. Thus what matters is whether we should tax future consumption more than current consumption. The results presented in the last two chapters seem to apply directly to this problem, since we may consider consumptions at various dates as as many different goods.

Ramsey's formula gives us a first guide. With a representative consumer, the Corlett-Hague result shows that a higher tax on future consumptions may be in order if they are more complementary to leisure than current consumption. This in principle is an empirically testable proposition: Does a permanent wage increase translate (for fixed utility) into an increase of future consumptions smaller than that in current consumption? Unfortunately, we have no convincing answer to this question. If future consumptions and current consumption are equally complementary to leisure but individuals are heterogeneous, then Ramsey's formula indicates that future consumption should be discouraged more if the rich tend to defer their consumption more than the poor. Observation shows convincingly that the rich have a higher propensity to save than the poor, which seems to provide us with a second argument for taxing capital.

However, we saw in chapter 4 that Ramsey's model in fact is very restrictive, as it only allows for proportional labor income taxation. Now turn to the Atkinson-Stiglitz result on the role of indirect taxation with an optimal nonlinear income tax. This theorem tells us that if the utility function of consumers is weakly separable, so that it can be written

$$U(C_1, \ldots, C_T, L_1, \ldots, L_T, w) = \tilde{U}(h(C_1, \ldots, C_T), L_1, \ldots, L_T, w)$$

then all consumptions should be taxed at the same rate and income from savings should not be taxed at the optimum. Under this separability hypothesis, the targeting principle applies: it may well be that the rich save more, but this is because they have higher incomes, and that comes from their higher productivity. Thus the optimal trade-off between equity and efficiency can be attained by taxing only labor income.

We raised some criticisms of the Atkinson-Stiglitz result in chapter 5. The fact that it neglects inherited wealth seems the most relevant here: if consumer-workers come to life with different productivities *and* different bequests, then the latter should be taxed at the optimum. There is indeed no relevant difference between endowments at birth, whether they consist in a higher productivity or a higher bequest. However, this argument neglects the effect of capital taxation on the decisions of the person who leaves the bequest. Taxation of bequests becomes more problematic if they are planned by altruistic donors.

6.2   The Overlapping Generations Model

Even if we accept all assumptions of the Atkinson-Stiglitz result, applying it directly to taxation of capital still is not wholly convincing. In a closed economy, savings equals investment, which renews the stock of productive capital. Factor incomes are not exogenous as in chapter 5; they depend on the taxation of capital through its accumulation process. Accumulation itself can only be studied in a dynamic model. The most often used model here is the overlapping generations model, which was invented by Allais, rediscovered by Samuelson (1958), and then applied to capital accumulation and public finance by Diamond (1965).

Remember that this model considers generations that follow each other over an infinity of periods. In the simplest model, which we will use in this chapter, each generation lives for only two periods and works only in the first period of its life. In period t, a generation is born; individual i in this generation works L_t^i and consumes C_{yt}^i during this period while he is "young." In period $(t+1)$ this individual is "old": he does not work any more, consumes $C_{o,t+1}^i$ using the income from his first-period savings, and dies. In this same period $(t+1)$ a new generation is born; it is $(1+n)$ times larger (which allows for demographic growth). Two generations, the young and the old, thus coexist within each period. Note that we can interpret the first period of life as working life and the second one as retirement. This interpretation is not flawless: thus only the young and active save in this model, which is a caricature of reality.[86] The value of this model lies more in its ability to illustrate the main economic mechanisms than in its descriptive aspects.

There is only one good (in addition to labor) in this model; as in the neoclassical growth model this good serves both as consumption good and as capital. Through savings the young finance their next-period consumption in old age, and their savings also allow the economy to accumulate capital. This capital is combined with labor to produce constant returns. Let Q denote production, net of the capital used (capital does not depreciate and therefore it can be reused in its entirety in production or consumption). Then we can write

$$Q = F(K, E) = Ef(k)$$

where f is concave, E is efficient labor (i.e., the sum of labor supplies weighted by their productivities)[87] and $k = K/E$ is capital intensity. This change of variable is perfectly identical to that in Solow's

---

86. In the real-world, saving is hump-shaped over the life cycle: the very young active borrow and the young retired save.

87. This implicitly assumes that all forms of labor are perfect substitutes in production.

model. As in the latter model, the wage rate per unit of efficient labor and the return to capital are given by

$$\begin{cases} w = f(k) - kf'(k) \\ r = f'(k) \end{cases}$$

6.3   The Zero Capital Taxation Result

The Atkinson-Stiglitz model is obtained by embedding the Ramsey model within Mirrlees's. Similarly, combining Mirrlees's model and Diamond's model allows us to study the optimal taxation of capital. Here Ordover-Phelps (1979) proved a remarkable result: if consumers have weakly separable utility functions and government has policy instruments that allow it to fix the capital stock at its socially optimal level, then the optimal tax rate on capital is zero.

The Ordover-Phelps (1979) model is rather complex, but Stiglitz (1985) gave a simple proof of the zero tax result. Assume that there are only two types, 1 and 2, of consumers in each generation. In period t there are thus $N_t^1 = N^1(1 + n)^t$ young of type 1, whose productivity is $v < 1$, and $N_t^2 = N^2(1 + n)^t$ young of type 2, of productivity 1. Given perfect competition of employers on the labor market, the relative wage of type 1 is v. With perfect substitutability of the skilled (type 2) and the unskilled (type 1) in production, labor can be measured in efficient units by

$$E_t = vN_t^1 L_t^1 + N_t^2 L_t^2$$

and production is $Q_t = F(K_t, E_t)$. We denote w_t the wage per unit of efficient labor. We write type i's utility function as $U^i(C_t^i, L_t^i)$ where $C_t^i = (C_{yt}^i, C_{o,t+1}^i)$ are his consumptions when he is young and when he is old.

The government collects taxes to finance its consumption R_t. Gross production therefore equals the sum of its uses, for private consumption, government consumption, and capital reinjected in production:[88]

$$F(K_t, E_t) + K_t = N_t^1 C_{yt}^1 + N_t^2 C_{yt}^2 + N_{t-1}^1 C_{o,t}^1 + N_{t-1}^2 C_{o,t}^2 + K_{t+1} + R_t$$

As in chapter 4 the government must choose a direct revealing mechanism $(C_t^1, Y_t^1, C_t^2, Y_t^2)$ under a self-selection constraint that

---

88. Recall our assumption that capital does not depreciate in production.

states that the skilled do not pretend to be unskilled so as to pay lower taxes. Type 2 may indeed claim to be type 1 by earning the same labor income Y_t^1, since government only observes incomes. To do this, he just has to work Y_t^1/w_t. The self-selection constraint then is

$$U^2\left(C_t^2, \frac{Y_t^2}{w_t}\right) \geq U^2\left(C_t^1, \frac{Y_t^1}{w_t}\right)$$

As usual, we will assume that the other self-selection constraint is slack at the optimum.

The government's objective is defined over utilities weighted by redistributive weights μ_t^i; government maximizes

$$W = \sum_{t=1}^{\infty} W_t = \sum_{t=1}^{\infty} (\mu_t^1 N_t^1 U_t^1 + \mu_t^2 N_t^2 U_t^2)$$

under the self-selection constraint and the scarcity constraint. The Lagrangian of this problem is $\mathscr{L} = \sum_{t=1}^{\infty} \mathscr{L}_t$, where

$$\mathscr{L}_t = W_t + \lambda_t^2\left(U^2\left(C_t^2, \frac{Y_t^2}{w_t}\right) - U^2\left(C_t^1, \frac{Y_t^1}{w_t}\right)\right)$$

$$+ \gamma_t(F(K_t, E_t) - N_t^1 C_{yt}^1 - N_t^2 C_{yt}^2 - N_{t-1}^1 C_{o,t}^1 - N_{t-1}^2 C_{o,t}^2 - K_{t+1} + K_t)$$

The policy instruments of government are the consumptions and the labor incomes of each type in each period, that is, for each t and each $i = 1, 2$,

$$C_t^i, Y_t^i$$

We also include the variables K_t as maximands. This amounts to assuming that the government has the means to fix the capital stock at its optimal level—we will see how later in this chapter.

Once again, it is simpler to maximize with respect to the labor supplies

$$\begin{cases} L_t^1 = \dfrac{Y_t^1}{w_t v} \\[2mm] L_t^2 = \dfrac{Y_t^2}{w_t} \end{cases}$$

We begin with the first-order conditions in C_t^2,

$$\frac{\partial \mathscr{L}}{\partial C_{yt}^2} = (N_t^2 \mu_t^2 + \lambda_t^2) \frac{\partial U^2}{\partial C_{yt}^2} (C_t^2, L_t^2) - N_t^2 \gamma_t = 0$$

and

$$\frac{\partial \mathscr{L}}{\partial C_{o,t+1}^2} = (N_t^2 \mu_t^2 + \lambda_t^2) \frac{\partial U^2}{\partial C_{o,t+1}^2} (C_t^2, L_t^2) - N_t^2 \gamma_{t+1} = 0$$

and the first-order condition in K_{t+1},

$$\frac{\partial \mathscr{L}}{\partial K_{t+1}} = \gamma_{t+1}(1 + F_K'(K_{t+1}, E_{t+1})) - \gamma_t = 0$$

It follows that

$$\frac{(\partial U^2 / \partial C_{yt}^2)(C_t^2, L_t^2)}{(\partial U^2 / \partial C_{o,t+1}^2)(C_t^2, L_t^2)} = \frac{\gamma_t}{\gamma_{t+1}} = 1 + F_K'(K_{t+1}, E_{t+1})$$

But the left-hand side is just the marginal rate of substitution of type 2 between current and future consumption, and this is equal to one plus the after-tax interest rate at the optimum of the consumer's optimization program. On the other hand, the marginal productivity of capital on the right-hand side equals the before-tax interest rate at the optimum of the producer's program. It follows immediately that at the social optimum, the government should not tax the interest income paid to type 2.

At this stage this result brings to mind the fact that the marginal tax rate on the labor income of the most productive agent is zero, which is not very surprising. It is still possible for the interest income paid to type 1 to be taxed. This is where the weak separability of utility functions comes into play. The first-order conditions in C_{yt}^1 and $C_{o,t+1}^1$ indeed are

$$\frac{\partial \mathscr{L}}{\partial C_{yt}^1} = N_t^1 \mu_t^1 \frac{\partial U^1}{\partial C_{yt}^1} (C_t^1, L_t^1) - \lambda_t^2 \frac{\partial U^2}{\partial C_{yt}^2} (C_t^1, L_t^1 v) - N_t^1 \gamma_t = 0$$

and

$$\frac{\partial \mathscr{L}}{\partial C_{o,t+1}^1} = N_t^1 \mu_t^1 \frac{\partial U^1}{\partial C_{o,t+1}^1} (C_t^1, L_t^1) - \lambda_t^2 \frac{\partial U^2}{\partial C_{o,t+1}^2} (C_t^1, L_t^1 v) - N_t^1 \gamma_{t+1} = 0$$

If we impose weak separability

$$U^i(C_t^i, L_t^i) = \tilde{U}^i(h(C_t^i), L_t^i)$$

then for all L and for each $i = 1, 2$,

$$\frac{\partial U^i(C_t^i, L)/\partial C_{yt}^i}{\partial U^i(C_t^i, L)/\partial C_{o,t+1}^i} = \frac{\partial h(C_t^i)/\partial C_{yt}^i}{\partial h(C_t^i)/\partial C_{o,t+1}^i}$$

The equation

$$\frac{\partial \mathscr{L}}{\partial C_{yt}^1} = 0$$

can then be rewritten as

$$\frac{\partial h(C_t^1)/\partial C_{yt}^1}{\partial h(C_t^1)/\partial C_{o,t+1}^1} \left(N_t^1 \mu_t^1 \frac{\partial U^1}{\partial C_{o,t+1}^1}(C_t^1, L_t^1) - \lambda_t^2 \frac{\partial U^2}{\partial C_{o,t+1}^2}(C_t^1, L_t^1 v) \right) = N_t^1 \gamma_t$$

and we get by substituting in the other first-order condition

$$\frac{\partial h(C_t^1)/\partial C_{jt}^1}{\partial h(C_t^1)/\partial C_{v,t+1}^1} = \frac{\gamma_t}{\gamma_{t+1}} = 1 + F_K'(K_{t+1}, E_{t+1})$$

This last equation means that the marginal rate of substitution of the consumer and its equivalent for the firm are equal. Thus at the social optimum, type 1 should not be taxed on his interest income, no more than type 2. Therefore the optimal taxation of interest income is zero.

Is this so surprising? We said earlier that the Atkinson-Stiglitz might fall when we take capital accumulation into account. But we assumed here, without justifying it, that the government can fix the capital stock at its optimal level. Can the government really do it? This is what we will look at now. To do so, we will have to learn more about Diamond's model.

6.4   Capital Accumulation

For simplicity, we assume that every generation has only one type of agent: redistributive considerations are not essential here since we focus on the capital accumulation process. As before, generations grow at rate n; labor supply is now assumed to be inelastic (each young person supplies one unit of labor). Capital does not depreciate, and there is no technical progress. We start the analysis by assuming that there is no taxation to begin with. Recall that we are in a closed economy, so savings must directly feed investment.

With an inelastic labor supply, the representative agent of generation t maximizes $U(C_{yt}, C_{o,t+1})$ under his budget constraint

$$\begin{cases} C_{yt} + S_t = w_t \\ C_{o,t+1} = (1 + r_{t+1})S_t \end{cases}$$

where S_t is the savings of generation t. We obtain the intertemporal budget constraint as

$$C_{yt} + \frac{C_{o,t+1}}{1 + r_{t+1}} = w_t$$

The first-order condition is

$$\frac{U_y'(C_t)}{U_o'(C_t)} = 1 + r_{t+1}$$

which generates demand functions $C(w_t, r_{t+1})$ and savings

$$S(w_t, r_{t+1}) = w_t - C_y(w_t, r_{t+1})$$

We still denote $F(K, L)$ production (net of capital), and we denote $f(k) = F(k, 1)$ net production per capita. As usual, profit maximization gives factor incomes:

$$\begin{cases} w_t = f(k_t) - k_t f'(k_t) \\ r_t = f'(k_t) \end{cases}$$

where we used the notation $k_t = K_t/L_t$.

Finally, equilibrium on the market for capital implies the equality between the savings of the young S_t and the capital stock in the next period.[89] Taking into account demographic growth, this gives

$$k_{t+1}(1 + n) = S(w_t, r_{t+1}) = S(f(k_t) - k_t f'(k_t), f'(k_{t+1}))$$

This equation defines the dynamics of the capital accumulation process. Unfortunately, it is very nonlinear, which raises several difficulties. First note that k_{t+1} appears on both sides of the equation, so the dynamics is only defined implicitly. We will assume here that we can in fact extract a dynamic mapping $k_{t+1} = g(k_t)$. Even then, this system may not be stable. Now assume that there exists a unique solution k^* of

$$k^*(1 + n) = S(f(k^*) - k^* f'(k^*), f'(k^*))$$

This solution is locally stable if

---

89. The capital stock of period t is recycled, and some of it may be consumed— remember that there is only one good in the economy.

$$|g'(k^*)| < 1$$

that is, if

$$\frac{-k^*f''(k^*)S'_w}{1 + n - f''(k^*)S'_r} < 1$$

Then the per capita capital stock converges (at least locally) to k^*, which defines the *steady state* equilibrium where capital intensity is constant and the stock of capital grows at the same rate n as the population.

We will always assume that the steady state is unique and locally stable, so as to look at its comparative statics. Simple computations show that if the savings function also depends on a parameter θ,

$$S_t = S(w_t, r_{t+1}, \theta)$$

then if the steady state is locally stable, the steady state capital intensity k^* is a function of θ whose sign is that of S'_θ: a variation of θ whose direct effect is to increase savings indeed leads to an increase in capital intensity.

The uniqueness and local stability assumptions imposed on the dynamic system are very strong: in general, one cannot exclude indeterminacies (several solutions in k_{t+1} for a given k_t) and/or cyclical or even chaotic dynamics.

Is the steady state optimal? Optimality is rather easy to define if we focus on stationary trajectories, where all per capita allocations are constant. Then all generations have the same utility, and we naturally seek to maximize the utility of any of them. Thus consider a stationary allocation with capital intensity k. Our old friend the benevolent and omniscient planner only faces one constraint: since he needs nk, given population growth, to keep the capital intensity unchanged, he only has $(f(k) - nk)$ to share between the old and the young in any given period. Since the old at each time are $(1 + n)$ times fewer than the young, we must therefore have

$$C_y + \frac{C_o}{1+n} = f(k) - nk$$

If we maximize $U(C_y, C_o)$ under this constraint, obviously we first need to maximize $(f(k) - nk)$, which gives

$$r = f'(k) = n$$

At the social optimum, capital intensity must be such that the interest rate equals the rate of growth of the population. This is called the golden rule, and it defines a capital intensity k^G.

Can we compare the optimum k^G and the steady state k^*? Unfortunately, there is no reason why these two capital intensities should coincide. Assume, for instance, that the utility has the Cobb-Douglas form

$$U(C_y, C_o) = a \log C_y + (1 - a) \log C_o$$

and that the production function also is a Cobb-Douglas:

$$F(K, L) = K^\alpha L^{1-\alpha}$$

Then

$$f(k) = k^\alpha$$

The consumption and savings functions are very simple:

$$\begin{cases} C_y = aw \\ C_o = (1+r)(1-a)w \\ S = (1-a)w \end{cases}$$

The dynamics of capital intensities is

$$k_{t+1}(1+n) = (1-a)(1-\alpha)k_t^\alpha$$

which indeed converges to a steady state given by

$$k^* = \left(\frac{(1-a)(1-\alpha)}{1+n} \right)^{1/(1-\alpha)}$$

The golden rule gives

$$\alpha(k^G)^{\alpha-1} = n$$

or

$$k^O = \left(\frac{\alpha}{n} \right)^{1/(1-\alpha)}$$

It is easily seen that k^G may be smaller or greater[90] than k^*. Moreover

---

90. The reader may check that $k^G > k^*$ seems more likely with "reasonable" values of a, α and n, but once again, this model is not particularly realistic.

no reasonable condition will make them equal: in general, the steady state is not optimal.[91]

When $k^G < k^*$, one can even improve the utility of all generations. Just assume that just after production at some date T, the government decides to release $(k^* - k^G)$ for consumption and to then maintain the capital intensity at k^G. The quantity of good available for consumption in period T is

$$f(k^*) + (k^* - k^G) - nk^G = f(k^*) - nk^* + (n+1)(k^* - k^G)$$

which is larger than $(f(k^*) - nk^*)$: both generations present at T can consume more. At later dates the quantity available for consumption is

$$f(k^G) - nk^G > f(k^*) - nk^*$$

by the definition of the golden rule, and here again all generations alive at these dates can consume more. With such excess accumulation of capital, we say that the economy is dynamically inefficient: there exists a reallocation that improves the utility of all generations.[92] Otherwise, we say that the economy is dynamically efficient—which does not mean that the level of capital is optimal, since $k^* \leq k^O$.

Let us now return to the taxation of capital. Any tax (or subsidy) on capital affects savings and therefore capital accumulation. If the steady state is not optimal, such a tax can thus bring the economy closer to the golden rule. If, for instance, we tax capital at rate τ and we redistribute the tax revenue to the young (with a transfer T_y) and to the old (with a transfer T_o), then the consumer's budget constraints become

$$\begin{cases} C_y + S = w + T_y \\ C_o = (1 + r(1 - \tau))S + T_o \end{cases}$$

or in the intertemporal form

$$C_y + \frac{C_o}{1 + r(1 - \tau)} = w + T_y + \frac{T_o}{1 + r(1 - \tau)}$$

---

91. This is no violation of the first welfare theorem: here we have an infinity of agents indexed with their date of birth $t = 1, \ldots, \infty$, whereas the proof of the first theorem heavily relies on the assumption that the number of agents is finite.
92. Abel et al. (1989) study empirically the accumulation process in the main developed countries. They conclude that the economy is dynamically efficient in each of these countries, which suggests that they have too little capital.

so that savings become

$$S = w + T_y - C_y \left(w + T_y + \frac{T_o}{1 + r(1 - \tau)}, r(1 - \tau) \right)$$

Transfers must, of course, balance the government's budget constraint, which is

$$T_y + \frac{T_o}{1 + n} = \frac{r\tau S}{1 + n}$$

since the tax collects $r\tau S$ on each old individual and the old are $(1 + n)$ times fewer than the young in each period.

Creating such a tax changes the capital accumulation process through

$$(1 + n)k = S$$

We could pursue with complicated computations, but let us focus on the effects involved instead. The creation of the tax has, as usual, two opposite effects on savings: the income effect increases savings, and the substitution effect reduces it.[93] A transfer to the old tends to reduce savings since it helps finance second-period consumption. Finally, a transfer to the young increases savings in the reasonable case where the marginal propensity to consume is below one. There are thus five effects to account for, and two independent instruments (since τ, T_y, and T_o are linked by the government's budget constraint).

For simplicity, return to the case where the utility function is Cobb-Douglas; then the income effect and the substitution effect cancel out and we have

$$S = (1 - a)(w + T_y) - \frac{aT_o}{1 + r(1 - \tau)}$$

First assume that the revenue from taxing capital is entirely given to the young: $T_o = 0$ and $T_y = r\tau S/(1 + n)$. Then we get

$$S = \frac{(1 - a)w}{1 - (1 - a)r\tau/(1 + n)}$$

which increases in τ. If we start from a dynamically inefficient economy, then the government can move closer to the golden rule by

---

93. There is here a third effect due to the discounting of the transfer to the old; this tends to reduce savings if T_o is positive.

discouraging savings. This is done here by subsidizing savings and by financing the subsidy through a lump-sum tax on the young. If the economy is dynamically efficient, the government should tax capital and transfer the revenue to the young.

The government can also move the economy closer to the golden rule without transferring money to or from the young, that is $T_y = 0$ and $T_o = r\tau S$. Then we compute

$$\left(1 + \frac{ar\tau}{1 + r(1 - \tau)}\right) S = (1 - a)w$$

and S now decreases in τ. If the economy is dynamically inefficient, the government now should tax capital and transfer the revenue to the old; if it is dynamically efficient, the right policy is to subsidize savings and raise a lump-sum tax on the old.

This example, of course, is purely illustrative: Cobb-Douglas functions may not be very realistic, and the two-period model where only the young save is a caricature.[94] However, it shows that the optimal way to tax capital depends heavily on how the tax revenue is used; for any given economy, one may want to tax or subsidize savings depending on whether the government balances its budget on the old or on the young. The intuition is simple: in this model the young save and the old dissave. Thus we encourage savings by making a transfer to the old and we discourage savings by making a transfer to the young.

Diamond's model therefore yields a rather ambiguous justification of capital taxation: the optimal policy may be a subsidy as well as a tax. In fact we will now see that the argument for taxing capital is even weaker than that: there are other ways to get closer to the golden rule, such as intergenerational transfers and the public debt.

We already implicitly studied the role of intergenerational transfers. Let us return to our analysis of capital taxation and assume that $\tau = 0$, so that capital is neither taxed nor subsidized. Then we must have

$$T_y + \frac{T_o}{1 + n} = 0$$

---

94. Several authors (e.g., see Auerbach-Kotlikoff 1987) use for simulation purposes more complex models that may have up to eighty generations living at each date. The central mechanisms, however, are the same as in our two-generation model.

But under reasonable assumptions, we know that savings S increases in T_y and decreases in T_o (this is clearly true for a Cobb-Douglas utility function, as we saw above). If the economy is dynamically inefficient, the government moves the economy closer to the golden rule by making a transfer from the young to the old: this discourages savings and thus reduces capital intensity. If, on the other hand, the economy is dynamically efficient, the government should make a transfer from the old to the young instead.

Note that transfers from the young to the old exist in many countries, where they finance (at least part of) Social Security and are known as pay-as-you-go pensions systems. The defining feature of such a system is that at each date, the social contributions paid by the young finance the pension benefits of the old. Thus a reasoned choice of the level of pension benefits may bring the economy closer to the golden rule.[95]

Intergenerational transfers are not the only way to move the economy closer to the golden rule. All governments finance part of their budget deficits by issuing public debt, that is, financial assets that are bought by private agents. We distinguish two forms of public debt, which do not have the same effects: external public debt, which is held by nonresidents, and internal public debt, which is held by agents who live in the country. Let us focus on internal public debt, since the agents live in a closed economy. Assume that debt is contracted for one period, and that it pays the same interest rate as capital—which must be true in equilibrium since there is no risk. Part of the savings of the young now is invested in government bonds to finance their consumption when they are old. Let b denote the per capita stock of public debt at the steady state. Since the per capita stock of debt must be constant, the government must issue exactly nb in new debt at each date, and it must pay rb interest on current debt. The difference $(r - n)b$ is financed by lump-sum taxes (possibly negative). If, for instance, these taxes are paid by the young, capital market equilibrium becomes

$$(k + b)(1 + n) = S(w - (r - n)b, r)$$

since savings now both funds investment and public debt. It is easy to see that public debt is a perfect substitute for intergenerational

---

95. Once again, this is a caricature: real-world social contributions are not lump sum. Since they are based on wages, they tend to discourage labor supply, which is inelastic in our version of Diamond's model.

transfers. We can indeed rewrite the equation as

$$(k + b)(1 + n) = w - (r - n)b - C_y(w - (r - n)b, r)$$

which we can identify as equivalent to the capital market equilibrium with intergenerational transfers:

$$k(1 + n) = w + T_y - C_y\left(w + T_j + \frac{T_v}{1 + r}, r\right)$$

where T_y and T_o are defined by[96]

$$\begin{cases} T_y = -b(1 + r) \\ T_o = (1 + r)(1 + n)b \end{cases}$$

These transfers are clearly balanced at each date since $T_y + T_o/(1 + n) = 0$. Thus internal public debt is equivalent to a transfer from the young to the old. The economy moves closer to the golden rule if public debt increases (resp. decreases) and the economy is dynamically inefficient (resp. efficient).

The conclusion suggested by this brief study of capital accumulation and government policy is rather mixed. As was shown by Atkinson-Sandmo (1980), whether capital taxation is of any use depends a lot on the policy instruments of government. Capital taxation may be a way to move the economy closer to the golden rule, but one may need a subsidy as well as a tax. Moreover the government may reach the same goal without taxing or subsidizing capital, but simply by setting the level of pension benefits or that of internal public debt. Of course, a more realistic study of the problem should take into account the distortions on labor supply induced by the income tax or social contributions.

6.5 Capital Taxation with an Infinite Horizon

We assumed until now that the agents had a finite horizon. Chamley (1986) and Judd (1985) have shown that if the agents have an infinite horizon, taxing capital cannot be optimal, whatever the preferences. We will illustrate this result using Chamley's model.

Chamley considers an economy with a representative consumer who lives an infinite number of periods and has a utility function

---

96. This is in addition to the fact that the young already balance the government's budget constraint.

$$V_t = \sum_{\tau=0}^{\infty} \delta^\tau u(C_{t+\tau}, L_{t+\tau})$$

Note that this does not imply weak separability à la Atkinson-Stiglitz, since the marginal rate of substitution between current and future consumption in general depends on labor supplies.

We again assume that there exists a single good, which is used as consumption good C, public consumption G, and capital good K. Production has constant returns with a technology $F(K, L)$. With no depreciation of capital, the scarcity constraint is

$$F(K_t, L_t) + K_t = C_t + G_t + K_{t+1}$$

Chamley assumes that the government can fix the capital stock at its optimal level. It can also raise proportional taxes on labor and capital income; we denote r_t and w_t the before-tax incomes of capital and labor and $\bar{r}_t$ and $\bar{w}_t$ their after-tax incomes. The government can also issue public debt b_t to finance the excess of its expenditure on its tax revenue R_t:

$$b_{t+1} = (1 + \bar{r}_t)b_t + G_t - R_t$$

As we know, this is one way for government to reach the optimal capital intensity.

Now tax revenue is given by

$$R_t = (r_t - \bar{r}_t)K_t + (w_t - \bar{w}_t)L_t$$

But since production has constant returns,

$$F(K_t, L_t) = r_t K_t + w_t L_t$$

and tax revenue becomes

$$R_t = F(K_t, L_t) - \bar{r}_t K_t - \bar{w}_t L_t$$

The government's budget constraint thus is

$$b_{t+1} = (1 + \bar{r}_t)b_t + \bar{r}_t K_t + \bar{w}_t L_t - F(K_t, L_t) + G_t$$

Note that by assumption, the government cannot use lump-sum taxes, which would of course be optimal. This is a Ramsey-type problem, and we know that in a finite-horizon model, the optimal level of capital taxation would depend on the preferences of the representative agent. We will now see that it is always zero when the horizon is infinite.

The consumer faces a trajectory of after-tax factor prices $\bar{r}_t$ and $\bar{w}_t$ and maximizes his utility under the budget constraint. We will not write the resulting equations; the important thing is that they (obviously) do not contain the capital stock.

At $t = 1$, the government must choose quantities and prices to maximize the objective

$$W = V_1$$

The government must take into account at each date t the scarcity constraint, to which we associate a multiplier λ_t, and its budget constraint, to which we associate a multiplier ξ_t. The Lagrangian also depends on terms linked to the consumer's program, which once again do not contain the trajectory of capital. As a matter of fact, the capital stock only appears in the two constraints. Using $r = F'_K$, the first-order condition in K_{t+1} is

$$-\lambda_t + \lambda_{t+1}(1 + r_{t+1}) + \xi_{t+1}(r_{t+1} - \bar{r}_{t+1}) = 0$$

Assume that the trajectories of all economic variables converge to a steady state. The multipliers represent the gain in social welfare, discounted in $t = 1$, from relaxing the scarcity constraint or the government's budget constraint. On a stationary trajectory they must decrease over time in a way that reflects the consumer's discount rate: λ_t and ξ_t must be proportional to δ^t. But at the optimum of the consumer's program, an Euler condition holds:

$$\frac{\partial u_t}{\partial C} = \delta(1 + \bar{r}_t)\frac{\partial u_{t+1}}{\partial C}$$

On a stationary trajectory, we must therefore have $\delta(1 + \bar{r}) = 1$, and we can write

$$\begin{cases} \lambda_t = \dfrac{\lambda}{(1 + \bar{r})^t} \\[2ex] \xi_t = \dfrac{\xi}{(1 + \bar{r})^t} \end{cases}$$

Therefore the first-order condition in K_{t+1} becomes on a stationary trajectory

$$(1 + \bar{r})\lambda = \lambda(1 + r) + \xi(r - \bar{r})$$

This equation has a simple interpretation: it says that the social value of a marginal increase in the capital stock is equal to the sum of the social value of the induced increase in production (recall that r is the marginal productivity of capital) and of the social value of the increase in taxes on capital (which depends on the difference in interest rates before and after the tax and must be weighted by the multiplier of the government's budget constraint).

It follows from this last equation that

$$(\lambda + \xi)(r - \bar{r}) = 0$$

But by construction, all multipliers are positive, and thus we must have $r = \bar{r}$: at the optimum, capital should not be taxed (or subsidized).

This result is very strong: as we already noted, it does not require in any way a weak separability assumption. The underlying intuition in fact is quite simple. Assume that at the steady state the capital is paid a before-tax return r and its tax rate is τ. Then capital taxation changes the relative price of consumption at date t and consumption at date $(t + T)$ by a factor

$$\left(\frac{1 + r}{1 + r(1 - \tau)}\right)^T$$

If τ is nonzero, this factor tends to zero or infinity (depending on the sign of τ) when T goes to infinity. Thus taxing (or subsidizing) capital would change in an explosive way the choice between current and future consumptions, which seems difficult to justify.

This result is interesting, but real-world consumers clearly do not live infinite lives. One simple way to interpret this model is to assume that the economy comprises generations that live only one period, consume C_t, work L_t, and save to leave a bequest to their children. Their motivation to do so is dynastic: the utility of the generation t-consumer depends directly on the utility of his children since $\delta > 0$. In these conditions the Chamley-Judd result shows that the optimal tax on bequests is zero, at least if these bequests are planned. Another way to interpret this result when agents live finite lives is to elaborate on the intuition given above: if the horizon is sufficiently far away, then it becomes difficult to justify a high tax rate on capital. Of course, this leaves room for quantitative disagreement.

6.6   The Incidence of Capital Taxation

We already studied the incidence of capital taxation in Harberger's model in chapter 1. However, that model assumes that the supply of capital is inelastic. We will now briefly look at the incidence of capital taxation when one takes into account its effects on capital accumulation.

The very stylized overlapping generations model we used until now is not adequate for this study, since it only has one consumer per generation. We adopt here the extension by Kaldor and Pasinetti of Solow's neoclassical growth model to an economy with both workers and capitalists. As in the rest of this chapter, we neglect capital depreciation and technical progress. The balanced growth equilibrium is given by

$$s(k)f(k) = nk$$

where $s(k)$ is the savings rate, the ratio of savings to production. Kaldor and Pasinetti endogeneized the way it depends on capital intensity by assuming the coexistence of two classes, workers and capitalists. Capitalists receive capital income $rk = f'(k)k$ and have a propensity to save s_r, while workers are paid wages $w = f(k) - kf'(k)$ and have a lower propensity to save $s_w < s_r$. This savings function obviously are rather ad hoc; they allow us nevertheless to model in a very simple way the heterogeneity of private agents.

Under these assumptions

$$s(k)f(k) = s_r f'(k)k + s_w(f(k) - kf'(k))$$

If we introduce a tax on capital at rate τ and redistribute the tax revenue $\tau f'(k)k$ to workers,[97] then the equilibrium is given by

$$s_r(1 - \tau)f'(k)k + s_w(f(k) - kf'(k) + \tau kf'(k)) = nk$$

With $s_r > s_w$ and for fixed k, the left-hand side decreases in τ. If the equilibrium is locally stable, decreasing savings imply a lower equilibrium capital intensity. As a consequence the gross return of capital $r = f'(k)$ increases and wages $w = f(k) - kf'(k)$ decrease: the tax is partly shifted to workers (whose income still increases since they receive the proceeds of the tax). As a matter of fact, if $s_w = 0$, we have

---

97. It would be rather strange to tax capital and return the proceeds to capitalists.

$$s_r(1 - \tau)f'(k) = n$$

and the net return of capital $(1 - \tau)f'(k)$ is unchanged by the tax: the tax is entirely shifted to workers.[98]

This reasoning is only valid in a closed economy. The polar opposite of a closed economy is a small open economy, which cannot influence world prices. Then with perfect capital mobility, the net return of capital cannot deviate from its world value:[99]

$$f'(k)(1 - \tau) = r^*$$

Then the tax on capital is entirely shifted on workers:[100] the before-tax return increases so as to leave unchanged the net return, and wages go down. Gordon (1986) relies on this as an argument against taxing capital in a small open economy: since taxing capital makes it fly abroad (which reduces capital intensity at home) and eventually is shifted to labor, it is better to tax labor directly. However, the assumption of perfect capital mobility is overdone: despite globalization, capital markets still are far from perfectly integrated.

6.7   Conclusion

As we have seen, there are several possible justifications for taxing capital. The first reason is that weak separability may be a bad assumption when it comes to the choice between current and future consumptions. Unfortunately, we lack empirical evidence to substantiate this claim. The second reason is that if agents inherit wealth that is not well taxed by the tax on bequests, then it may be optimal to tax capital income. Note in this regard that if these bequests were planned by the donors, then the Chamley-Judd result goes the other way.

The second justification for capital taxation resides in the suboptimality of capital accumulation in the economy. In the likely case

---

98. This sentence is not completely true: production per capita and capital intensity also decrease, which reduces the income of capitalists $r(1 - \tau)k$. On the other hand, workers have unchanged incomes, as the proceeds of the tax exactly compensate the decrease in wage income.

99. If, for instance, the net return were lower than abroad, capital would flee the economy; this would reduce k and thus increase the net return until it becomes equal to its value abroad.

100. But see note 98.

in which our economies suffer from too little capital, we saw that if, for instance, agents have a Cobb-Douglas utility function, it may be useful to tax capital and to transfer the tax revenue to the young. Note, however, that the same result may be achieved by raising a lump-sum tax on the old and using it to subsidize capital. Moreover one may dispense with taxing or subsidizing capital altogether and just use intergenerational transfers or change the level of the public debt.

Thus none of these arguments seem to provide a very secure footing for taxing capital (and certainly none of them supports the layman's opinion that capital and labor should be taxed at the same rate). However, there is another argument. We assumed until now that the relative wages of the various individuals were exogenous. In Stiglitz's model of capital taxation we thus assumed that the skill premium was equal to the relative productivity v. If this relative wage in fact depends on capital intensity, then $v = v(K_t)$. It is easy to see that the derivative of the Lagrangian in K_{t+1} then would be

$$\gamma_{t+1}(1 + F'_K(K_{t+1}, E_{t+1})) - \gamma_t - \lambda_{t+1}^2 \frac{\partial U^2}{\partial L_{t+1}^2} v'(K_{t+1}) = 0$$

whence

$$\frac{\gamma_t}{\gamma_{t+1}} = 1 + F'_K(K_{t+1}, E_{t+1}) - \frac{\lambda_{t+1}^2}{\gamma_{t+1}} \frac{\partial U^2}{\partial L_{t+1}^2} v'(K_{t+1})$$

Given existing empirical evidence (e.g., see Krusell et al. 2000), there are good reasons to think that unskilled labor is more substitutable to capital than skilled labor. In other words, it is easier to replace unskilled labor with machines than to do the same with skilled labor. Then an increase in the capital intensity in the economy tends to increase the relative wage of skilled labor, so that $v(K)$ is a decreasing function. It follows immediately from the equation[101] above that the aftertax interest rate is smaller than the before-tax interest rate, meaning that capital should be taxed.

This argument is quite general: one could check that in the Chamley-Judd model, such a configuration of elasticities of substitution would also lead to taxing capital. Of course, this effect remains to be quantified. Note also that some authors think that the increasing role

---

101. Remember that utility decreases in L.

of computers in production could make skilled labor a better substitute for capital.

This chapter set aside some points that are nevertheless important. Thus we always assumed full employment. It is not clear how unemployment would affect our results; in any case, that certainly would depend on the causes of unemployment. We also assumed that financial markets were perfect. If some agents in fact find it easier to borrow than others, then such a market imperfection makes the allocation of capital among competing projects inefficient. In particular, if the rich find it easier to borrow, it is reasonable to think that this would justify some taxation of capital. Even without such considerations, Chamley (2001) shows that when agents are constrained on their borrowing, it may be optimal to tax capital. To see this, assume that future wages are affected by idiosyncratic shocks (independent across agents). Since it is difficult to borrow, each consumer will build up precautionary savings to guard against times when his wage will be low. In general, consumption at one given date will be positively correlated with accumulated savings. Then taxing this accumulated savings to finance a uniform lump-sum transfer effectively redistributes from high consumption states of the world to low consumption states of the world. This smooths consumption across states and thus increases the expected utilities of consumers. Once again, the tax here acts as an insurance device.

Finally, note that all that we said so far also applies to the taxation of human capital: under some conditions that we needn't repeat, the return to human capital should not be taxed. Only the innate productivity of agents should be taxed. This recommendation may seem abstract, but one can derive practical consequences from it. For a start, assume that the tax on labor income is proportional. Then a student who must decide whether to study one more year compares the value of his forgone wages to the increase in future wages that a higher diploma will give him. With a proportional tax, the tax rate appears on both sides and drops out so that the tax is neutral. In practice, the tax is usually progressive and thus it discourages the accumulation of human capital. Moreover investments in human capital are not limited to forgone wages. We should also include tuition fees, which therefore should be deductible from taxes. Similarly taxes paid to finance public education expenditures should be deductible from taxable income, given the arguments in this chapter.

References

Abel, A., G. Mankiw, L. Summers, and R. Zeckhauser. 1989. Assessing dynamic efficiency: Theory and evidence. *Review of Economic Studies* 56: 1–20.

Atkinson, A., and A. Sandmo. 1980. Welfare implications of the taxation of savings. *Economic Journal* 90: 529–49.

Auerbach, A., and L. Kotlikoff. 1987. *Dynamic Fiscal Policy.* Cambridge University Press.

Chamley, C. 1986. Optimal taxation of capital income in general equilibrium with infinite lives. *Econometrica* 54: 607–22.

Chamley, C. 2001. Capital income taxation, wealth distribution and borrowing constraints. *Journal of Public Economics* 79: 55–69.

Diamond, P. 1965. National debt in a neoclassical growth model. *American Economic Review* 55: 1126–50.

Gordon, R. 1986. Taxation of investment and savings in a world economy. *American Economic Review* 76: 1086–1102.

Judd, K. 1985. Redistributive taxation in a simple perfect foresight model. *Journal of Public Economics* 28: 59–83.

Krusell, P., L. Ohanian, J.-V. Rios-Rull, and G. Violante. 2000. Capital-skill complementarity and inequality: A macroeconomic analysis. *Econometrica* 68: 1029–53.

Ordover, J., and E. Phelps. 1979. The concept of optimal taxation in the overlapping generations model of capital and wealth. *Journal of Public Economics* 12: 1–26.

Samuelson, P. 1958. An exact consumption-loan model of interest with or without the social contrivance of money. *Journal of Political Economy* 66: 467–82.

Stiglitz, J. 1985. Inequality and capital taxation. IMSSS Technical Report 457, Stanford University.

7   Criticisms of Optimal Taxation

We devoted four chapters to optimal taxation. Some economists would think that this is way too much, for reasons that we will briefly discuss in this chapter.

A first category of criticisms comes from within the theory itself. Even if we accept the viewpoint of optimal taxation, we may find some of its assumptions weak. Thus we assumed that the economy consisted of isolated individuals, each of whom was a taxable unit. In practice, the taxable unit often is the family, and even when taxation is individual, members of a household partially pool incomes. Consider, for instance, a simple example where each household is a childless couple who can be given a utility function that depends on total income and on both labor supplies. Then we can rewrite the optimal direct taxation program by denoting (w_1, w_2) the productivities of the two members of the couple and by looking for the optimal tax schedule $T(w_1L_1, w_2L_2)$. Boskin-Sheshinski (1983) studied this problem. Their analysis suggests that in so far as labor supply of married women is much more elastic than that of men, the labor income of women should be taxed at a lower rate than that of men.

One may also wonder whether it is realistic to attribute such sophisticated preferences as a Bergson-Samuelson functional to government. This implicitly assumes that the government is able to compare numerically the social cost of one dollar of tax raised on two given individuals. Consider, for instance, the following problem: should government take fifty dollars from a person who earns 50,000 dollars a year to give ten dollars to a minimum wage earner? Simple introspection shows that it is difficult to answer such questions. Rather than to assume that government can do it, we may attribute to it preferences that are both simpler and possibly more politically realistic. Thus Kanbur-Keen-Tuomala (1994) assume that government tries to minimize a measure of poverty. They show that the optimal tax schedule subsidizes the labor supply of the poorest individuals; however, their simulations suggest that this effect is weak in practice.

Finally, in these earlier chapters we focused on taxes that are linear on goods and nonlinear on income. Guesnerie-Roberts (1984) show that if a nonlinear income tax cannot be used, it may be useful to resort to quantitative controls. To see this, consider Ramsey's model with two goods (plus labor) and a representative consumer with a quasi-linear utility function:

$$X_1 + u_2(X_2) - v(L)$$

Assume, as usual, that production only uses labor with constant returns so that we can normalize producer prices to $p_1 = p_2 = 1$. We also normalize the consumer price system by $q_1 = 1$. The consumer's demand for good 2 is given by

$$u_2'(X_2(q)) = q_2$$

If government forces the consumer to buy $(X_2(q) + \varepsilon)$ instead of $X_2(q)$, the consumer must reduce his demand for good 1 by $q_2\varepsilon$ to stay on his budget line. To the first order, his change in utility is

$$(u_2'(X_2(q)) - q_2)\varepsilon$$

which is zero. But the taxes collected by government increase by $t_2\varepsilon$. Thus, if $t_2 > 0$ (resp. $t_2 < 0$), the government can improve social objectives by forcing the consumer to buy more (resp. less) of good 2 than he spontaneously would. The intuition is simple: when a good is taxed, consumers tend to buy too little of it, and a positive quota partly counters this tax-induced distortion.

We will devote the rest of this chapter to three categories of criticisms that are more external to the theory of optimal taxation:

• the literature on optimal taxation is only concerned with vertical equity and largely neglects horizontal equity

• in the real-world, reformers cannot set aside the existing tax system to reconstruct ex nihilo a better system, as optimal taxation seems to imply

• as was mentioned repeatedly, there should be reintegrated in the analysis the administrative costs of taxes as well as political constraints.

7.1   Horizontal Equity

Recall that we distinguished two concepts of equity. Vertical equity sums up all characteristics of individuals in their earning capacities. The central question, which is at the heart of optimal taxation, then is how to trade off efficiency and redistribution between the rich (who have a higher earning capacity) and the poor.

In theory, one may justify the exclusive focus of optimal taxation on vertical equity by assuming that taxable units only differ by their productivity—for instance, they are all young bachelors in good health. In practice, decision-makers cannot abstract from other differences between units: family composition, disabilities, but also differences in tastes. Thus horizontal equity concerns are central to many current debates.

Unfortunately, horizontal equity is a rather evasive concept. One may define it approximately by specifying that the effect of the tax system on individuals should not vary with respect to irrelevant individual characteristics. The difficulty, of course, is how to decide which characteristics should be deemed irrelevant. A concern for liberalism (in the philosophical meaning) would suggest that differences in tastes should be included in this category. But the horizontal equity principle then excessively restricts the choice of the tax system. It is easy to see that even a uniform tax on goods violates this definition of horizontal equity if demands do not have the same price elasticity; similarly a proportional income tax would be excluded. On the other hand, age or gender clearly are irrelevant characteristics. But even in that case, serious difficulties arise. Should, for instance, female pensioners receive the same benefits as men, even though they live longer and thus receive a larger discounted amount? Most tax systems discriminate (one way or the other) between married couples and common-law couples: Is it good or bad?

Let us now look in a more detailed way at the consequences of horizontal equity for direct taxation when families have varying compositions. To simplify again, we just compare the tax treatments of a bachelor and a couple. We apply the horizontal equity principle in the following way: if two families have the same before-tax utility, they must have the same aftertax utility. This implicitly assumes that we can define the utility of a family, not only that of its members. For a bachelor, it is easy to define utility as $U_b(C, L)$ if he consumes C

and works L. We assume that we can write the utility of a couple as $U_c(C, L_1, L_2)$, where C denotes the total amount available for the consumptions of its two members, and L_i is the labor supply of member i. Note that this definition makes the strong assumption that how the consumption is shared within the couple does not affect its utility.

Let us assume that a couple whose two members have productivities w_1 and w_2 has the same before-tax utility as a bachelor with productivity w:

$$\max_L U_b(wL, L) = \max_{(L_1, L_2)} U_c(w_1 L_1 + w_2 L_2, L_1, L_2)$$

Horizontal equity implies that after taxation, the utilities of the bachelor and the couple still coincide:

$$\max_L U_b(wL - T_b(wL), L)$$

$$= \max_{(L_1, L_2)} U_c(w_1 L_1 + w_2 L_2 - T_c(w_1 L_1, w_2 L_2), L_1, L_2)$$

where $T_b(Y)$ is the tax paid by a bachelor with before-tax income Y and $T_c(Y_1, Y_2)$ is the tax paid by a couple whose two members have before-tax incomes Y_1 and Y_2.

This is still a very complex problem. To simplify it even more, assume that labor supplies are inelastic: whatever the level of taxes, each individual supplies one unit of labor. Finally, assume that the utilities of the bachelor and the couple can be compared through an equivalence scale: the couple must have an income N times greater than the bachelor to enjoy the same standard of living:

$$\forall R, \quad U_b(R) = U_c(NR)$$

The equality of before-tax utilities then gives

$$U_b(w) = U_c(w_1 + w_2) = U_b\left(\frac{w_1 + w_2}{N}\right)$$

or

$$w = \frac{w_1 + w_2}{N} \tag{1}$$

After taxation, we must have the equality

$$U_b(w - T_b(w)) = U_c(w_1 + w_2 - T_c(w_1, w_2))$$

$$= U_b\left(\frac{w_1 + w_2 - T_c(w_1, w_2)}{N}\right)$$

from which it follows that

$$w - T_b(w) = \frac{w_1 + w_2 - T_c(w_1, w_2)}{N} \qquad (2)$$

Combining equalities (1) and (2) finally gives

$$T_m(w_1, w_2) = NT_c\left(\frac{w_1 + w_2}{N}\right)$$

To preserve horizontal equity, the government should therefore tax the incomes of the two members of the couple jointly after applying a coefficient read from the equivalence scale. This is exactly the *income-splitting* system applied for the income tax in France. Still, it rests on a number of very restrictive assumptions. Moreover the implicit equivalence scale used in the French income tax schedule is rather different from the OECD equivalence scale.

For childless couples, the income-splitting system gives incentives for marrying: since the income tax is progressive, the function T_b is convex and thus

$$T_c(w_1, w_2) = 2T_b\left(\frac{w_1 + w_2}{2}\right) < T_b(w_1) + T_b(w_2)$$

In other countries, which do not apply income splitting, marriage may be penalized or encouraged, depending on whether the incomes of the two members are close or not. Such is the case in the United States, where the personal income tax paid by a family of N members, M of them children, and with total income R, is given by

$$T(R - D - NE) - MC$$

where D is a standard deduction, E a personal exemption, and C a child credit. In general, it is easy to see that the only income tax that taxes married couples as a function of their total income and does not change incentives to marry must have a constant marginal rate, which is of course very restrictive. This special case again shows the basic conflict between vertical equity and horizontal equity.

7.2   Tax Reforms

Many authors have criticized optimal taxation for the reason that it implicitly assumes that the tax system can be reconstructed ab initio (e.g, see Feldstein 1976). A strict application of the Atkinson-Stiglitz result, for instance, would imply setting up the optimal direct tax and abolishing all nonuniform indirect taxes. In practice, the political machine moves less abruptly: tax reforms are piecemeal and gradual. Moreover any reform creates both winners and losers,[102] and the latter usually complain loudly. Thus one should look for "directions of tax reform" that are Pareto-improving, that is, incremental changes of the tax system that create no losers and some winners.

The literature on these *tax reforms* is usually fairly technical. We will only give here a brief sketch of the methods involved; the reader can go to Myles (1995, ch. 6) or Guesnerie (1995) for more detail. We study here indirect taxation, using the notation of chapter 3. The economy thus comprises I consumer-workers whose Marshallian net demand functions are $X_i(q, R)$, where q denotes consumer prices and R is a uniform lump-sum transfer. The aggregate production set is described by

$$F(y) \leq 0$$

and we denote $X = \sum_{i=1}^{I} X_i$ the aggregate excess demand. We once again assume that profits are taxed at a 100 percent rate, and that there exist producer prices p that support the equilibrium (this last assumption can be justified rigorously).

Start from an equilibrium (p, q, R) that is productively efficient, namely

$$F(X(q, R)) = 0$$

We consider an infinitesimal tax reform that changes consumer prices and the uniform lump-sum transfer $dz = (dq, dR)$. This reform induces a change in the aggregate excess demand dX, and it is feasible only if the economy stays within the aggregate production set. Thus we must have

$$F' \cdot dX \leq 0$$

But since p supports the equilibrium, F' must be proportional to p.

---

102. In the absence of compensating lump-sum transfers.

Moreover we have

$$dX = \frac{\partial X}{\partial q} \cdot dq + \frac{\partial X}{\partial R} \, dR$$

Thus the reform is feasible only if $A \, dz \leq 0$, where A is the vector

$$A = \left(p \frac{\partial X}{\partial q}, \, p \frac{\partial X}{\partial R} \right)$$

Moreover it increases the indirect utility of consumer i by

$$\frac{\partial V_i}{\partial q} \cdot dq + \frac{\partial V_i}{\partial R} \, dR$$

which, given Roy's identity, can also be written as

$$\frac{\partial V_i}{\partial R} (dR - X_i \, dq)$$

For the tax reform to be Pareto improving, it must be that for each consumer i, $B_i \, dz > 0$, where

$$B_i = (-X_i, 1)$$

Thus we just have to find a vector dz such that[103]

$$A \, dz \leq 0 \quad \text{and} \quad B_i \, dz > 0 \qquad \text{for all } i = 1, \ldots, I,$$

Using Farkas's lemma (or the theorem of the alternative), one may show that such a feasible, Pareto-improving tax reform exists if A does not belong to the cone B generated by the B_i's, that is,

$$B = \left\{ \sum_{i=1}^{I} \lambda_i b_i, \, \lambda_i \geq 0 \text{ and } b_i \in B_i \, \forall i \right\}$$

To interpret this condition, note that by differentiating the budget constraint

$$q \cdot X_i(q, R) = R$$

we get

$$q \cdot \frac{\partial X_i}{\partial q} + X_i = 0 \quad \text{and} \quad q \cdot \frac{\partial X_i}{\partial R} = 1$$

---

103. As in chapter 3, Walras's law implies that the budget constraint of the government is satisfied.

Denote $t = q - p$ the vector of taxes; we can rewrite these equalities as

$$p\frac{\partial X_i}{\partial q} = -X_i - t\frac{\partial X_i}{\partial q} \quad \text{and} \quad p\frac{\partial X_i}{\partial R} = 1 - t\frac{\partial X_i}{\partial R}$$

from which it follows that

$$A = \sum_{i=1}^{I} B_i - \left(t\frac{\partial X}{\partial q}, t\frac{\partial X}{\partial R} \right)$$

In particular, if $t = 0$, then $A = \sum_{i=1}^{I} B_i$ belongs to the cone B, and as could be expected, there is no Pareto-improving tax reform when the original economy only has lump-sum taxes. Now assume that all consumers are identical so that $B_1 = \cdots = B_I$ and B is simply the half-line generated by B_1. Then it is easy to see that if t is nonzero, A does not belong to B and thus there exist feasible, Pareto-improving tax reforms.

Figure 7.1 illustrates this result. For simplicity, we pictured an economy with two goods and two consumers $(n = I = 2)$, and we assumed $dR = 0$. Good 1 is leisure, which is in excess supply in equilibrium, and good 2 is a consumption good produced from labor. The vectors B_1 and B_2 then belong to the bottom-right part of the graph. We assumed that A does not belong to B, so that there exist feasible, Pareto-improving tax reforms: vector dq is an example. Note that it is easy to construct such a reform; the only knowledge required is that of demands and their local elasticities.

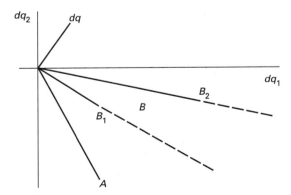

Figure 7.1
Tax reform

We formulated the problem in an indirect tax setup, but it is possible to extend this approach to mixed taxation, with linear taxes on goods and a nonlinear income tax. Konishi (1995) shows that in this case there always exists a feasible and Pareto-improving tax reform. The intuition for this result is that the nonlinearity of the income tax leaves a lot of elbow room. If a tax reform that only affects tax rates on goods harms some consumers, then it is always possible to compensate the losers by manipulating the income tax.

Finally, note that while this literature may seem abstract, some of its conclusions have significant economic content. The papers by Corlett-Hague (1953), Christiansen (1984), and Naito (1999) illustrated this in earlier chapters. Guesnerie (1995, ch. 4) gives other examples.

7.3   Administrative and Political Issues

We alluded several times to the importance of administrative costs. These come into three main categories:

• evasion makes it necessary to increase the tax rates on honest taxpayers and thus makes taxation less acceptable. Note that one should distinguish between evasion, which is an illegal activity, and avoidance, which is simply fiscal optimization by taxpayers fortunate enough to be in a position to use loopholes.[104]

• administrative costs *stricto sensu* are the costs of collecting and processing tax revenue, for instance, including the budget of the tax authority

• one should also take into account the compliance costs incurred by taxpayers while searching for the most tax-favored investments, paying for professional advice (especially for firms and the richer taxpayers), and losing time while filling up forms.

The sum total of these costs is not trivial: estimates for the United States are close to 7 percent of tax revenue, or more than a hundred billion dollars a year. However, one should realize that part of the complexity in the system is unavoidable due to equity concerns. After all, the least costly system would be to rely on voluntary contributions, but it would hardly be fair (and probably not very effective either). The largest costs may not be the more obvious. Thus,

---

104. It is often said that "the poor evade, the rich avoid."

having several tax brackets hardly complicates the task of taxpayers, who can merely look up tables. The flowering of exemptions and other tax expenditures probably induces much more serious costs.

Still, these costs should be considered when setting up or reforming a tax system. As we already noted in chapter 4, VAT is an excellent tax in that regard. With the subtraction method, each firm must declare both its purchases and its sales, which is a fairly simple task: the difference is noninvested value added, which is the basis for VAT. Thus the report of firm A, which bought a computer from firm B, allows the tax authority to check the sincerity of the report of firm B. This system effectively discourages evasion. Similarly the generalization of pay-as-you-earn (source-withholding) income taxation allows the fight against tax evasion to focus on nonwage income.

As a conclusion, remember that the whole optimal taxation literature rests on the fictitious benevolent planner. As Schumpeter (1949, p. 208) already noted:

Policy is politics; and politics is a very realistic matter. There is no scientific sense whatever in creating for one's self some metaphysical entity to be called "The Common Good" and a not less metaphysical "State," that, sailing high in the clouds and exempt from and above human struggles and group interests, worships at the shrine of the Common Good.

It is not necessarily true that each government must be captured by interest groups that twist the tax system their way. Still, it is certainly true that governments are carried into power by coalitions that hope for some sort of improvement in their economic lot. If the arrival in power of a new government only means that the social objective function changes, then the optimal taxation literature can accomodate political changes. Things become more thorny if the new government wishes to favor some horizontal groups: civil servants, the steel industry, farmers, and so on.

Despite the recent developments in political economy there is no generally agreed way for economic theory to endogeneize the tax system. Most existing models rely on the median voter theorem, which more or less reduces the political agenda to a unidimensional choice. Still, one may note that the usual criteria of economists may be turned around by politicians. Thus economists have held since Adam Smith that the incidence of a good tax should be clear. But, if the incidence is clear, then the losers are very likely to create an opposition lobby. From a political viewpoint, it is much better to create taxes whose incidence is so opaque that popular protest remains diffuse.[105] In this sense, it is no wonder that targeted tax expenditures are so beloved of politicians: they create grateful voters (the beneficiaries) and dilute the costs among a mass of undifferentiated voters who find it very hard to mobilize. More generally, the study of decision-making on tax issues should be a part of the curriculum of every good specialized economist.

Given the temptation for every government to bend the tax system so as to favor the interest groups that carried it into power, Brennan-Buchanan (1977) suggest that taxpayers can protect themselves by setting up a "tax constitution" that constrains all future governments. Of course, it will be hard to agree on such a constitution once lobbies have emerged. Brennan-Buchanan therefore appeal to the fictitious "veil of ignorance," by assuming that agents design a social contract before they know their future position in society. They then choose constraints c that will apply to all future tax systems. As agents learn their identities, the government is formed, and the government chooses a tax system T that must respect the constraints c.[106] Brennan-Buchanan also assume that the government can appropriate a proportion $(1 - \alpha)$ of the tax revenue to satisfy its clientele or overpay civil servants. Then the government chooses T so as to maximize tax revenue $R(c, T)$. Ex ante, taxpayers thus must choose the level of production of the public good G, then the constraints c, so as to achieve

$$\alpha \max_t R(c, T) = G$$

Brennan and Buchanan show that in this setup, tax constitutions should prefer a narrow tax base to a wider one, since otherwise the government would find it too easy to abuse its discretionary power to tax.

References

Boskin, M., and E. Sheshinski. 1983. Optimal tax treatment of the family: Married couples. *Journal of Public Economics* 20: 281–97.

105. Jean-Baptiste Colbert, minister of finance to Louis XIV in France, used to say: "Taxation is the art of plucking the goose so as to obtain the largest amount of feathers with the smallest amount of hissing."
106. The constraints c might, for instance, define the taxable basis and T the tax rate.

Brennan, G., and J. Buchanan. 1977. Towards a tax constitution for Leviathan. *Journal of Public Economics* 8: 255–73.

Christiansen, V. 1984. Which commodity taxes should supplement the income tax? *Journal of Public Economics* 24: 195–220.

Corlett, W., and D. Hague. 1953. Complementarity and the excess burden of taxation. *Review of Economic Studies* 21: 21–30.

Feldstein, M. 1976. On the theory of tax reform. *Journal of Public Economics* 6: 77–104.

Guesnerie, R. 1995. *A Contribution to the Pure Theory of Taxation*. Cambridge University Press.

Guesnerie, R., and K. Roberts. 1980. Effective policy tools and quantity controls. *Econometrica* 52: 59–86.

Kanbur, R., M. Keen, and M. Tuomala. 1994. Optimal nonlinear income taxation for the alleviation of poverty. *European Economic Review* 38: 1613–32.

Konishi, H. 1995. A Pareto-improving commodity tax reform under a smooth nonlinear income tax. *Journal of Public Economics* 56: 413–46.

Myles, G. 1995. *Public Economics*. Cambridge University Press.

Naito, H. 1999. Re-examination of uniform commodity taxes under a nonlinear income tax system and its implication for production efficiency. *Journal of Public Economics* 71: 165–88.

Schumpeter, J. 1949. The Communist manifesto in sociology and economics. *Journal of Political Economy* 57: 199–212.

III   Some Current Debates

The last part of this book uses the material presented in the first two parts to throw light on some current debates on tax policy. I chose to discuss income support programs, the consumption tax, and environmental taxation, but there are other topics in the news, like tax competition, which is hotly debated in the European Union.

Given the complexity of these issues, the reader should not hope to find here clear-cut conclusions. At some point one must stop relying on theorems and examine a whole array of theoretical, empirical, and institutional arguments. Ideally each reader should build his own judgment after studying these arguments and weighing their relative strengths. This may seem to be a difficult discipline, but remember what the inventor of Peter's principle wrote:

Some problems are so complex that you have to be highly intelligent and well-informed just to be undecided about them.

Even in a perfectly competitive economy, without any governmental intervention or any other distortion, the free play of the market may leave some agents with low income. First, some low-productivity individuals are only offered low wages; second, some agents whose disutility of labor is relatively large to their offered wage may refuse to work. Even in such an idealized economy there appear two groups of poor: the working poor and the nonemployed poor. Of course, the distortions in real-world economies affect the sizes of these two groups. Thus monopsony power by employers may push wages down and some workers into poverty. Moreover market imperfections that create unemployment also create nonemployed poor. Finally, tax policy itself may open "poverty traps," as we will see.

The existence of pockets of poverty in a developed economy is generally considered unbearable. Politicians of the left and the right alike agree that poverty should be reduced, even though they diverge greatly on what means should be used. All components of public action may play a role in reducing poverty. For example, a macroeconomic policy aiming at full employment or labor market reforms may increase employment and thus thin the ranks of the nonemployed poor. It is nevertheless clear that tax policy has a crucial role to play in treating the symptoms and also the causes of poverty. This notion has led most modern developed nations to create a complex system of means-tested benefits. International organizations also encourage developing countries to set up a "safety net" for their populations.

The study of current tax systems in developed countries shows that their redistributive effects are largely due to their benefit component. Taxes in themselves are mostly progressive for high incomes only, while benefits are by their nature concentrated on low incomes: they can raise incomes by as much as 50 to 100 percent in the bottom quintile of the income distribution. Some of these benefits, such as family benefits, partly answer horizontal equity concerns. But most of them were designed to fight poverty and to implement solidarity in the face of various social risks (health, unemployment, etc.). The aim of this chapter is to examine how the tax system does and should support low incomes.

8.1   Measuring Poverty

Defining poverty is a dificult task, both for conceptual and technical reasons. Several approaches coexist, none of which is perfectly convincing. The first approach defines poverty in absolute terms: a family is poor if its consumptions of certain "essential" goods fall below what is considered to be the minimum acceptable standard. This criterion in principle is multidimensional, but usually it is reduced to the single criterion of income: then a family is classified as poor if its income does not allow it to purchase these minimum consumption levels. This is the approach used in the United States, where the *poverty line* is about 11,000 dollars per year for a childless couple, or a bit more than a full-time minimum wage.

European countries adopted a relative approach that has more to do with inequality than with poverty. One first defines "consumption units" to be the number of equivalent adults in the family, using an equivalence scale.[107] Then a family is classified as poor if its income per consumption unit is below half of the median (or sometimes average) income per consumption unit. With this measure one may, of course, imagine situations where all families have more income per consumption unit and yet the percentage of "poor" increases. This definition thus implicitly considers that poverty is a relative notion, which depends on the average income in society. In France, for instance, the poverty line is about 580 euros per month and per consumption unit. About 10 percent of families then are poor.

Whether the measure adopted is absolute or relative, it is in most cases instantaneous: a family is poor in a given year if its income

---

107. The equivalence scale used attributes one consumption unit to the first adult in the family, 0.5 to each other adult, and 0.3 to each child.

falls below the poverty line in that year. This family may in fact leave poverty the next year and not be poor over its life cycle. Instantaneous poverty indexes therefore should be complemented with measures of income mobility, which unfortunately are harder to come by. Some studies suggest that about a quarter of the (traditionally defined) poor in fact are only transitorily poor.

Once a poverty line is defined, poverty can be measured in several ways. The simplest one is the percentage of families that fall below the poverty line (the *head count*). One also often uses the *poverty gap*, which measures the average amount of money that should be given to each poor family in order to bring it up to the poverty line. This second definition thus takes into account the distribution of income among the poor. Some studies tried to axiomatize the measure of poverty; thus Sen (1976) obtains a more complex formula that relies on the head count, the poverty gap, and the Gini index.[108]

If poverty and income distribution are identified, then one may use social welfare functions. Atkinson (1970) and Dasgupta-Starrett (1973) thus show that if one compares two income distributions with equal average income, then distribution A is preferred to distribution B for all strictly quasi-concave and symmetric social welfare functions if and only if the Lorenz curve for A is closer to the diagonal than the Lorenz curve for B. This is a usual definition of a more egalitarian income distribution; still, it clearly defines a very partial order only.

8.2   Private Charity and Public Transfers

One may wonder a priori why government should be concerned with fighting poverty. After all, social preferences reflect (somewhat opaquely) private preferences. If government must fight poverty, it is probably because the standard of living of the poor enters every citizen's utility function. Since citizens are altruistic, then why should not the fight against poverty be left to private charity?

This argument has another component that deserves attention. Once we recognize that private charity can play a role, we may fear that public transfers substitute for private charity and thus do not improve in fact the welfare of the poor. We will now examine these two questions by adapting a model due to Warr (1982).

---

108. The Gini index is twice the surface between the diagonal and the Lorenz curve.

To make things as simple as possible, we assume that there are only two types of agents in the economy. The m "poor" have gross income y and a utility function $u(c)$, where c is their aggregate consumption and u is increasing and concave. The n "rich" have a gross income $Y > y$ and altruistic preferences given by

$$u(C) + \beta u(c)$$

where C represents the consumption of a rich agent and $\beta > 0$ his altruism index. In this economy the Pareto optimum associated to a social weight of each poor agent $\lambda > 0$ is the solution to the program

$$\max_{c,C}(\lambda m u(c) + n(u(C) + \beta u(c)))$$

under the scarcity constraint

$$mc + nC \leq my + nY$$

The first-order condition of this program is

$$\frac{\lambda m + \beta n}{m} u'(c) = u'(C)$$

The corresponding solution can be implemented through a gift of D^* from each rich agent, where D^* is defined by

$$u'(Y - D^*) = \frac{\lambda m + \beta n}{m} u'\left(y + \frac{nD^*}{m}\right)$$

In practice, such gifts are by definition voluntary. We will therefore focus on the Nash equilibrium of the game in which each rich agent decides how much to give in order to reduce poverty. The rich agent i then takes the voluntary contributions $\sum_{j \neq i} D_j$ of the other rich agents as given and solves

$$\max_{D_i}\left[u(Y - D_i) + \beta u\left(y + \frac{D_i + \sum_{j \neq i} D_j}{m}\right)\right]$$

In the symmetric equilibrium, all D_i are equal to some D^E given by

$$u'(Y - D^E) = \frac{\beta}{m} u'\left(y + \frac{nD^E}{m}\right)$$

It is easy to see by comparing the equations that define D^* and D^E that $D^E < D^*$: the voluntary contributions of the rich are too small to implement the Pareto optimum. The reason is that just as in the subscription equilibrium for financing public goods (see Salanié 2000, ch. 4), each agent only takes into account part of the positive consequences of his contribution. This is easily seen in the limit case where $\lambda = 0$, so that social preferences coincide with those of the rich. Even then, each rich agent neglects the effect that his gift has on the utility of the other rich agents (through their concern for the poor); this leads to underefficient contributions.

This result seems to open the door for government intervention. Thus assume that the government institutes a compulsory lump-sum transfer T from the rich to the poor. Then each rich agent chooses his voluntary contribution D_i so as to maximize

$$u(Y - D_i - T) + \beta u\left(y + \frac{D_i + \sum_{j \neq i} D_j + nT}{m}\right)$$

which leads at the *interior* symmetric equilibrium to a contribution D^T given by

$$u'(Y - D^T - T) = \frac{\beta}{m} u'\left(y + \frac{n(D^T + T)}{m}\right)$$

Obviously this equation exactly coincides with the previous one once we replace D^E with $(D^T + T)$. It follows that

$$D^T = \max(D^E - T, 0)$$

So long as the compulsory transfer T is smaller than D^E, the rich adjust their voluntary contributions so as to keep the total transfer equal to D^E: private charity is fully crowded out by public transfers. On the other hand, if T goes above D^E, then voluntary contributions D^T are zero and the total transfer is T, which may be set at the optimal level $D^* > D^E$; this implements the Pareto optimum.

Note that the optimum D^* can also be reached by creating a subsidy to voluntary contributions financed by a tax on the consumption of the rich. Thus assume that we tax the consumption of the rich at the rate t and we subsidize their gifts at the rate s. Then the consumption of the rich agent i is

$$C_i = (Y - D_i)(1 - t) + sD_i$$

and he chooses his voluntary contribution D_i so as to maximize

$$u((Y - D_i)(1 - t) + sD_i) + \beta u\left(y + \frac{D_i + \sum_{j \neq i} D_j}{m}\right)$$

which gives at the symmetric equilibrium

$$(1 - t - s)u'((Y - D)(1 - t) + sD) = \frac{\beta}{m}u'\left(y + \frac{nD}{m}\right)$$

It is easy to see that if we fix t and s so as to achieve both

$$1 - t - s = \frac{\beta}{\beta n + \lambda m}$$

and the government's budget balance

$$t(Y - D) = sD$$

then $D = D^*$: it is possible to implement the Pareto optimum through a balanced combination of taxes and of subsidies. This type of policy does exist in reality, since the personal income tax includes deductions for charitable giving in many countries. However, in this simple model the optimal subsidy rate is

$$s^* = \frac{Y - D^*}{Y}\left(1 - \frac{\beta}{\beta n + \lambda m}\right)$$

Fix the proportion of poor in the population so that we can fix β; then when n and m become large, the subsidy rate goes to $(Y - D^*)/Y$. This value is equal to the proportion of the income of the rich that they keep for themselves at the Pareto optimum, so it implies a rather large subsidy rate. Such a generous tax expenditure would probably encourage abuses. A system of public transfers may be profitable even though it crowds out private charity.

This very simplified model neglects several elements in favor of a policy of public transfers. First, some rich agents may be less altruistic than others, and only the government can make them contribute as much as the others. Second, the government may be able to exploit more economies of scale than private charities in the administration of charitable giving. Third, poverty is often linked to random events against which public insurance may be the only resort, given the difficulties raised by asymmetric information.

8.3   The Main Benefits

Two types of transfers can be used to reduce poverty: in-kind benefits and cash benefits. We call a benefit "in-kind" when it can only be spent on one particular category of goods. In the United States, for instance, food stamps are given to poor households and can only be used to buy food. Several countries have housing benefits that can only be used to pay the rent. Economists tend to be wary of in-kind benefits. First, this type of program is costly to administer—for instance, the US government must make sure that food stamps are not traded for money. Second, a standard microeconomics exercise shows that a consumer reaches lower utility when he is given an in-kind benefit than when he gets the same amount in cash: in the latter case he can reallocate his consumption between all goods according to his preferences. It is also true that economists are by training distrustful of what interferes with the freedom of choice of individuals.

As the American example shows, these arguments against in-kind benefits have not convinced the laymen. The public seem to rely on a paternalistic approach that holds that individuals, when left to themselves, do not consume enough of some essential goods (called *merit goods*) like food and housing. Then the government must intervene to modify their choices.[109] One might justify this idea economically by assuming that the consumption of merit goods by the poor exerts a positive externality on the utility of all citizens: we had rather live in a society where our neighbors (and especially their children) are well-housed and well-fed, even though they would prefer to consume other goods instead.

The bulk of benefits nevertheless is in cash; we will focus now on the most often used types of cash benefits.

8.3.1   Guaranteed Minimum Income

One first approach is to guarantee to each family a minimum income G. Then the benefit given is a function of gross income Y given by

$$\max(G - Y, 0)$$

The first use of such a system in history was in England with the "Speenhamland system" between 1795 and 1834. Such a system has an obvious shortcoming: it induces a 100 percent taxation rate for its beneficiaries, that is when gross income Y is smaller than G.

---

109. An oft-quoted example is that of school cafeterias. In some countries the replacement of free tickets with a cash benefit has led some parents to save on their children's lunches. This situation was perceived as intolerable and many local authorities returned to the free ticket system.

These families get a benefit $(G - Y)$ that decreases dollar-for-dollar with gross income. This may have large disincentive effects on labor supply.[110] Moreover it may encourage its beneficiaries to evade the system by working in the underground economy or by understating their income. However, this type of "differential allocation" was in use in the United States until 1996 with the *Aid for Families with Dependent Children* (AFDC) and still is in France with the *Revenu Minimum d'Insertion*. Sometimes guaranteed minimum income benefits are also given to special classes of beneficiaries, such as old people without a pension or disabled persons.

8.3.2   The Negative Income Tax

Many economists of very diverse political leanings, among them the conservative Milton Friedman and the Keynesians James Tobin and James Meade, have argued in favor of a negative income tax. This is defined as the combination of a uniform transfer G and taxation of income from the first dollar. This proposal is often combined to that of a constant marginal tax rate (e.g., see Atkinson 1995); the suggested tax schedule then is

$$T(Y) = -G + tY$$

so that families whose gross income Y is smaller than G/t indeed pay a negative income tax.

For its promoters the negative income tax ensures all families a minimal standard of living, while avoiding large disincentive effects on labor supply. No large country has adopted the negative income tax so far, but as we will see, some limited experiments have been carried out in the United States.

8.3.3   Low-Wage Subsidies

A third group of measures against poverty aims at making work more attractive by subsidizing the wage of individuals who hold a low-paying job. The main existing examples are the British WFTC and especially the American EITC; France has also recently adopted a more timid system with the *prime pour l'emploi*.

The United States adopted in 1975, and considerably extended in the 1990s, the *Earned Income Tax Credit* (EITC) program. The EITC

---

110. This is indeed why the Speenhamland system was abolished in England.

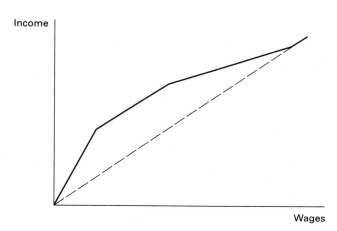

Figure 8.1
Earned income tax credit

benefits about 20 percent of all American families; it costs about 30
billion dollars a year, which makes it a very large tax expenditure.
Its name is confusing, since it is not only a tax credit for families who
pay the income tax but is also paid to families who do not pay tax.
Its mechanism is summarized on figure 8.1, where the benefit paid
is the amount between the solid line and the dashed line. The EITC is
given by government on top of wages so long as these are below a
ceiling. For a couple with one child, for instance, the subsidy is 34
cents per dollar of wages (it is the *phase in*) until wages of 6,700
dollars per year;[111] then it stabilizes at 2,300 dollars per year, and
finally it decreases with wages (it is the *phase out*) with a marginal
tax rate of 16 percent until the benefit becomes zero at wages of
about 27,000 dollars per year. The EITC is slightly more generous for
families with more children; on the other hand, it pays very small
amounts to childless families.

The corresponding program in the United Kingdom is that of
Family Credit created in 1971, which became *Working Families Tax
Credit* (WFTC) in 1999. In the long run, it should benefit 1.5 million
people and cost 0.6 percent of GDP. WFTC is paid at a full rate to
families whose gross income is smaller than 90 pounds per week,[112]

---

111. The minimum wage is about 10,000 dollars per year in the United States, and the
poverty line is 14,000 dollars per year for a couple with one child.
112. The minimum wage adopted in April 1999 in the United Kingdom is 140 pounds
per week.

provided one member of the family works at least 16 hours per week. Its value then is 60 pounds per week, plus 20 pounds per child. This value then is reduced as a function of gross income, with a fairly high tax rate of 55 percent. Thus the income of a childless family with one minimum wage earner who works full time (resp. half time) increases from 70 to 130 pounds per week (resp. from 140 to 170 pounds per week) thanks to the WFTC.

By definition, low-wage subsidies are designed to encourage work. By definition too, they cannot help the nonemployed poor, at least if they do not take a job. Thus they must be complemented by a safety net aimed at the nonemployed.

8.3.4   The Minimum Wage

Many countries in the world have (more or less recently) adopted a minimum wage that covers all or part of the wage-earning population. The minimum wage does not belong to the tax system *stricto sensu*. Yet it finds its place in this chapter for two reasons. First, because it was often conceived as a way to fight poverty. Second, because it can reduce employment of the low-skilled, who also constitute most of the beneficiaries of social minima and other means-tested benefits. Thus it is important to study how it interacts with these transfers.

The laws that govern the minimum wage differ widely across countries; sometimes they exempt some subpopulations such as the young. The level of the minimum wage is also very variable. One should distinguish here the gross minimum wage and the net minimum wage. Consider as examples two low-minimum wage countries, the United States and the United Kingdom, and a high-minimum wage country, France. The net minimum wage is about the same in these three countries: in 1999, it was 820 euros per month in France, 140 pounds per week in the United Kingdom, and 5.15 dollars per hour in the United States. On the other hand, take the ratio of the employer's cost of the minimum wage to the employer's cost of the median wage. This measures how much the minimum wage weighs on the wage distribution, from the employer's viewpoint; it also eliminates the effect of exchange rate fluctuations. This turns out to be one-third higher in France than in the United States or the United Kingdom, since social contributions are much higher in France.

8.4   The Lessons from Theory

Apart from the minimum wage, the various systems of low-income support described above can be analyzed as nonlinear income taxes. Thus we can apply to them the theory of optimal taxation, as developed in the second part of this book. We will now see in what measure this theory, and more generally economic theory, can throw light on the form of these benefits.

8.4.1   The Negative Income Tax

The case of the negative income tax seems to be the simplest one. We saw in chapter 4 that the optimal nonlinear direct tax schedule $T(Y)$ has a marginal rate between zero and one. Moreover one can prove that if the government does not need to collect too much net tax revenue, then $T(0) < 0$, and simulations show that such is the case for all reasonable values of the parameters. Thus theory seems to justify a negative income tax, at least under its most general form. But what about the *basic income/flat tax* advocated, inter alia, by Atkinson (1995)? In this system (which I denote BI/FT) the tax is characterized by a *basic income G* paid to each individual and a proportional tax on each dollar earned at a rate t (the *flat tax*), so that the resulting tax schedule is

$$T(Y) = -G + tY$$

We will divide the population in two groups; it is not necessary right now, but it will be useful later. Thus assume that a fraction γ of the population (group A) has a zero earning ability, for a variety of possible reasons.[113] Let $u(C, L)$ denote the utility function of each individual. Then members of group A do not work, receive the basic income G, and get an indirect utility

$$V(0, G) = u(G, 0)$$

Group B, with a proportion $(1 - \gamma)$ of the population, has productivities distributed according to a probability distribution function f on $[0, +\infty[$. An individual in this group who has productivity w chooses his labor supply $L \geq 0$ so as to maximize

$$u(wL(1 - t) + G, L)$$

---

113. They may be retirees, disabled persons, or simply people who are not productive enough to earn the minimum wage.

Let $L(w(1-t), G)$ denote the solution of this program and $V(w(1-t), G)$ its value (which is simply the indirect utility). Note that $L(w(1-t), G)$ may be zero, so that the nonemployed population contains both group A and perhaps the least productive members of group B.

If the government has redistributive objectives represented by a Bergson-Samuelson functional Ψ and it wishes to collect tax revenue R, then it will choose the pair (G, t) so as to maximize

$$\gamma \Psi(V(0, G)) + (1 - \gamma) \int_0^\infty \Psi(V(w(1-t), G)) f(w)\, dw$$

under the budget constraint

$$(1 - \gamma) \int_0^\infty twL(w(1-t), G) f(w)\, dw \geq R + G$$

Let $\lambda \geq 0$ denote the multiplier associated to the budget constraint. First consider the first-order condition in G. It can be written

$$\gamma \Psi' V_G' + (1 - \gamma) \int \Psi' V_G' f = \lambda \left(1 - (1 - \gamma) \int twL_G' f\right)$$

With our usual notation, V_G' is the marginal utility of income α and $\Psi' V_G'$ is the social marginal utility of income β. The left-hand side thus is just the expectation of β on the population. Since $w = 0$ for group A, we may write, by rearranging terms,

$$E\left(\frac{\beta}{\lambda} + twL_G'\right) = 1$$

But the integrand is simply what we called in chapter 3 the net social marginal utility of income b. We finally obtain the equality

$$Eb = 1$$

It is not surprising that this should hold here, since we already derived it in a similar context in chapter 5.

Let us now focus on the first-order condition in t. It is

$$\int \Psi' V_t' f + \lambda \int (wL + twL_t') f = 0$$

By the Roy identity,

$$V_t' = -\alpha w L$$

Moreover Slutsky's identity gives us (as in chapter 2)

$$L_t' = -wS - wLL_G'$$

where

$$S = \left(\frac{\partial L}{\partial w}\right)_u \geq 0$$

is the usual term of the Slutsky matrix. We obtain by rearranging terms and reusing the net social marginal utility of income b,

$$\int (1 - b)wLf = \int w^2 tSf$$

Let us now introduce the compensated elasticity of labor supply

$$\varepsilon^C = \frac{w(1 - t)S}{L} \geq 0$$

Then the right-hand side becomes

$$\frac{t}{1 - t} \int wL\varepsilon^C f$$

and since $Eb = 1$, the left-hand side is minus the covariance of b and wL. We finally have

$$\frac{t}{1 - t} = -\frac{\text{cov}(b, wL)}{E(wL\varepsilon^c)}$$

This classical formula gives the rate of the optimal linear direct tax. The denominator of this fraction is positive; its numerator is usually negative since the gross income wL increases in w while the net social marginal utility of income b decreases in w. Thus the rate of the optimal tax is between zero and one. It is larger when labor supply is less elastic (ε^C is small) and when the government is more averse to inequality (so that b decreases rapidly with w). To illustrate this formula, consider quasi-linear individual preferences

$$u(C, L) = C - AL^{1+1/\varepsilon}$$

so that ε^C is constant and equals ε. Also assume that government is "charitable conservative": it only wishes to redistribute between group A and group B. Thus it attributes a net social marginal utility of income b_0 to each individual in group B and ab_0 to each individual in group A, where a is larger than one. Then

$$E(wL\varepsilon^C) = \varepsilon E(wL)$$

and

$$-\text{cov}(b, wL) = E(1 - b)wL = (1 - b_0)E(wL)$$

Moreover $Eb = 1$ implies that

$$\gamma ab_0 + (1 - \gamma)b_0 = 1$$

whence

$$b_0 = \frac{1}{\gamma a + 1 - \gamma}$$

We finally obtain

$$\frac{t}{1 - t} = \frac{1}{\varepsilon} \frac{(a - 1)\gamma}{\gamma a + 1 - \gamma}$$

Thus the tax rate decreases in ε and increases in γ. When $a = 1$, the government is utilitarian and $t = 0$: as expected, with such individual preferences the optimal linear tax is a uniform lump-sum transfer. On the other hand, when $a = +\infty$, the government is Rawlsian, and we get the classical formula

$$\frac{t}{1 - t} = \frac{1}{\varepsilon}$$

This is also easily obtained by maximizing the value of the basic income G under the government's budget constraint, provided that $L_G' = 0$. Any value of t that is larger than $1/(1 + \varepsilon)$ lies beyond the top of the Laffer curve that plots tax revenue as a function of t. In such a situation the government could both reduce t and increase G to achieve a Pareto-improving tax reform.

The main objection to this system is that simulations suggest that the only way to pay a decent basic income G is to raise tax at a high rate t. If such a reform were adopted, part of the middle classes would face an increased marginal tax rate, which would discourage its labor supply—not to mention the political difficulties this would entail. Assume, for instance, that the government wishes to collect a proportion r of gross income and also to pay a basic income G that is a proportion s of the average gross income. Then the tax schedule is

$$T(Y) = -sEY + tY$$

and the government's budget constraint is

$$rEY = ET(Y)$$

which leads to $t = r + s$. If, for instance, $s = 0.4$ and $r = 0.1$, we get $t = 0.5$, which seems high. To alleviate this difficulty, Akerlof (1978) suggesting resorting to *tagging*, that is varying the transfer G with the observable characteristics of individuals. Thus assume that the members of group A are readily identified, for instance, because they are old or disabled. Then one may reserve the basic income G for these people; the tax schedule becomes

$$T(Y) = tY$$

for members of group B and the government's budget constraint this time leads to $t = r + sy$, which may be much lower. More generally, it is easy to see that if the government can identify the members of group A, then it is generally optimal to give them a larger basic income than to the members of group B: $G_A > G_B$. To see this, assume for simplicity that preferences are quasi-linear, which implies that labor supply does not depend on income. Then the triplet (G_A, G_B, t) should be chosen so as to maximize

$$\gamma \Psi(V(0, G_A)) + (1 - \gamma) \int_0^\infty \Psi(V(w(1 - t), G_B)) f(w) \, dw$$

under the budget constraint

$$(1 - \gamma) \int_0^\infty twL(w(1 - t)) f(w) \, dw \geq R + \gamma G_A + (1 - \gamma) G_B$$

The first-order condition in G_A is

$$\Psi'(V(0, G_A)) V_G'(0, G_A) = \lambda$$

and the first-order condition in G_B is

$$\int_0^\infty \Psi'(V(w(1 - t), G_B)) V_G'(w(1 - t), G_B) f(w) \, dw = \lambda$$

Since Ψ is concave and the marginal utility of income V_G' is one with quasi-linear preferences, we find that

$$\int_0^\infty \Psi'(V(w(1-t), G_B)V_G'(w(1-t), G_B)f(w)\,dw < \Psi'(V(0, G_B))$$

The two first-order conditions lead to

$$\Psi'(V(0, G_A)) < \Psi'(V(0, G_B))$$

Once again, the concavity of Ψ allows us to conclude that $G_A > G_B$.

The intuition for this result is simple. In the optimal taxation problem, the government wishes to help the nonemployed poor. Its ability to do so is limited by the risk that more productive agents quit their job to receive means-tested benefits. But, if the poor can be identified, then the incentive constraint is relaxed and it is easier to give the poor a large benefit.

In practice, tagging obviously cannot be perfect: group membership is not perfectly observable, and if $G_A > G_B$, the members of group B are tempted to pretend that they belong to group A. Gruber (2000) thus shows that when the benefit for disabled persons increased in Canada, the number of people who claimed disability benefits went up significantly. Salanié (2002) nevertheless proves that even with (exogenous) classification errors of both types, it remains optimal to pay a larger basic income to the tagged population.

8.4.2   Low-Wage Subsidies

By definition, a low-wage subsidy contributes a negative marginal rate to the tax schedule (about -30 percent for the EITC). It may in fact be that for some income classes the resulting tax schedule has a negative marginal rate. Such is the case in the United States for a family that only receives the EITC (in its phase-in stage) on top of its wages and pays no income tax.

This phenomenon seems contrary to theory, since we saw in chapter 4 that the optimal marginal tax rate is always positive. Some variants of the model may, however, overturn this theoretical result. We already mentioned in chapter 7 the result by Kanbur-Keen-Tuomala (1994) that a government that seeks to minimize a measure of poverty should apply a negative marginal tax rate to the least productive indivduals if they work at the optimum. We indeed know that the optimal tax rate obtained by Mirrlees has a zero marginal tax rate for the least productive individual if that individual works. If we now replace the objective of maximizing a social welfare function by the aim of minimizing poverty, then labor disutility does not enter the government's objectives anymore. It thus seems natural that such a government should wish to create negative marginal rates so as to encourage people to work and thus to break out of poverty.

Mirrlees's model considers labor supply behavior on its intensive margin, that is, through infinitesimal changes in continuous variables such as hours or effort. Saez (2000) studies the extensive margin, that is, participation decisions. He shows that it may then be optimal to subsidize the labor supply of the least productive individuals. To see this, assume that the population is split into groups of productivities $w_1 < \cdots < w_n$. An individual of type i may take a job with fixed hours that pays w_i, pay a tax T_i, and consume $C_i = w_i - T_i$, or he may refuse to work and consume $C_0 = -T_0$. Each individual compares these two possibilities and chooses to work or not, given his disutility of labor. We assume that the proportion of individuals of type i who decide to work is a function H_i that is increasing and differentiable in $(C_i - C_0)$.

Consider an infinitesimal increase dT_i in the tax paid by the working individuals in group i. If they number N_i, the tax paid will increase mechanically (without any labor supply adjustment) by $N_i H_i \, dT_i$. Let us denote b_i as the social net marginal utility of income of the working members of group i. Then the social value of this mechanical increase in taxes is

$$M_i = (1 - b_i) N_i H_i \, dT_i$$

Given this increase in T_i, agents in group i will react by reducing their participation H_i. Let η_i denote the elasticity of the function H_i; then since $(C_i - C_0)$ varies by $-dT_i$, we have

$$\frac{dH_i}{H_i} = -\eta_i \frac{dT_i}{C_i - C_0}$$

which induces a variation in tax revenue of $(T_i - T_0) N_i \, dH_i$. Since the individuals concerned are by definition at the margin between working and not working, their utility is unchanged at the first order, and the social value of this increase in tax revenue is simply

$$B_i = -N_i H_i \eta_i \, dT_i \frac{T_i - T_0}{C_i - C_0}$$

At the optimum the mechanical effect M_i and the behavioral effect B_i must cancel out so that

$$\frac{T_i - T_0}{C_i - C_0} = \frac{1 - b_i}{\eta_i}$$

But we know that the average of the b_i's is one; since b_i usually decreases in w_i and η_i is positive, it follows that T_i must be lower than T_0 for the least productive workers.[114] Thus the government should subsidize the wages of the poorest workers. There is no risk that this would induce more productive workers to take low-paying jobs, since without variations in hours, workers reveal their productivity. The main problem here is to make participation large enough, which justifies low-wage subsidies.

Saez's model does not explain how the H_i and the b_i are determined, even though they are endogenous. Thus the argument does not apply with Rawlsian preferences, since then the b_i are zero for $i > 0$. Choné-Laroque (2001) adopt a more rigorous approach. They consider a population of individuals whose productivities w and labor disutilities v are a priori unknown. If a person takes a job, then his productivity is observed and he receives a net wage $(w - T(w))$. Otherwise, he receives an income $(-T(0))$. The number of people with productivity w who choose to work thus is proportional to

$$\Pr(v \leq w - T(w) + T(0) \mid w)$$

Choné and Laroque show that if the preferences of the government are Rawlsian, then for fixed $T(0)$, $T(w)$ is the value t that maximizes

$$(t - T(0)) \Pr(v \leq w - t + T(0) \mid w)$$

Assume for simplicity that w and v are independently distributed; let G denote the cumulative distribution function of v in the population, and $g = \ln G$. Then by taking the logarithm and differentiating, we obtain

$$\frac{1}{T(w) - T(0)} = g'(w - T(w) + T(0))$$

or by differentiating in w:

---

114. No individual of type i would work if $C_i < C_0$.

$$-\frac{T'(w)}{(T(w) - T(0))^2} = g''(w - T(w) + T(0))(1 - T'(w))$$

It is easy to show that as usual, $T'(w) \leq 1$. Thus T' can be negative if g is convex, which happens if, for instance, many individuals have a disutility of labor close to some value v_0.

8.4.3   The Guaranteed Minimum Income

The guaranteed minimum income raises a polar problem: it induces a marginal tax rate of 100 percent, which is difficult to reconcile with theory with a positive marginal disutility of labor. Besley-Coate (1995) nevertheless show that a guaranteed minimum income may be a component in an optimal antipoverty program if it is complemented by *workfare*, that is, by the obligation for beneficiaries to work in public interest jobs. This result breaks down when the government has Bergson-Samuelson objectives, however.

8.4.4   The Minimum Wage

The minimum wage can be modeled within the optimal taxation problem as a constraint that the government imposes on private agents. Several papers have tried to find conditions under which it is optimal to impose such a constraint (e.g., see Boadway-Cuff 2001). Since all employees, by construction, must have a productivity larger than the minimum wage, its existence improves the information of the government and thus may increase social welfare. This argument, however, sounds rather technical, and the most usual justification for the minimum wage relies on the monopsony power of employers.

If the employer has market power on the labor market, he will pick a wage rate and employment level that are both lower than their competitive levels. Creating a minimum wage between the monopsony wage and the competitive wage then increases both employment and wages, thus bringing the economy closer to the social optimum. Figure 8.2 illustrates this argument. In a competitive labor market, equilibrium would be at point C. The monopsony reduces its demand for labor so as to avoid an increase in wages; equilibrium then is at point M. At this point wages and employment are lower than at the competitive equilibrium; as the marginal productivity of labor is larger than its marginal disutility, the level of

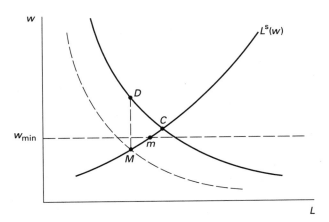

Figure 8.2
Monopsony and the minimum wage

employment is not socially optimal at the monopsony equilibrium, which leads to a social welfare loss measured by the triangle *CMD*. Now assume that the government introduces a minimum wage between the monopsony wage and the competitive wage. Then the equilibrium wage coincides with the minimum wage. The monopsony thus faces a fixed wage, as in the competitive equilibrium, but since its ability to hire is limited by the supply of labor, the new equilibrium is in *m*. At this point both wages and employment are larger than in the monopsony equilibrium, and the social welfare loss is smaller. Obviously the optimal policy is to set the minimum wage exactly at the competitive level. Note that this argument in no way justifies a minimum wage larger than the competitive wage. Moreover the quantitative force of this justification for the minimum wage depends on the elasticity of labor supply, which we know is fairly small for men for instance.

Models of wage bargaining offer another version of this argument. Consider an employer who bargains with an employee whose productivity is ρ and who has a reservation wage r. Without a minimum wage, the wage w may be determined by generalized Nash bargaining

$$\max_{w}(\rho - w)^{1-\alpha}(w - r)^{\alpha}$$

which implies that the worker is hired if $\rho > r$ and then gets wage

$$w^* = \alpha\rho + (1 - \alpha)r$$

If the government creates a minimum wage m, then maximization takes place under the constraint $w \geq m$. Simple computations show that if $\rho > r$, there are three cases:

1. if $\rho < m$, the worker will not be hired
2. if $w^* < m < \rho$, he will be hired at the minimum wage m
3. if $w^* > m$, he will be hired at the wage w^*.

In case 3 the minimum wage has no effect. In case 1 it classically reduces employment. On the other hand, case 2 is where the monopsony power comes into play: the minimum wage increases the wage of an intermediate category of workers. Depending on the form of the redistributive objectives of government, the creation of a minimum wage may increase the welfare of workers as a whole.[115]

8.5   Empirical Evaluations

A good system of low-income support should increase the incomes of the poor at an acceptable cost for the community. One way to do so is to design the system so that it discourages labor supply as little as possible or even encourages it; such a system would minimize the transfers of public money to the poor. Therefore empirical evaluations of the various policies have looked very closely at their effects on labor supply.

We already mentioned that no country has ever implemented the negative income tax in its BI/FT form as an actual national tax system. Some experiments have, however, taken place in the United States in the last thirty years. In each of these experiments, a few thousands of low- and middle-income families were selected and taxed under BI/FT over several years, instead of the current US tax system. The analysis of these experiments (see Robins 1985) shows that the negative income tax has disincentive effects on labor supply, especially for women. This conclusion seems rather robust; it can be explained both by the unfavorable income effect of the basic income and by the need to raise the rate of the flat tax high enough that it can finance the system.[116]

---

115. Such is never the case with Rawlsian objectives, since the minimum wage can never increase the utility of the least favored workers.
116. See the theoretical analysis in section 2.1.2.

Several studies have focused on the effect of the EITC in the United States. Eissa-Liebman (1996) thus compare the changes in participation rates of single mothers and of childless single women. The former are the main beneficiaries of the EITC, while the latter receive much smaller EITC benefits. Eissa and Liebman show that during the expansion in the EITC, the participation rate of single mothers increased much more than that of childless single women. This suggests that the EITC had a positive effect on participation of single mothers. On the other hand, it seems to have reduced the participation of married women: many of them are in the phase-out stage of the EITC where the EITC increases the marginal tax rate. On the whole, the EITC has probably had positive effects on labor supply.

The minimum wage was often studied through its employment effects. There are three main approaches. The first one regresses the employment rate of a category of workers (often teenagers) on the level of the minimum wage, perhaps weighted by the percentage of this category who is paid the minimum wage. Such regressions use time series at national, regional, or industry level. They often obtain negative effects of the minimum wage on the employment rate of the categories most at risk (e.g., teenagers). The estimated results, however, do not seem to be very robust. Macroeconomic data in fact are probably not adequate for measuring the effects of the minimum wage on employment. Changes in the minimum wage indeed are fairly small and only induce changes in employment that are dwarfed by the changes induced by other macroeconomic shocks. Thus it is very difficult to identify the employment effects of the minimum wage at the macroeconomic level.

The second approach uses the natural experiments method. It was illustrated by Card-Krueger (1994), who used the fact that the value of the minimum wage differs across states in the United States. In particular, New Jersey increased its minimum wage in 1992, while the minimum wage was unchanged in the neighboring state of Pennsylvania. Card and Krueger measured the change of employment in fast-food joints[117] in these two states in the months following the New Jersey increase. They found that employment in fact increased more in New Jersey than in Pennsylvania; they concluded that in this case at least, an increase in the minimum wage appeared to *increase*

---

117. Fast-food joints hire unskilled people who are often paid the minimum wage.

employment. This sudy is very controversial (e.g., see the discussion by Neumark-Wascher 2000 and the reply of Card-Krueger 2000). The natural experiments method is always sensitive to the criticism that the control group (here fast-food joints in Pennsylvania) could have faced shocks different from those of the treatment group (fast-food joints in New Jersey). The method used by Card and Krueger (1994), by construction, imputes the whole differential change in employment between New Jersey and Pennsylvania in 1992 to the increase in the minimum wage, but data reproduced by Card and Krueger (2000) show that the relative employment in fast-food joints in Pennsylvania and in New Jersey fluctuates a lot, even in periods when the minimum wage is unchanged in both states.

A third approach uses individual household data. This is illustrated on French and US data by Abowd et al. (2001). These authors compare the probabilities of two groups keeping a job when the cost of the minimum wage increases from s_0 to s_1: the employees who were paid a wage between s_0 and s_1 before the minimum wage increase, and a control group who were paid a wage larger than s_1. Their results show that the probability of keeping a job is significantly higher for the second group.

The paper by Laroque-Salanié (2002) adopts a more structural approach to model the interaction between the minimum wage and the tax-benefit system in France. Laroque and Salanié start from a labor supply model for women that takes into account most of the tax-benefit system. In this model a woman works only if, by doing so, she gets a sufficient increase in net income, given the taxes she has to pay and the benefits she receives. Laroque and Salanié moreover specify that a woman who wants to work can only do so if her market wage is larger than the minimum wage. Their model allows them to simulate the employment effects of various policies. They find that an increase in the minimum wage has strong negative effects on women's employment. The contrast between these results and those obtained in the United States by Card and Krueger is probably due to the fact that the cost of the minimum wage for the employer is much larger in France than in the United States.

The effects of a guaranteed minimum income on employment have been mostly studied in the United States, where the AFDC had this form between 1982 and 1996. Moffitt (1992) presents this literature. The negative effect on labor supply of the 100 percent marginal tax rate induced by the AFDC seems to have been significant. However, the labor supply of the concerned individuals would probably have been low even without the AFDC, since many of them were single mothers. This is a peculiarity of US welfare recipients that makes it hard to transpose these results to other countries.

8.6   Recent Reforms

Several countries have made large changes in their low-income support systems in the 1990s. The movement started in the United States, where the explosion in the AFDC caseloads in the 1970s had made this program very unpopular. American administrations reacted against the perceived disincentive effects of the AFDC by turning to programs that aimed at stimulating workforce participation of their beneficiaries. This translated into a strong expansion of the EITC in the 1990s and into the welfare reform of 1996. The latter abolished the AFDC and replaced it with a *Temporary Aid to Needy Families* (TANF) that has some new characteristics. First, the precise design of this program is left to each state, which can use to that effect a block grant by the federal government. Second, the aid is temporary: no beneficiary should receive it for more than five years. Finally, the states receive financial incentives to make sure that as many beneficiaries as possible take a job. The 1996 reform has lead to a spectacular fall in the number of welfare recipients.

The success of the EITC[118] has encouraged the United Kingdom to adopt a similar system, with the WFTC. The main differences are that the WFTC is more generous for childless families and that it is only paid to families where one member at least works at least 16 hours a week. This last condition tries to avoid subsidizing very part-time work. As in the United States, the WFTC is expected to especially stimulate the labor supply of single mothers.

Canada recently created an experiment called the Self-sufficiency Project (SSP). It is a subsidy limited in time (to three years) that pays each beneficiary half of the difference between a ceiling and his gross income. Thus the SSP generates a marginal tax rate of 50 percent. It is reserved to single parents who work at least 30 hours a week and who have had some kind of welfare payment for a year at least. Card (2000) estimates that the effect of this program on labor supply was

---

118. The EITC is estimated to have pulled four million people out of poverty. Meyer and Rosenbaum (2001) find that it was the main factor behind the recent increase in the labor supply of single mothers in the United States.

spectacular, and that the condition on hours worked played a big role.

The two other systems studied in this chapter have not played a central role in these reforms. The minimum wage is still fairly low in the United States, and the level chosen when it was created in the United Kingdom in 1999 was also low. The fear that large increases may have negative employment effects probably explains it, as does the realization that the minimum wage does not target the poor very well. Many minimum wage earners live with their parents or other family members who may have larger wages, and benefits introduce a wedge between wages and income. Moreover in countries where unemployment is high, the poor are often unemployed or inactive.

As a conclusion, it is very important to note that the main objective of low-income support systems is not job creation but the reduction of poverty. Job creation is only an intermediate goal that allows to limit the social cost of transfers to the poor. Simple computations show that even policies such as the EITC have a cost per job created that is much larger than the value of a job for the economy. These policies should be evaluated by comparing the induced reduction in poverty and their cost, but this is clearly a very difficult task.

References

Abowd, J., F. Kramarz, D. Margolis, and T. Philippon. 2001. The tail of two countries: Minimum wage and employment in France and the United-States. IZA Working Paper 203.

Akerlof, G. 1978. The economics of "tagging" as applied to the optimal income tax, welfare programs, and manpower planning. *American Economic Review* 68: 8–19.

Atkinson, A. 1970. On the measurement of inequality. *Journal of Economic Theory* 2: 244–63.

Atkinson, A. 1995. *Public Economics in Action: The Basic Income/Flat Tax Proposal.* Oxford University Press.

Besley, T., and S. Coate. 1995. The design of income maintenance programs. *Review of Economic Studies* 62: 187–221.

Boadway, R., and K. Cuff. 2001. A minimum wage can be welfare-improving and employment-enhancing. *European Economic Review* 45: 553–76.

Card, D. 2000. Reforming the financial incentives of the welfare system. IZA Working Paper 172.

Card, D., and A. Krueger. 1994. Minimum wages and employment: A case study of the fast-food industry in New Jersey and Pennsylvania. *American Economic Review* 84: 772–93.

Card, D., and A. Krueger. 2000. Minimum wages and employment: A case study of the fast-food industry in New Jersey and Pennsylvania: Reply. *American Economic Review* 90: 1397–1420.

Choné, P., and G. Laroque. 2001. Optimal incentives for labor force participation. CREST Discussion Paper 2001-25.

Dasgupta, P., and D. Starrett. 1973. Notes on the measurement of inequality. *Journal of Economic Theory* 6: 180–87.

Eissa, N., and J. Liebman. 1996. Labor supply response to the earned income tax credit. *Quarterly Journal of Economics* 111: 605–37.

Gruber, J. 2000. Disability, insurance benefits and labor supply. *Journal of Political Economy* 108: 1162–83.

Kanbur, R., M. Keen, and M. Tuomala. 1994. Optimal nonlinear income taxation for the alleviation of poverty. *European Economic Review* 38: 1613–32.

Laroque, G., and B. Salanié. 2002. Labor market institutions and employment in France. *Journal of Applied Econometrics* 17: 25–48.

Meyer, B., and D. Rosenbaum. 2001. Welfare, the earned income tax credit, and the labor supply of single mothers. *Quarterly Journal of Economics* 116: 1063–1114.

Moffitt, R. 1992. Incentive effects of the US welfare system: A review. *Journal of Economic Literature* 30: 1–61.

Neumark, D., and W. Wascher. 2000. Minimum wages and employment: A case study of the fast-food industry in New Jersey and Pennsylvania: Comment. *American Economic Review* 90: 1362–96.

Robins, P. 1985. A comparison of the labour supply findings from the four negative income tax experiments. *Journal of Human Resources* 20: 567–82.

Saez, E. 2000. Optimal income transfer programs: Intensive vs. extensive labor supply responses. NBER Working Paper 7708.

Salanié, B. 2000. *The Microeconomics of Market Failures*. MIT Press.

Salanié, B. 2002. Optimal demogrants with imperfect tagging. *Economics Letters* 75: 319–24.

Sen, A. 1976. Poverty: An ordinal approach to measurement. *Econometrica* 44: 219–31.

Warr, P. 1982. Pareto optimal redistribution and private charity. *Journal of Public Economics* 19: 131–38.

9   The Consumption Tax

As we saw in chapter 6, the standard models of capital accumulation suggest that the optimal tax rate on capital is zero. This is clearly subject to some reservations: as the conclusion to that chapter showed, there are alternative models that point toward a nonzero optimal tax rate. Still, we have little idea of what the tax rate on capital should be in these alternative models. From Mill to Fisher, Kaldor and Meade, many economists have therefore neglected these reservations and pleaded for substituting a consumption tax for the income tax as we know it. They argued that the economy suffers from too little capital and that such a reform, by increasing savings, would bring the economy closer to the golden rule. This would increase consumption per capita and ultimately social welfare.[119] They also point out that by equalizing (to zero) the tax rate on all forms of capital, a consumption tax would restore the neutrality of the tax system toward investment decisions. Finally, they also suggest that this neutrality would make the tax simpler to administer and reduce its compliance costs.

This debate has not kept to economists alone. It has started influencing policy debates, particularly in the United States, but also in the United Kingdom with the 1978 Meade Report. Let us start by recalling a few equivalences.

9.1   Equivalences between Taxes

We focus here on ideal taxes that are both proportional and comprehensive (with no special provisions). Then a first equivalence

---

119. We know from chapter 2 that the uncompensated elasticity of savings to the interest rate seems to be small, but remember that the welfare loss from the capital tax depends on the *compensated* elasticity.

links a uniform tax on incomes of all factors and a uniform VAT on all goods. As we saw in chapter 1, a uniform VAT indeed has exactly the same economic effects as a uniform factor tax of the same rate. This result must be slightly modified in the many countries whose VAT allows firms to deduct investment from value added (just as they do with intermediate consumptions). Then VAT bears on non-invested value added, and it is equivalent to a tax on that part of income that is not invested, or again to a consumption tax.

In a world where financial markets are perfect, we can write the intertemporal budget constraint of a consumer-worker who lives T periods, receives a bequest H_1, and leaves a bequest S_T as

$$\sum_{t=1}^{T} \frac{C_t}{(1+r)^{t-1}} + \frac{S_T}{(1+r)^T} = \sum_{t=1}^{T} \frac{w_t L_t}{(1+r)^{t-1}} + H_1$$

This equality shows that if there are no bequests, then a consumption tax is exactly equivalent to a wage tax—which is not an income tax since it does not tax income from savings. More generally, a tax on both consumption and bequests left is equivalent to a tax on both wages and bequests received.

Recall that these equivalences only hold for uniform, comprehensive, and proportional taxes, whereas actual taxes are neither of these three. Still, they throw some light on the debate on the consumption tax.

9.2   The Comprehensive Income Tax

The income tax as we know it is a rather hybrid construction: it taxes income from various forrms of savings in a very unequal way and relies on a concept of income that satisfies few economists. Since the work of Haig and Simons in the 1930s, economists indeed have leaned toward a definition of *comprehensive income* as the total amount that can be allocated to consumption or savings in a given period. To understand this, consider the equation that sums up the changes in an agent's wealth. During a period t, the agent receives wage income, consumes, and gets a rate of return r_t on its beginning-of-period wealth A_t. His end-of-period wealth A_{t+1} then is

$$A_{t+1} = A_t(1 + r_t) + w_t L_t - C_t$$

This equality allows us to define comprehensive income Y_t as

$$Y_t = C_t + (A_{t+1} - A_t) = w_t L_t + r_t A_t$$

Thus comprehensive income is the sum of the agent's consumption and the increase in his wealth. Said differently, it is the amount the agent may consume without reducing his wealth (for $A_{t+1} = A_t$, we get $C_t = Y_t$). The equality above shows that comprehensive income can also be defined as the sum of wage income and return on wealth $r_t A_t$. If the return on wealth is entirely accounted for by interest and dividends, then it is included in the usual definition of income and thus comprehensive income coincides with national accounts income. On the other hand, national accounts income only accounts for capital gains (the appreciation of stocks, housing, etc.) when they are realized, that is, just before the underlying asset is sold. Comprehensive income accounts for these capital gains even when they are latent, that is, before the agent even considers selling the asset. Take a bullish period on the stockmarket; then consumers who own shares will probably boost their consumption since they perceive a higher wealth. Comprehensive income explains this, while national accounts income does not even register the latent capital gains.

Several economists start from this more satisfactory definition of income to argue that the income tax should be a comprehensive income tax. This amounts to saying that the income tax should also tax latent capital gains. This is not a trivial change, as many families own stocks and even more own their house. Beyond the argument above, the proponents of a comprehensive income tax note that the current income tax creates a *lock-in* effect: since it only taxes capital gains when they are realized (and not at all when the owner of the asset dies), it provides incentives for owners to keep the asset for longer than they would in a world without taxes. These economists also insist on the importance of accounting for inflation properly. Recall that comprehensive income is the sum of consumption and the *real* increase in wealth, so that a comprehensive income tax would only tax real income from savings. On the other hand, the current income tax taxes the nominal income from savings. In inflationary periods it also taxes pseudo-income that contributes nothing to consumption or increases in wealth. Thus a 50 percent tax rate on income from savings in fact confiscates the whole real return from savings when inflation is 2 percent and the nominal interest rate is 4 percent.

The creation of a comprehensive income tax would imply a notable extension of the taxable basis, since this would include latent
capital gains and all the income from various sources of savings that
are currently tax-favored.[120] Advocates of a consumption tax go
to the polar opposite, since they would exempt all income from
savings, whether it consists of interests, dividends, or capital gains
(latent or realized).

9.3   The Consumption Tax in Practice

One often hears that a consumption tax would be unjust, since the
rich consume less (as a proportion of income) than the poor. We will
see that by using judiciously the equivalences recalled above, one
may conceive a consumption tax that is as progressive as one likes.
The frequent assimilation of the consumption tax to a renunciation
to progressivity is a confusion that partly result from the fact that in
the United States many proponents of the consumption tax indeed
favor a proportional income tax: the *flat tax*.

A proportional (income or consumption) tax would have obvious
administrative advantages. First, it would simplify (marginally) the
tax returns.[121] It would also eliminate one of the anomalies of progressive taxes: with such schedules a taxpayer pays more tax when
his income varies over time than when it is constant. Finally, it
would make pay-as-you-earn withholding systems much simpler
when the taxpayer has several sources of income.

Despite these advantages most voters estimate that taxes should
be progressive. Thus the tax acts proposed in the United States usually comprise a personal exemption that takes the poorer families
off the tax rolls; this clearly detracts from the advantage of strict
proportionality.[122]

There are many ways to make a consumption tax progressive. In
general, a consumption tax is the combination of a corporate tax and

---

120. The most spectacular exemption in many—but not all—current income tax systems concerns fictitious rents, that is, the rental value of an owner-occupied house.
These rents are implicitly received by the owner and in fact constitute income from the
savings materialized in the house.
121. Several presidential candidates in the United States have taken to waving a
postcard as the promise of a much simpler tax return.
122. As we saw in chapter 4, this type of tax schedule was already the favorite of
classical authors, from Smith to Mill.

a personal tax.[123] The corporate tax often is a proportional tax on noninvested value added. Since investment is deducted from the taxable basis, this amounts to allowing for immediate depreciation of all capital investment, which is a simple if radical way of equating fiscal depreciation and economic depreciation. It also restores the neutrality toward all forms of investments, which is a radical change on current income taxes. In the best-known blueprint, due to Hall-Rabuschka (1995), wages paid by firms are deducted from non-invested value added before computing the corporate tax; the personal tax then is a tax on all wage income received by families. Changing the schedule of this personal wage tax allows the government to achieve any degree of progressivity. Opponents of the consumption tax justly remark that such a wage tax would exempt people who have had the good fortune of a large bequest and live off it without working. Most people find this immoral, so the wage tax should be complemented with a progressive tax on bequests.

Another possibility (the *Unlimited Savings Allowance* or *USA Tax*; see Seidman 1997) consists in taxing families in a progressive manner on the difference between the money flows they receive (whether it is labor income or capital income) and their savings, since this difference by definition equals their savings. The USA Tax was inspired by the writings of Irving Fisher; it supposes that families keep proper accounts of their money flows (in and out) that are not linked to consumption. To make it equivalent to a tax on wages and bequests received, the USA Tax should also tax the bequests left by taxpayers.

Proponents of the consumption tax predict a large positive effect on savings and, since the economy is assumed to have too little capital, on welfare. There have been many quantitative studies on this topic. They usually do obtain a positive effect on welfare, but with very variable figures. One of the most serious problems of such a reform arises when moving from an income tax to a consumption tax. The unfortunate taxpayers who have saved while paying the income tax, hoping to live off the income from their savings without paying any more tax, now have to pay the consumption tax. This

---

123. Some proponents of the consumption tax seek to abolish all personal taxes by relying on a tax on (noninvested) value added, which is the same as a consumption tax as we know. The disadvantage of this method is that it makes it hard to make the tax progressive.

could represent a large welfare loss for them. The proposed reforms thus all contain more or less satisfactory clauses to account for this so-called *old wealth* problem.

References

Hall, R., and A. Rabushka. 1995. *The Flat Tax*. Hoover Institution Press.

Seidman, L. 1997. *The USA Tax: A Progressive Consumption Tax*. MIT Press.

10   Environmental Taxation

There are at least three reasons to discuss environmental taxation in this book. First, there has been a lot of discussion of economic aspects of environmental policy in recent years, both at national level and in international conferences such as the 1997 Kyoto conference on global warming. Second, the share of tax revenue generated by environmental taxation has increased over time, and it now brings about 6 percent of tax revenues in the OECD.[124] Finally, and most important for our purposes, environmental taxation has some specific features. It is aimed at preserving or improving the quality of the environment, but the quality of the environment is a public good (it is nonrival in that my enjoying the environment does not reduce the utility you may derive from it). As a public good it is influenced by the uncoordinated economic decisions of a large number of agents. Since there is no market that coordinates these decisions, they induce externalities. Pollution indeed is one of the classical examples of negative externalities.

Thus the study of environmental taxation largely boils down, in theoretical terms, to the study of taxation in an economy with externalities. The main difference in the approach of this book is that in the absence of taxes, an economy with an externality is not efficient, since the externality itself creates a distortion. On the other hand, this distortion can be corrected by using a tax that brings the economy back to the first-best: this is the idea behind Pigovian

---

124. Scandinavian countries have been particularly keen to use "green taxes" on sulphur and CO_2 inter alia; they bring about 9 percent of tax revenue in Denmark, for instance. On the other hand, the United States has been much more reluctant and only collects about 3 percent of tax revenue through environmental taxes.

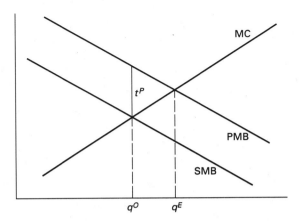

Figure 10.1
Pigovian tax

taxation.[125] In partial equilibrium the argument is very simple. Consider a "dirty" good, one whose consumption reduces the quality of the environment (an illustration for this chapter is how car travel pollutes the air). Then consumption of the good creates both a private marginal benefit (PMB) whose valuation is given by the inverse demand function and a marginal loss due to pollution. The algebraic sum represents the social marginal benefit (SMB), which lies below PMB in the supply and demand figure 10.1. The social optimum lies at the intersection of SMB and the marginal cost (MC) curve; it determines a production q^O of the dirty good. On the other hand, market equilibrium is given by the intersection of MC and the private marginal benefit (PMB) curve, and it generates too much production (and pollution) since $q^E > q^O$. Now let government raise a specific tax on the consumption of the dirty good and fix the value of this tax as

---

125. Pigou (1960 [1920]; ch. IX, §13) wrote:

It is plain that divergences between private and social marginal product of the kinds we have so far been considering cannot.... be mitigated by a modification of the contractual relation between any two contracting parties, because the divergence arises out of a service or disservice rendered to persons other than the contracting parties. It is, however, possible for the State, if it so chooses, to remove the divergence in any field by "extraordinary encouragements" or "extraordinary restraints" upon investments in that field. The most obvious forms which these encouragements and restraints may assume are, of course, those of bounties and taxes.

$$t^P = SMB(q^O) - PMB(q^O)$$

Then market equilibrium corresponds to a production q such that

$$PMB(q) - t^P = MC(q)$$

which clearly holds for $q = q^O$: the Pigovian tax t^P brings the economy back to the first-best optimum. It is obvious from the formula that t^P is just the marginal loss due to pollution; we say that the tax internalizes the externality.

This simple story raises several difficulties which we will discuss in the rest of this chapter. We would like to know what happens in general equilibrium when other taxes exist and induce their own distortions. It might be, for instance, that substitutes of dirty goods should be subsidized in order to reduce pollution. On the other hand, dirty goods may be bad targets for taxation if, for instance, they are heavily consumed by the poor. In general equilibrium the social value of a green tax depends on how the revenue it collects is used. A notion popularized by Pearce (1991), for instance, states that this green tax revenue can be used to cut other, distortionary taxes such as the tax on labor income. This would reduce distortions and thus have an indirect positive effect of welfare. Thus green taxation would yield a "double dividend": the first dividend would be the improvement in the quality of the environment, while the reduction in the distortions induced by other taxes would generate a second dividend. We will discuss whether general equilibrium analysis supports this rosy view of environmental taxation.

Environmental taxation clearly raises many other interesting issues. These have to do with tax incidence, for instance, or the estimation of marginal benefits from taxing pollution, or international aspects of regulating pollution. More generally, there is an old and fascinating debate on the choice of instruments to regulate pollution: in addition to taxes, one may use standards, tradable quotas, subsidies for abatement, or rely on negotiation as suggested by Coase (1960). The reader should look at good recent treatments of the topic such as Sandmo (2000) or Bovenberg-Goulder (2002).

All of this chapter uses the general equilibrium model introduced in chapter 3 when we discussed indirect taxation. Remember that in this model, I consumer-workers of utility functions $U_i(X^i, L^i)$ who all have identical productivities face linear taxes at rates t_k on the n goods and at rate τ on labor. Firms j produces one unit of good j

from one unit of labor. Thus, if we normalize the wage to one, the producer price of good j is one and its consumer price is $(1 + t_j)$. Agent i faces a budget constraint

$$\sum_{k=1}^{n} (1 + t_k)X_k^i = (1 - \tau)L^i + T_i$$

if he receives a lump-sum transfer T_i from the government. Government needs to raise taxes in order to finance its lump-sum transfers and pay G units of labor.

We now assume that good 1 is a dirty good whose total consumption deteriorates the quality of the environment e. We denote

$$X_k = \sum_{i=1}^{I} X_k^i$$

then we define $e = f(X_1)$ where f is a smooth decreasing function. Of course, the quality of the environment only matters in so far that agents care, so we rewrite the utility functions as $U_i(X^i, L^i, e)$, where each U_i increases in e. Once again, think of X_1 as car travel, which brings private utility but also pollutes the air. We assume that I is large, so that each agent neglects his own impact on e. Note that we assume for simplicity that production sets are not affected by the quality of the environment. We call all goods with $k > 1$ "clean goods."

10.1   Optimal Green Taxes

10.1.1   The First-Best Case
We start with the marginal conditions for the first-best optimum. These are obtained by choosing a set of Pareto weights (v_i) and maximizing

$$\sum_{i=1}^{I} v_i U_i(X^i, L^i, e)$$

given $e = f(X_1)$ and the production constraint, which is just $\sum_{k=1}^{n} X_k + G \leq \sum_{i=1}^{I} L^i$. Let μ denote the multiplier on the production constraint. Then the first-order condition on X_1^i is

$$v_i \frac{\partial U_i}{\partial X_1^i} + \sum_{j=1}^{I} v_j \frac{\partial U_j}{\partial e} f'(X_1) = \mu$$

For other goods $(k > 1)$ the first-order condition is

$$v_i \frac{\partial U_i}{\partial X_k^i} = \mu$$

Finally, the first-order condition on L^i is

$$v_i \frac{\partial U_i}{\partial L^i} + \mu = 0$$

Substituting this last condition in the first two, we obtain for the clean goods

$$-\frac{\partial U_i/\partial X_k^i}{\partial U_i/\partial L^i} = 1$$

which is the standard condition that the marginal rate of substitution between goods and leisure should equal the technical marginal rate of substitution. On the other hand, we obtain for the dirty good

$$-\frac{\partial U_i/\partial X_1^i}{\partial U_i/\partial L^i} - \left(\sum_{j=1}^{I} \frac{\partial U_j/\partial e}{\partial U_j/\partial L^j} \right) f'(X_1) = 1$$

This condition differs from the usual one since the marginal rate of substitution between the dirty good and leisure is corrected for the marginal disutility induced by the deterioration of the environment when the consumption of the dirty good increases. The left-hand side of this equation is called the social marginal rate of substitution; more generally, the marginal conditions for a Pareto optimum in the presence of externalities state the equality of social marginal rates of substitution and social technical marginal rates of substitution.

Assume that the government is able to redistribute arbitrarily by using differentiated lump-sum transfers. Then the Pareto optimum characterized above can be decentralized by using an appropriate tax system. Consider indeed the marginal conditions for an equilibrium with consumer prices q and net wage $(1 - \tau)$. These state that for all i and k,

$$-\frac{\partial U_i/\partial X_k^i}{\partial U_i/\partial L^i} = \frac{q_k}{1 - \tau}$$

As in chapter 3, focus on the case where $\tau = 0$ and $q_k = 1 + t_k'$, where t_k' is the tax rate on good k. Then we can choose $t_k' = 0$ for $k > 1$ and

$$t_1' = \left(\sum_{j=1}^{I} \frac{\partial U_j / \partial e}{\partial U_j / \partial L^j} \right) f'(X_1)$$

computed at the Pareto optimum under study. It is easily seen by substitution that such a tax system decentralizes the Pareto optimum. Note that since U_j decreases in L^j and f is decreasing, t_1' is positive. It is the value of the Pigovian tax in general equilibrium when the government can use arbitrary lump-sum transfers.[126] Note also that its value differs across Pareto optima, as the marginal benefit of reducing pollution presumably is larger when pollution is high. The Pigovian tax embodies the same idea as in partial equilibrium: it internalizes the externality by making polluters bear the social cost of pollution.

10.1.2   The Second-Best Case

As argued repeatedly in this book, it is not realistic to assume that the government can redistribute arbitrarily by using lump-sum transfers. Informational problems make it difficult for the government to go beyond uniform lump-sum transfers. Then the government cannot implement the first-best optimum any more. The best it can do is to choose a vector of tax rates on goods t' (where we again normalize the tax rate on wages at zero) and a uniform lump-sum transfer T so as to maximize a Bergson-Samuelson functional of indirect utilities

$$W(V^1, \ldots, V^I)$$

under the government's budget constraint

$$IT + G \le \sum_{k=1}^{n} t_k' X_k$$

Here each indirect utility $V^i(q, e, T)$ is defined by maximizing $U^i(X^i, L^i, e)$ given the budget constraint

$$q \cdot X^i \le L^i + T$$

This is a very similar problem to the one we studied in chapter 3. For

---

126. If the quality of the environment depends on the consumption of the dirty good by each consumer rather than on the total consumption, then the government must use personalized Pigovian taxes, where $f'(X_1)$ is replaced in the formula by $f_i'(X_1^1, \ldots, X_1^I)$ for consumer i.

simplicity, we will study the case of separable externalities, where the utility functions can be written as

$$U^i(X^i, L^i, e) = \tilde{U}^i(h^i(X^i, L^i), e)$$

for some scalar function h^i. Then the demand functions for the various goods are independent of the quality of the environment e.

The first-order condition in q_k reads

$$\sum_{i=1}^{I} \frac{\partial W}{\partial V^i}\left(\frac{\partial V^i}{\partial q_k} + \frac{\partial V^i}{\partial e}f'(X_1)\frac{\partial X_1}{\partial q_k}\right) = -\lambda\left(X_k + \sum_{l=1}^{n} t_l'\frac{\partial X_l}{\partial q_k}\right)$$

As usual, denote by α_i the marginal utility of income of consumer i and by β_i his social marginal utility of income:

$$\beta_i = \alpha_i \frac{\partial W}{\partial V^i}$$

The result is

$$\sum_{i=1}^{I} \beta_i X_k^i = \lambda\left(X_k + \sum_{l=1}^{n} t_l'\frac{\partial X_l}{\partial q_k}\right) + \left(\sum_{i=1}^{I} \frac{\partial W}{\partial V^i}\frac{\partial V^i}{\partial e}\right)f'(X_1)\frac{\partial X_1}{\partial q_k}$$

Now denote

$$\Gamma = \frac{1}{\lambda}\sum_{i=1}^{I} \frac{\partial W}{\partial V^i}\frac{\partial V^i}{\partial e}$$

and define a new tax system on goods by $t_k'' = t_k'$ for $k > 1$ and

$$t_1'' = t_1' + \Gamma f'(X_1)$$

Then the first-order condition above becomes

$$\sum_{i=1}^{I} \beta_i X_k^i = \lambda\left(X_k + \sum_{l=1}^{n} t_l''\frac{\partial X_l}{\partial q_k}\right)$$

which is exactly the equation we obtained in chapter 3, with the difference that t' is replaced with t''. If we denote

$$t_1^P = -\Gamma f'(X_1)$$

which is again positive, it follows that the optimal tax rates t' only differ from the Ramsey optimal tax rates t^R by the addition of the Pigovian tax t_1^P to the tax rate on the dirty good:

$$t_1' = t_1^R + t_1^P \quad \text{and} \quad t_k' = t_k^R \qquad \text{for } k > 1$$

This "additivity property" was first derived by Sandmo (1975). Remarkably it implies that the government should not attempt to deter pollution by taxing more heavily goods that are complements of the dirty good, even in the second-best optimum. Still, raising a Pigovian tax on the dirty good does discourage the consumption of its complements and encourage the consumption of its substitutes. Indeed, the formula for the optimal discouragement indexes obtained in chapter 3 holds for t'':

$$-\frac{\sum_{j=1}^{n} t_j'' \sum_{i=1}^{I} S_{kj}^i}{X_k} = 1 - \bar{b} - \bar{b}\theta_k$$

This can also be written

$$-\frac{\sum_{j=1}^{n} t_j' \sum_{i=1}^{I} S_{kj}^i}{X_k} = 1 - \bar{b} - \bar{b}\theta_k - t_1^P \frac{\sum_{i=1}^{I} S_{k1}^i}{X_1}$$

Since t_1^P is positive and S_{k1}^i is positive for substitutes of good 1 and negative for its complements, it follows that the government should discourage more the consumption of goods that are more complementary to the dirty good.

Given the Atkinson-Stiglitz theorem of chapter 5, one may wonder whether these results also hold when the government can choose a nonlinear income tax optimally. Cremer-Gahvari-Ladoux (1998) show that the additivity property still holds in that setting, even though the optimal indirect taxation in the absence of externality may be uniform (if the utility is weakly separable in goods and leisure). On the other hand, the optimal income tax schedule is affected by the externality in nontrivial ways.

10.2   Is There a Double Dividend?

Given that the green tax presumably brings revenue to the government, a natural idea is to recycle this revenue by cutting other taxes in the economy. We will now examine one such tax reform that increases the green tax and cuts the tax on labor so as to maintain government revenue constant. We start from the equilibrium corresponding to arbitrary tax rates on goods t and on labor τ, and we increase t_1 and reduce τ. Note that we do not assume that the tax system is optimal to begin with. Since consumer heterogeneity complicates the computations without changing anything important, we simplify by assuming that there is only one consumer and no lump-sum transfer. Let $U(X, L, e)$ denote his utility function, so that the consumer maximizes $U(X, L, e)$ under the budget constraint

$$\sum_{k=1}^{n} (1 + t_k) X_k = (1 - \tau) L$$

Since $de = f'(X_1) dX_1$, the tax reform changes utility by

$$dU = U_X' \cdot dX + U_L' dL + U_e' f'(X_1) dX_1$$

Now, if α is the marginal utility of income, the first-order conditions of the consumer's program give

$$U_X' = \alpha(1 + t) \quad \text{and} \quad U_L' = -\alpha(1 - \tau)$$

So we have, by dividing by α,

$$\frac{dU}{\alpha} = (1 + t) \cdot dX - (1 - \tau) dL - t_1^P dX_1$$

where t_1^P is the Pigovian tax

$$t_1^P = -\frac{U_e' f'(X_1)}{\alpha}$$

Now the production constraint is $\sum_{k=1}^{n} X_k + G = L$. It follows that

$$\sum_{k=1}^{n} dX_k = dL$$

so that the normalized change in utility is

$$\frac{dU}{\alpha} = t \cdot dX + \tau \, dL - t_1^P dX_1$$

In this formula, $-t_1^P dX_1$ represents the improvement in the quality of the environment; it is called the first dividend of the tax reform. The other part of the formula,

$$t \cdot dX + \tau \, dL = \sum_{k=1}^{n} t_k \, dX_k + \tau \, dL$$

is called the second dividend. The question we will now study is whether this second dividend is positive, as in the double-dividend story mentioned in the introduction to this chapter. To do this, we will evaluate the second dividend in a simple case. However, it is easy to get the intuition of the results. To see this, first assume that taxes are optimal. Then by definition, $dU = 0$. But since the first dividend is always positive, this implies that the second dividend is in fact negative. Now assume that we start from Ramsey-optimal tax rates (i.e., they would be optimal if there were no externality). Then by definition the second dividend is zero. It follows that the second dividend can only be positive when the original tax system favors the polluting good even more than in the Ramsey-optimal tax system.

To make this more precise, let us return to the second dividend,

$$D = \sum_{k=1}^{n} t_k \, dX_k + \tau \, dL$$

The government's budget constraint is $G = \sum_{k=1}^{n} t_k X_k + \tau L$. Since only t_1 and τ are modified and revenue must not change, we have

$$dt_1 X_1 + \sum_{k=1}^{n} t_k \, dX_k + \tau \, dL + L \, d\tau = 0$$

so that

$$D = -X_1 \, dt_1 - L \, d\tau$$

We cannot conclude at this point, since $dt_1 > 0$ and $d\tau < 0$. The algebra in fact gets rather messy at this stage. To simplify things, let us assume that externalities are separable (the utility function is separable in (X, L) and e) and that the utility function over (X, L) takes the Cobb-Douglas form, so that

$$U(X, L, e) = \tilde{U}\left(\prod_{k=1}^{n} X_k^{\gamma_k} (1 - L)^{1-\gamma}, e \right)$$

where $\gamma = \sum_{k=1}^{n} \gamma_k$. Then easy computations show that

$$L = \gamma$$

and thus does not depend on tax rates (such is the beauty of Cobb-Douglas functions) and for each k,

$$X_k = \gamma_k \frac{1 - \tau}{1 + t_k}$$

Differentiating, we get

$$dX_k = -X_k \frac{dt_k}{1 + t_k} - \gamma_k \frac{d\tau}{1 + t_k}$$

Substituting in the differentiated government budget constraint, it follows that

$$dt_1 X_1 - t_1 X_1 \frac{dt_1}{1 + t_1} - \sum_{k=1}^{n} \frac{\gamma_k t_k}{1 + t_k} d\tau + \gamma \, d\tau = 0$$

or, using $\gamma = \sum_{k=1}^{n} \gamma_k$,

$$X_1 \frac{dt_1}{1 + t_1} + \sum_{k=1}^{n} \frac{\gamma_k}{1 + t_k} d\tau = 0$$

Now substitute

$$-X_1 \, dt_1 = d\tau(1 + t_1) \sum_{k=1}^{n} \frac{\gamma_k}{1 + t_k}$$

in the expression for D. Using $\gamma = \sum_{k=1}^{n} \gamma_k$ again, this finally gives

$$D = d\tau \sum_{k=1}^{n} \gamma_k \frac{t_1 - t_k}{1 + t_k}$$

Note that with a Cobb-Douglas utility function, the optimal Ramsey taxes are uniform: all t_k's are equal. If the government has already translated its environmental concerns into a green tax, then $t_1 > t_k$ for all $k > 1$. Since $d\tau$ is negative, it follows that the double dividend is negative in this simple case. This result can be generalized somewhat to slightly more general utility functions (see Bovenberg-de Mooij 1994). In any case, the lesson from this exercise is that the double-dividend story is seriously misleading. The intuition is fairly clear: Ramsey taxation is by definition the most efficient way to collect revenue by taxing goods. The Pigou tax is good for the environment (this is the first dividend), but it it is more distortionary than the labor tax. To put things differently, the indirect utility depends both on the quality of the environment e and on the real wage, which is easily seen to be

$$w_R = \frac{1 - \tau}{\prod_{k=1}^{n} (1 + t_k)^{\gamma_k/\gamma}}$$

When the government increases t_1 and reduces τ to keep tax revenue constant, the numerator goes up but the denominator goes up by more, so that the real wage decreases: this is another way to state that the second dividend is negative. Of course, it may still be welfare-improving to increase the green tax: the first dividend may be larger than the second one (in absolute values). But calculations on computable general equilibrium models reported by Bovenberg-Goulder (1996) show that this is more than a theoretical fine point and that in the presence of distortionary taxes, the optimal green tax may fall noticeably short of the Pigovian level.

To conclude this discussion, I should mention two caveats. First, it may be (e.g., in less developed countries) that the starting point of the tax reform has $t_1 < t_k$ for some $k > 1$, so that the existing tax system in fact subsidizes the dirty goods relative to some other clean goods. Then the second dividend may be positive, as shown by the formula for D. Second, in economies with unemployment an "employment dividend" may be generated, at least in the short run, by taxing dirty goods if the sectors that produce them are particularly capital intensive, but this is quite a different argument.

References

Bovenberg, L., and R. de Mooij. 1994. Environmental levies and distortionary taxation. *American Economic Review* 84: 1085–89.

Bovenberg, L., and L. Goulder. 1996. Optimal environmental taxation in the presence of other taxes: General equilibrium analyses. *American Economic Review* 86: 985–1000.

Bovenberg, L., and L. Goulder. 2002. Environmental taxation and regulation. In *Handbbok of Public Economics*, vol. 3, A. Auerbach and M. Feldstein, eds. North-Holland.

Coase, R. 1960. The problem of social cost. *Journal of Law and Economics* 3: 1–44.

Cremer, H., F. Gahvari, and N. Ladoux. 1998. Externalities and optimal taxation. *Journal of Public Economics* 70: 343–64.

Pearce, D. 1991. The role of carbon taxes in adjusting to global warming. *Economic Journal* 101: 938–48.

Pigou, A. 1920 [1960]. *The Economics of Welfare*. Macmillan.

Sandmo, A. 1975. Optimal taxation in the presence of externalities. *Swedish Journal of Economics* 77: 86–98.

Sandmo, A. 2000. *The Public Economics of the Environment*. Oxford University Press.

Appendixes

A   Some Basic Microeconomics

I will only remind the reader here of the few results that are necessary for reading this book. For more details on consumer theory, the reader could go to Deaton-Muellbauer (1980), and to MasColell-Whinston-Green (1995) for microeconomics more generally. I thank Philippe Choné for writing a first draft of this appendix.

A.1   Consumer Theory

We take as given a quasi-concave utility function U based on N arguments $(X_1, \ldots, X_N)$.

A.1.1   Hicksian and Marshallian Demands

The consumer must allocate his income R between the N goods. We denote the price vector $q = (q_1, \ldots, q_N)$ and the basket of goods $X = (X_1, \ldots, X_N)$. The consumer's program is

$$\max_{q \cdot X \leq R} U(X) \tag{A.1}$$

The solution of this program is the Marshallian or uncompensated demand, which we denote $g(q, R)$. The value of the maximum is the indirect utility $V(q, R)$. The functions g and V are 0-homogeneous in (q, R): there is no monetary illusion.

The dual program is

$$\min_{U(X) \geq U} q \cdot X \tag{A.2}$$

The solution of this program is the Hicksian or compensated demand, which we denote $h(q, U)$. The value of the minimum is the expenditure function $e(q, U)$. Note that the expenditure function is concave in q since it is the minimum of a family of linear functions.

Since the two programs above are dual, we have the following two identities:

$$V(q, e(q, U)) = U \quad \text{and} \quad e(q, V(q, R)) = R.$$

Let us introduce the Lagrange multiplier λ associated with the budget constraint in the primal program (A.1); then

$$V(q, R) = U(g(q, R)) - \lambda(q \cdot g(q, R) - R)$$

Now differentiate this equation and use the envelope theorem; since at the optimum

$$q \cdot g(q, R) = R$$

it follows that

$$\frac{\partial V}{\partial R} = \lambda \quad \text{and} \quad \forall i, \quad \frac{\partial V}{\partial q_i} = -\lambda g_i \tag{A.3}$$

Thus the multiplier can be interpreted as the marginal utility of income. By taking the ratio of the two equalities, we get Roy's identity:

$$\forall i, \quad g_i = -\frac{\partial V / \partial q_i}{\partial V / \partial R}$$

The expenditure function e is 1-homogeneous in q and the Hicksian demand functions h are 0-homogeneous in q. By the envelope theorem,

$$\frac{\partial e}{\partial q_i} = h_i(q, U)$$

Let s_{ij} denote the derivatives of the Hicksian demand functions that hold utility constant:

$$s_{ij} = \frac{\partial h_i}{\partial q_j} = \left(\frac{\partial X_i}{\partial q_j}\right)_U$$

Note that

$$s_{ij} = \frac{\partial^2 e}{\partial q_i \partial q_j}$$

so the matrix formed by the (s_{ij})'s is symmetric and (since e is concave in q) negative semi-definite. We call it the Slutsky matrix, denoted S here.

We denote e_{ij}^* as the corresponding "Hicksian" or "compensated" elasticities:

$$e_{ij}^* = \frac{q_j}{h_i} s_{ij} = \frac{q_j}{h_i} \frac{\partial h_i}{\partial q_j}$$

Euler's equations state the homogeneity of the functions e and h:

$$e = \sum_j q_j h_j \quad \text{and} \quad \sum_j q_j s_{ij} = 0, \qquad \text{for all } i$$

The last equation can also be written $Sq = 0$ or, in terms of compensated elasticities:

$$\sum_j e_{ij}^* = 0$$

A.1.2   The Slustky Equations

The Slutsky equations link the price derivatives of the demand functions for constant utility (s_{ij}) and for constant income. They follow from differentiating the equation

$$h(q, U) = g(q, e(q, U))$$

with respect to q. Since the compensated demand functions h are the derivatives of the expenditure function with respect to prices

$$\frac{\partial h_i}{\partial q_j} = \frac{\partial g_i}{\partial q_j} + h_j \frac{\partial g_i}{\partial R}$$

which we rewrite as

$$\frac{\partial X_i}{\partial q_j} = \left(\frac{\partial X_i}{\partial q_j} \right)_U - X_j \frac{\partial X_i}{\partial R}.$$

The Slutsky equations make it possible to write the derivatives if the Hicksian demand functions include only the behavioral parameters that can be estimated, as in

$$s_{ij} = \frac{\partial g_i}{\partial q_j} + g_j \frac{\partial g_i}{\partial R}$$

The symmetry constraints $s_{ij} = s_{ji}$ and the Euler equation $Sq = 0$ also imply restrictions on the Marshallian elasticities that can be tested. Denote

$$e_i = \frac{R}{g_i} \frac{\partial g_i}{\partial R}$$

and

$$e_{ij} = \frac{q_j}{g_i} \frac{\partial g_i}{\partial q_j}$$

the uncompensated elasticities with respect to income and prices; then

$$e_{ij}^* = e_{ij} + w_j e_i$$

where $w_j = q_j g_j / R$ is the budget share of good j. It follows, for instance, that

$$\forall i, j, \quad e_{ij} + w_j e_i = e_{ji} + w_i e_j$$

A.1.3 Interpretation
Let us use the notation of *hat calculus*, that is, the logarithmic derivatives

$$\hat{z} = \frac{dz}{z}$$

Assume that prices change by $\hat{p}_i$ and income by $\hat{R}$. Then demands change by

$$\hat{g}_i = \sum_j e_{ij} \hat{q}_j + e_i \hat{R} = \sum_j e_{ij}^* \hat{q}_j + e_i \left(\hat{R} - \sum_j w_j \hat{q}_j \right)$$

and utility changes by (see A.3)

$$dV = -\lambda \sum_j q_j g_j \hat{q}_j + \lambda R \hat{R} = \lambda R \left(\hat{R} - \sum_j w_j \hat{q}_j \right)$$

Thus, if $\hat{R} = \sum_j w_j \hat{q}_j$, then $dV = 0$, and the change in utility is second-order. The quantity $\hat{R} = \sum_j w_j \hat{q}_j$ therefore is the change in income necessary to compensate the consumer for the change in prices, that is, to hold his utility constant. As an absolute variation (not a relative one any more), this change in income is $dR = R\hat{R} = \sum_j g_j \, dq_j$.

A.2 Producer Theory

We focus in the two-input case, with labor and capital as our inputs. Capital K is paid a return r and labor L is paid a wage w. The production function we denote as $F(K, L)$.

A.2.1 The Producer's Problem

The producer chooses his input mix so as to minimize his costs; given perfect competition on markets for inputs, this amounts to

$$\min_{F(K,L) \geq Y} (rK + wL)$$

We denote the demands for inputs $K(r, w, Y)$ and $L(r, w, Y)$, and the cost function $C(r, w, Y)$. The cost function is concave in (r, w), since it is the minimum of a family of linear functions. Denote λ the Lagrange multiplier associated to the production constraint $F(K, L) \geq Y$; we derive

$$C(r, w, Y) = rK + wL - \lambda(F(K, L) - Y)$$

By the envelope theorem and using $F(K, L) = Y$ at the optimum, it follows that

$$C'_Y = \lambda \quad \text{and} \quad r = \lambda F'_K, \quad w = \lambda F'_L. \tag{A.4}$$

If the market for the firm's product is competitive and the price is p, then the maximization of profit $(pY - C(Y, r, w))$ gives

$$p = C'_Y = \lambda \quad \text{and} \quad F'_K = \frac{r}{p}, \quad F'_L = \frac{w}{p}$$

The inputs are paid their marginal productivities.

A.2.2 Factor Demands

The cost function is 1-homogeneous in (r, w) and the factor demands are 0-homogeneous in (r, w). By the envelope theorem,

$$K = \frac{\partial C}{\partial r} \quad \text{and} \quad L = \frac{\partial C}{\partial w}$$

The Euler equations that state the 1-homogeneity of the cost function can be written

$$C = rK + wL = r\frac{\partial C}{\partial r} + w\frac{\partial C}{\partial w}$$

Denote s_{Kr}, s_{Kw}, s_{Lr}, and s_{Lw} the derivatives of the factor demands with respect to input prices, for instance $s_{Kr} = \partial K / \partial r$. These terms are the second derivatives of the cost function; therefore we have, for instance, $s_{Kw} = s_{Lr}$ and $s_{Kr} < 0$, $s_{Lw} < 0$ (from the concavity of C). From the 0-homogeneity of factor demands, we obtain

$$r s_{Kr} + w s_{Kw} = 0 \quad \text{and} \quad r s_{Lr} + w s_{Lw} = 0$$

Denote the price elasticities of factor demands e_{Kr}, e_{Kw}, e_{Lr}, and e_{Lw}. For instance,

$$e_{Kr} = \frac{\partial \ln K}{\partial \ln r} = \frac{r s_{Kr}}{K}$$

Then we have

$$e_{Kr} + e_{Kw} = 0 \quad \text{and} \quad e_{Lr} + e_{Lw} = 0$$

Taking the logarithmic derivative of the demand for capital (holding production constant) and using the notation of hat calculus, we get, for instance,

$$\hat{K} = e_{Kr}(\hat{r} - \hat{w}) \quad \text{and} \quad \hat{L} = e_{Lw}(\hat{r} - \hat{w})$$

It follows that

$$\hat{K} - \hat{L} = -(e_{Kw} + e_{Lr})(\hat{r} - \hat{w}).$$

Define the elasticity of substitution between capital and labor as

$$\sigma^* = -\frac{\partial \ln L/K}{\partial \ln w/r}$$

or, to use hat calculus again,

$$\hat{K} - \hat{L} = -\sigma^*(\hat{r} - \hat{w}),$$

then we obtain

$$\sigma^* = e_{Kw} + e_{Lr} = -(e_{Kr} + e_{Lw}) > 0.$$

When the relative price of labor increases by 1 percent, the capital-labor input mix shifts by σ^* percent towards capital.

Moreover differentiating $Y = F(K, L)$ gives

$$dY = F_K' \, dK + F_L' \, dL = \frac{r}{p} dK + \frac{w}{p} dL$$

or with hat calculus:

$$\hat{Y} = \frac{rK}{pY}\,\hat{K} + \frac{wL}{pY}\,\hat{L}.$$

A.2.3   The Special Case of Constant Returns

Now assume that the production function F is 1-homogeneous in the pair (K, L). Then it is easily seen that both the cost function and the factor demands are 1-homogenous in Y. Using the equations above and denoting $c(r, w)$ the unit cost, we can write

$$C(r, w, Y) = c(r, w)Y, \quad K(r, w, Y) = c'_r(r, w)Y \quad \text{and}$$

$$L(r, w, Y) = c'_w(r, w)Y.$$

Recall that by homegeneity, $rc'_r + wc'_w = c$. Thus the unit cost is the sum of unit factor demands, weighted by their respective input prices.

References

Deaton, A., and J. Muellbauer. 1980. *Economics and consumer behaviour*. Cambridge University Press.

MasColell, A., M. Whinston, and J. Green. 1995. *Microeconomic Theory*. Oxford University Press.

B

Optimal Control

This appendix presents Pontryagin's maximum principle used in chapters 4 and 5 to solve optimal control problems. Mathematically, an optimal control problem consists in determining the function that maximizes a given functional under some constraints on the function and its derivatives. This type of problem can also be solved by using the calculus of variations. The originality of optimal control is that it rests on an analogy with engineering. Consider therefore a system that changes in time between $t = a$ and $t = b$. This system is characterized by a vector of *state variables* $x(t) \in \mathbb{R}^n$ that are influenced by *control variables* $u(t) \in \mathbb{R}^p$. The state variables evolve according to

$$x'(t) = g(x(t), u(t), t)$$

The system may also obey some constraints on the endpoint values of some state variables:

$$x_i(a) = \underline{x}_i \qquad \text{for } i \in I_a$$

and

$$x_i(b) = \bar{x}_i \qquad \text{for } i \in I_b$$

where I_a and I_b are two subsets of $\{1, \ldots, n\}$ with empty intersection.

Finally, the control variables can be freely chosen in some subset U of $\mathbb{R}^p$. In the variant we focus on here,[127] optimal control consists in choosing the values of these control variables so as to maximize an objective

---

127. Kamien-Schwartz (1991) is a technically simple reference that contains much more detail than I can give here.

$$\int_a^b f(x(t), u(t), t) \, dt$$

under the constraints listed above, with f a given function.

To solve this problem, we define the Hamiltonian as a dynamic analogue of the Lagrangian:

$$\mathscr{H}(x, u, t, \lambda) = f(x, u, t) + \lambda \cdot g(x, u, t)$$

where $\lambda \in \mathbb{R}^n$ is a vector of multipliers that depend on t. Let (x^*, u^*) denote the solution to the problem. Pontryagin's principle states that given some technical conditions,[128] the solution and the associated multipliers λ^* (which are functions of time) satisfy the following:

• for all t, $u^*(t)$ maximizes the Hamiltonian[129] $\mathscr{H}(x^*(t), u, t, \lambda^*(t))$ over $u \in U$

• for all t where u^* is continuous, λ^* is a solution of the differential equation

$$\lambda^{*\prime}(t) = -\frac{\partial \mathscr{H}}{\partial x}(x^*(t), u^*(t), t, \lambda^*(t))$$

• the *transversality conditions* hold

if $i \notin I_a$,   then $\lambda_i^*(a) = 0$

and

if $i \notin I_b$,   then $\lambda_i^*(b) = 0$

We in fact need a slightly more general form of the optimal control problem where the solution must also verify an integral constraint (called *isoperimetric*):

$$\int_a^b h(x(t), u(t), t) \, dt = 0$$

To stay within the first class of problems, we just have to define a new state variable $y(t)$ by $y(a) = y(b) = 0$ and

$$y'(t) = h(x(t), u(t), t)$$

---

128. For instance, x^* should be piecewise continuously differentiable and u^* should be piecewise continuous.
129. This is why the principle is called Pontryagin's *maximum* principle.

Let $\mu(t)$ denote the multiplier associated to this new differential equation and define the new Hamiltonian

$$\mathcal{H}(x, y, u, t, \lambda, \mu) = f(x, u, t) + \lambda \cdot g(x, u, t) + \mu h(x, u, t)$$

Then we can apply Pontryagin's principle. In particular, we must have

$$u'(t) = -\frac{\partial \mathcal{H}}{\partial y} = 0$$

so that μ is constant.

Of course, it does not matter whether the variable t represents time or any other index. We apply in this book Pontryagin's principle to optimal taxation problems, which have a formally equivalent mathematical structure.

Reference

Kamien, M., and N. Schwartz. 1991. *Dynamic Optimization: The Calculus of Variations and Optimal Control in Economics and Management.* North-Holland.

Index